DO ECONOMIC SANCTIONS WORK?

Do Economic Sanctions Work?

Makio Miyagawa
Deputy Director, Russian Division
Ministry of Foreign Affairs, Japan

St. Martin's Press

First published in Great Britain 1992 by
THE MACMILLAN PRESS LTD
Houndmills, Basingstoke, Hampshire RG21 2XS
and London
Companies and representatives
throughout the world

A catalogue record for this book is available
from the British Library.

ISBN 0–333–55275–X

Printed in Great Britain by
Ipswich Book Co Ltd
Ipswich, Suffolk

First published in the United States of America 1992 by
Scholarly and Reference Division,
ST. MARTIN'S PRESS, INC.,
175 Fifth Avenue,
New York, N.Y. 10010

ISBN 0–312–08544–3

Library of Congress Cataloging-in-Publication Data
Miyagawa, Makio, 1951–
Do economic sanctions work? / Makio Miyagawa.
p. cm.
Includes bibliographical references and index.
ISBN 0–312–08544–3
1. Economic sanctions. I. Title.
HF1413.5.M59   1992
337—dc20   92–14516
                              CIP

To my Father and Mother

Contents

PART THREE   CONCLUSION

List of Tables and Maps

Table

Map

Preface and Acknowledgements

Economic sanctions – are they in fact effective diplomatic weapons, or mere attempts at self-satisfaction? This book seeks to answer that question through the investigation of the role of economic sanctions in the international community today.

First, I identify the general principles and characteristics common to most applications of economic sanctions by analysing more than thirty recent examples of the last half-century or so, the most recent case being that of the United Nations sanctions against Iraq. Second, I evaluate the use of economic sanctions by the United States and its allies against Iran after American Embassy staff were taken hostage in November 1979, by tracing in detail the process of the imposition of sanctions: their impact upon the Iranian economy and upon Iran's political decision-making process, Iran's efforts to reduce that impact, the difficulty the United States had in obtaining the cooperation of its allies and the main factors leading to an eventual settlement.

It was towards the end of 1980 when I first came across this subject. Oxford was experiencing a rare blizzard, and the university was almost deserted as dons and students had returned to their home towns and villages for the Christmas holidays. I was left alone then, looking for an appropriate thesis subject. I was casually listening to the radio in the common room, when a news programme happened to report the possible release of the American hostages in Iran, and discussed what contributions economic sanctions might make to a resolution of the crisis. Without that radio news, this book could not have been completed.

Since that day I have been fortunate, as a graduate student there, a member of the Japanese embassy in London and then of the Japanese Foreign Ministry in Tokyo, to have had a number of opportunities to discuss and analyse this subject with many members of the diplomatic profession.

In the course of my research I have benefited from discussion and even argument with a variety of people who are too numerous to mention. However, I owe a great debt of thanks particularly to the following people for the help they have given me in the writing of this book. I should first like to express my very sincere thanks to Mr Wilfred Knapp of St Catherine's College for his detailed and painstaking guidance and criticism and his many extremely stimulating suggestions – also his very kind encouragement, without which this book must never have reached completion. I also owe a great debt to the late Professor Hedley Bull of Balliol College, whose frequent advice continued until his last illness. He began by pointing me in the right direction as to how best to proceed with such a study, later suggesting many valuable improvements and enabling me to overcome what threatened to be an almost insuperable organizational 'log-jam' when the thesis was in its final stages. I must also thank Professor Margaret P. Doxey, whom I have only once had a chance to interview, for her invaluable early advice on approaches to this subject.

I am extremely grateful, in particular, to two of my bosses during my career in the Japanese Government, who showed a most generous understanding towards my continued research and writing on this subject. They are The Hon. Ichiro Ozawa, and Yukio Satoh, without whose tolerance and encouragement this book could have never been completed.

I wish here to record my gratitude to the excellent help of Mr James Feagan for 'dethesifying' and streamlining my original text into a book. His help was absolutely essential. I should like to thank Charles and Lynn MacGregor, Steven Smith, James and Caroline Noble, Masatoshi Hirofuji, Kyoichi Sasayama, George Kendall, Fusae Sasahara, Louisa Rubinfien and Susan Hitch for their friendship, encouragement and advice. I am especially indebted to Mary R. Mortimer for her unfailing encouragement, friendship and devotion, typing almost the whole of my original text and arranging various interview appointments.

The staff of the Bodleian Library, the Royal Institute of International Affairs, the International Institute of Strategic Studies, the Japanese Diet Library and the Foreign Ministry's Library helped me immeasurably. I also thank Mrs Belinda Holdsworth, Editor at Macmillan, for her extensive advice, and Mrs Anne Rafique who provided me with valuable editorial suggestions.

Finally, I should like to express my gratitude to my father (who died before he could see the book in anything even close to completed form) and to my mother, who waited very patiently and supported and encouraged me in my writing throughout the last six years. My wife Yuko has given me many suggestions and shown remarkable cooperation and tolerance with my continued involvement in writing this book after and sometimes before my daily work hours in the diplomatic service.

This volume in no way represents the official views of the Ministry of Foreign Affairs in Japan; the thoughts are my own.

Part One

Economic Sanctions: the Historical Experience

1 Introduction

On 12 March 1933, six British engineers of Metropolitan-Vickers Ltd were suddenly arrested in Moscow and their office there raided by the Soviet secret police. Considerable anxiety was felt in Britain, as on 15 March the secret police were given expanded powers to impose all forms of punishment without trial and the news from Moscow was that some 35 Soviet officials had already been shot without being tried. A public trial began on 12 April, but there seemed to be no hope of the engineers getting a fair and impartial hearing before the Soviet courts.

The British government decided to suspend the commercial negotiations in progress with the Soviet Union, and on 19 April, the day after two of the engineers were sentenced to imprisonment and the other four to expulsion, it banned imports of most Russian goods. The Soviet government then declared a counter-embargo on British goods. However, negotiations to settle the matter were eventually successful. The two engineers were released on 1 July and the embargoes lifted.

This incident has not attracted a great deal of attention, occurring at a time when the world faced graver problems: the Depression was getting worse; disarmament disputes were dragging on; Hitler was gaining power in the Weimar Republic. From 22 April, the British Prime Minister, Ramsay MacDonald, was in the United States for discussions with President Roosevelt, but the topics given major importance in their discussions had to do with how the World Monetary and Economic Conference might revitalize the world economy or how the Disarmament Conference might create an international arrangement to eliminate competitive militarization.

Nearly half a century later, there occurred in Tehran an incident which did attract world-wide attention. On 4 November 1979, the American Embassy was suddenly raided and its staff seized by a group of heavily armed Iranian students, who accused the Embassy staff of espionage. The US chargé d'affaires repeatedly requested help, but no Iranian police were sent to free them or give them protection. It soon became obvious that Ayatollah Khomeini himself endorsed the students' action.

The US government banned imports of Iranian oil and froze all official Iranian assets. It also called on its allies to participate in the ban and for collective sanctions by the United Nations. Although the UN Security Council failed to decide on collective economic measures, the United

States' allies joined in the sanctions. The hostages were eventually released on 20 January 1981.

Between the two cases, in both of which economic coercive measures would seem indisputably to have contributed to settlement of the dispute, and also up to the present, economic sanctions have been employed on numerous occasions, by various states and by international organizations, and the methods have developed considerably. Sometimes the end the imposer(s) desired was attained, sometimes not. In any event, such measures have undeniably come 'centre stage' in international relations, and have recently attracted wide academic attention in the study of international politics.

They are not a particularly new phenomenon. Early in the nineteenth century, for instance, the then British Foreign Secretary Castlereagh suggested that in order to make the prohibition of slavery effective, the Powers should agree to boycott the colonial products of any country failing to prohibit the slave-trade effectively. Also early in the nineteenth century, the 'Pig War' occurred when Austro–Serbian antagonism led to the non-renewal of the commercial treaty between the two countries, Austria closing her markets to Serbian products.

However, economic sanctions have been an increasingly conspicuous feature of international affairs since the end of World War I, owing largely, perhaps, to the world's growing economic interdependence and the decreasing legitimacy of the use of force. With World War I it became generally recognized that modern warfare meant the mass destruction of human life and property and the wholesale devastation of nations' cultural heritage. The end of the War brought the end of the untramelled right of states to resort to war, till then seen as more or less absolute and legitimate. The Covenant of the League of Nations provided for sanctions against those resorting to war in disregard of the Covenant.

The day when the international community can enforce rules amongst its members by applying sanctions seems still far distant. But a country cannot merely do nothing if it becomes the target of what it considers an unlawful, rule-breaking act on the part of another state. Nevertheless, the Charter of the United Nations requires member states to settle any dispute by peaceful means and to refrain from the threat or use of force in their relations with others. Economic sanctions have, therefore, come to be regarded as the most acceptable and attractive alternative, although there still exists scepticism regarding their efficacy. Otto Wolff von Amerongen states in his article 'Economic Sanctions as a Foreign Policy' that economic sanctions 'resemble a tiger without teeth or claws, a tiger unable to do more than growl a little'.

What are economic sanctions? What means are available? In what circumstances can economic sanctions be effective? In which cases have economic sanctions actually been effective? When were they not effective? Even in cases in which they may be thought to have had considerable effect, did the state, organization or grouping imposing them really attain its objectives? If it did, was it because of the economic sanctions or for some other reason? If economic sanctions can rarely attain their objectives, why have states etc. resorted to them so frequently? Do economic sanctions perhaps have some hidden merits?

This book attempts to investigate the role of economic sanctions in the international community today and their importance for the study of international politics. The book has two objectives. The first is to identify the general principles and characteristics common to most cases of the use of economic sanctions, by analysing in detail more than thirty of the most significant examples of the last half century or so, the means used, the circumstances conducive to effectiveness, factors limiting effectiveness, the declared, the hidden and the 'real' goals. The second is to evaluate the use of economic sanctions by the United States and its allies against Iran after American Embassy staff were taken hostage in November 1979, by tracing the process of the imposition of sanctions, their impact upon the Iranian economy and upon Iran's political decision-making process, Iran's efforts to reduce the impact, the difficulty the United States had in obtaining the cooperation of its allies and the main factors leading to settlement of the incident.

2 What are Economic Sanctions?

Economic sanctions take a variety of forms, ranging from a mere refusal to renew trade agreements to a total export and import embargo. Therefore, any attempt to address the subject necessarily requires delimitation of the scope of the study by advancing a satisfactory definition of the term 'economic sanctions'.

What are 'sanctions'? 'Sanction' is defined in the *Oxford English Dictionary* as (a) 'the specific penalty enacted in order to enforce obedience to a law', and (b) 'a consideration which operates to enforce obedience to any law or rule of conduct; a recognized motive for conformity to moral or religious law, operating either through the agent's desire for some resultant good or through his fear of some resultant evil'.

Be they lawyers, theologians, businessmen, men or women in any walk of life, all know sanctions as defined above. Teachers discipline their pupils when they do not behave. A person driving without a licence is fined. In daily life various kinds of sanction are used to enforce rules of behaviour considered desirable in a society.[1]

The strength of rules in a society depends essentially upon the consent, or at least the acquiescence, of those who live under them. Where the consent is conscious and universal, there will be hardly any need to enforce the rules with sanctions. But the human race has probably never experienced such a situation. There is always at least a minority that does not obey the rules, and when the rules are flouted by one of that minority, whether deliberately or not, those rules must be upheld by sanctions.

It is, however, everywhere desirable that whenever rules are flouted, sanctions should be applied with the general authority of the 'society' in question, not by individual members acting without reference to such authority. In the international community, however, where there as yet exists hardly any central authority, the term 'sanction' is used not only to describe positive and negative measures to influence individual members to conform to the desired behaviour, but even one kind of retaliatory action adopted by individual members.[2]

It sometimes happens that State A applies sanctions against State B merely because State B has turned hostile to State A. In such a case, sanctions do not constitute punishment for a breach of law or the rules of conduct within the 'society', but retaliation for the unfriendly change in the other state's policy. One may feel rather hesitant about including such retaliatory action in the concept of sanctions. But bearing in mind the cardinal characteristics which distinguish the international community from other communities – its lack of a government, absence of centralization of authority – and also in view of the fact that the imposing state will tend to insist that the unfriendly alteration of the target's policy amounts to a breach of a widely accepted principle of 'friendship', such retaliatory acts are here counted as sanctions.

One point which merits attention is that not all sanctions are punitive; some are preventive. Circumstances may arise in which forceful action is necessary in order to prevent rule-breaking. Such 'police' actions are (a) action taken to prevent the commission of an act transgressing 'society's' rules, or (b) measures taken after the commission of such an act in order to prevent the offender from attaining his object, or, at least, from enjoying the fruits of his ill-doing.

Taking all this into account, 'economic sanctions' may be defined as:

> The use of economic capacity by one international actor, be it a state or international organization, or by a group of such actors, against another international actor, or group of actors, with the intention of (a) punishing the latter for its breach of a certain rule or (b) preventing it from infringing a rule which the party applying sanctions deems important.[3]

Here, 'certain rule' refers not only to legal rules embodied in international agreements or generally accepted international law, but also to political principles etc., whose acceptance is less general, which perhaps only those imposing the sanctions may consider to be rules.

The words 'the use of economic capacity' require further definition. This can be described as coercive economic action which is intended to deny a certain economic advantage to the target by, for instance, denying the target access to valuable markets, preventing the target's purchase of goods or hampering investment in the target. Also, the purpose of the use of economic capacity is not economic benefit but attainment of a given political goal by forcing the target to alter its policy or behaviour, whether in the long or short term.

The scope of this book is determined by this definition, in the light of which the cases of economic sanctions analysed below have been chosen. However, four points relating to the choice of cases should be mentioned.

First, is it meaningful to distinguish between economic sanctions in peacetime and similar economic measures in wartime? Three important factors should be taken into consideration here:

(a) Historically many of the coercive economic measures adopted in peacetime have also been applied in wartime.

(b) Coercive economic measures in wartime presuppose the parallel use of military force against the enemy and are used to supplement military action. The immediate purpose of these economic measures is to undermine the enemy's economic capacity to wage war, rather than to force the enemy to give in.

(c) In wartime, each side enjoys absolute freedom to apply any coercive economic measures against the other, whereas in peacetime certain, quite constraining, criteria must be satisfied before such measures may be used.

Like all kinds of power, economic power can be used for the attainment of various wartime objectives. Napoleon's 'Continental Blockade' was aimed at severing Britain's economic links with the continent of Europe. Likewise, Britain's continental blockade in World War I was also an attempt to deny Germany food and raw materials. Are such blockades employed in wartime to damage the enemy's war effort to be regarded as 'economic sanctions'?

The above two cases of economic blockade are not to be categorized as economic sanctions, since such measures in wartime are geared to destroying the enemy's wartime economy and production, etc., in the hope of causing serious damage to the enemy's capability to prosecute the war. Their immediate purpose is not coercion related to a more specific political goal or 'rule'.

Nevertheless, in view of both the similiarities and the differences between coercive economic measures in peacetime and those in wartime, we shall not exclude from discussion all such measures adopted in wartime, but, rather, refer to them only where the context justifies it.

Secondly, should economic counter-measures adopted mainly to protect one's own economic interest be regarded as economic sanctions? These measures include the introduction of protective import tariffs designed to protect the economic interests of domestic producers, or to reduce unemployment in one's own country.

Article 23 of the General Agreement on Tariffs and Trade (GATT) provides that, if any benefit accruing to a contracting party under the GATT is being nullified or impaired as a result of the failure of another contracting party to carry out its obligations under the GATT, the representatives of all the member countries may authorize the contracting party whose benefits are nullified or impaired to suspend the application to the other contracting party of such concessions or other obligations under the GATT as the representatives may determine to be appropriate. Any GATT member country, therefore, is allowed to take protective action, when its economic interests under that agreement are jeopardized by a violation of the agreement by another member country, if the representatives of all the contracting countries consider that the circumstances are serious enough to justify such action.

The essence of sanctions is to punish the rule-breaker, to prevent him from attaining his objective, and to change his policy; they are not ends in themselves, designed to protect the economic interests of the imposer. If import tariffs are imposed to penalize a country which has disregarded the widely accepted international free-trade order, they may be seen as economic sanctions. But, where import tariffs are introduced merely to protect one's own economic interests, this action should be seen as falling outside the boundary of economic sanctions. Economic sanctions are coercive economic measures which aim at a particular political goal.

The third doubtful area is where economic measures, though aimed at attainment of a political goal, come within the ambit of ordinary commercial intercourse. They are not then to be regarded as an application of economic sanctions. For instance, in the late 1960s the United States was troubled by increasing illegal use of heroin smuggled in from abroad, about 8 per cent of which came from Turkey. In May 1971 the United States concluded an agreement with the Turkish government which enabled the United States to buy the entire poppy crop with a view to rooting out smuggling. This ultimately compelled Turkish farmers to switch to less lucrative crops.

In this particular case the United States did not force the Turkish government to conclude the agreement, though it might have indicated that a refusal would affect American policy towards Turkey in other matters. Generally speaking, in so far as a political goal is attained through normal diplomatic intercourse, the action involved should not be held to constitute economic sanctions.

Lastly, how should economic aid be viewed? Obviously, the suspension of economic aid constitutes a use of economic power. But can a decision to supply economic aid to the target's rival with a view to punishing the target be counted as an instance of economic sanction?

It would seem that it could, for example in such cases as that of the economic aid (accompanied by military aid) the United States gave Pakistan to show its displeasure with India. However, so far as aid is concerned, it seemed wiser to restrict the text to brief reference to some typical examples of the *severance* of economic aid, in view of the very great difficulty of establishing reliably the ramifications of economic pressure in the third, and sometimes fourth, countries involved. An additional complication is that in such cases it would be necessary to consider the political and economic relations between, say, the different pairs of countries involved. This would unduly extend the bounds of the present study.

With all these factors under consideration, the analysis in Part One looks at the following significant cases of economic sanctions:

1. 1933: UK against the USSR.
   Action: Import embargo.
   Cause: Soviet refusal to release two imprisoned British citizens.
   Result: Success (the two British citizens were eventually released).[4]

2. 1935: League of Nations against Italy.
   Action: Trade embargo and financial restrictions.
   Cause: Italian invasion of Abyssinia.
   Result: Failure.[5]

3. 1939–41: USA, UK and others against Japan.
   Action: Trade boycott and financial restrictions.
   Cause: Desire to prevent Japan from moving towards southern Indo-China.
   Result: Failure.[6]

4. 1946 onwards: The Arab League against the Zionist Movement in Palestine/Israel (the state of Israel was established in 1948).
   Action: Trade embargo.
   Cause: Opposition to the creation of an Israeli state.
   Result: Failure.[7]

5. 1947: The West against the Soviet bloc.
   Action: Prohibition of all sales of 'strategic goods'.
   Cause: Soviet Union's forbidding East European states to accept American economic aid.
   Result: Uncertain (still continuing, or 'overtaken' by events).[8]

6. 1948–58: USSR and other Cominform countries against Yugoslavia.
   Action: Trade embargo and discontinuing of economic aid.
   Cause: Yugoslavia's assertion of its independence of the Eastern bloc.
   Result: Failure.[9]

7. 1951: UK against Iran.
   Action: Oil import boycott.
   Cause: Iran's nationalizaton of the Anglo-Iranian Oil Company.
   Result: Qualified success.[10]

8. 1954: USSR against Australia.
   Action: Wool import boycott.
   Cause: Australia's refusal to extradite a defecting Soviet citizen.
   Result: Failure.[11]

9. 1956: USA against UK and France.
   Action: Blocking financial assistance by the International Monetary Fund.
   Cause: UK and France's attempt to reoccupy the Suez Canal.
   Result: Success.[12]

10. 1958: USSR against Finland.
    Action: Virtual trade embargo (the Soviet Union suspended negotiations for renewal of annual trade contracts for 1958).
    Cause: Two pro-Soviet political parties not represented in newly formed Finnish cabinet.
    Result: Success.[13]

11. 1960: USA (from 1964, the Organization of American States also) against Cuba.
    Action: Trade embargo and cessation of economic aid.
    Cause: Cuba's drawing closer to the Soviet Union and nationalization of American-owned oil refineries.
    Result: Failure.[14]

12. 1960: USSR against China.
    Action: Trade embargo and cessation of economic aid.
    Cause: China's publicizing of its independence of Moscow at the Third Conference of Communist states in Bucharest, June 1960.
    Result: Failure.[15]

13. 1961: USSR against Albania.
    Action: Virtual trade embargo (the Soviet Union delayed trade negotiations and Comecon expelled Albania) and halting of loans and technical assistance.

> *Cause*: Albania's open support of Peking against Moscow at the
> Third Conference of Communist states (see case 12).
> *Result*: Failure.[16]

14. 1961: Organization of American States (OAS) against the Dominican
    Republic.
    Action: Trade embargo, particularly on oil, oil products and trucks.
    Cause: Revelation that the virtual dictator of the Dominican Repub-
    lic, Trujillo, had plotted the assassination of the President of
    Venezuela, Raoul Betancourt.
    Result: Qualified success.[17]

15. 1962: West Germany against the USSR.
    Action: Restrictions on trade.
    Cause: Construction of the Berlin Wall by East Germany in August
    1961.
    Result: Failure.

16. 1965: UN against Portugal.
    Action: Resolution calling for a ban on the sale or shipment of
    arms and military equipment.
    Cause: Suppression by Portugal of independence movements in
    Portugal's overseas African territories.
    Result: Failure.[18]

17. 1966 and 1968: UN against Rhodesia.
    Action: Trade embargo.
    Cause: Unilateral Declaration of Independence and racial discrim-
    ination policy pursued by the Smith regime.
    Result: Qualified success, in that, although sanctions did not bring
    down the Rhodesian government, they did constitute a
    useful bargaining counter.[19]

18. 1971: France against Algeria.
    Action: Oil-import boycott.
    Cause: Nationalization of a French oil company by Algeria.
    Result: Failure.

19. 1973: Arab members of OPEC (Organization of Petroleum Exporting
    Countries) against the USA, West European countries, Japan,
    etc.

Action: Oil export boycott.
Cause: US resupply of Israel with arms during the Yom Kippur War.
Result: Partial success.[20]

20. 1977: UN against South Africa.
    Action: Arms embargo, as a result of a UN Security Council resolution declaring that the arms trade with South Africa was a 'threat to peace' under Article 39 of the UN Charter.[21]
    Cause: South Africa's continued ignoring of calls by the UN to abandon apartheid.
    Result: Partial success.[22]

21. 1980: USA against USSR.
    Action: Grain export embargo.
    Cause: Soviet invasion of Afghanistan.
    Result: Partial success.

22. 1981–2: USA, UK, Japan and others against USSR and Poland.
    Action: Financial restrictions imposed and trade embargo commodity list expanded.
    Cause: Polish declaration of martial law, presumed to be the consequence of Soviet pressure.
    Result: Partial success.[23]

23. 1982: EEC countries against Argentina.
    Action: Trade embargo (British also imposing financial restrictions).
    Cause: Landing of Argentinian forces in the Falkland Islands.
    Result: Qualified success.[24]

24. 1990: USSR against Lithuania
    Action: Trade embargo.
    Cause: Lithuania's unilateral declaration of independence.
    Result: Success.

25. 1990: UN against Iraq.
    Action: Trade embargo and financial restrictions.
    Cause: Iraq's invasion and occupation of Kuwait.
    Result: Still continuing.

In addition there are brief studies of the following cases of the discontinuing of economic aid:

1. 1948: USA against the Netherlands.
    Action: Suspension of aid under the Marshall Plan.
    Cause: Dutch refusal to grant independence to Indonesia.
    Result: Success.[25]

2. 1963: USA against Sri Lanka.
    Action: Suspension of long-term loans.
    Cause: Nationalization by the Bandaranaike government of a number
    of American and British petrol stations in Sri Lanka.
    Result: Qualified success, in that after a new government took
    power in 1965, compensation was paid to the companies in
    exchange for $30 million aid per year.

3. 1965: West Germany against Egypt.
    Action: Suspension of aid.
    Cause: Egypt's moves towards recognition of East Germany.
    Result: Failure.

4. 1965: France against Cuba.
    Action: Suspension of delivery of a fertilizer plant under an economic
    aid scheme.
    Cause: Cuban nationalization of a French firm.
    Result: Failure.

5. 1971: USA against Chile.
    Action: Suspension of economic aid.
    Cause: Chilean nationalization of US assets.
    Result: Qualified success, in that the action contributed to (a) de-
    stabilization and (b) the Pinochet coup.

6. 1989: USA, EC, Japan and others against China.
    Action: Suspension of economic aid.
    Cause: Pro-democracy demonstrations in Tiananmen Square met by
    military force resulting in great loss of life.
    Result: Uncertain.

In this chapter economic sanctions have been defined, and significant
historical cases since World War I selected for study. In the rest of Part
One general principles and characteristics are identified which are considered common to the cases of economic sanctions chosen – the methods
available and actually used, circumstances conducive or otherwise to

effectiveness, factors tending to limit efficacy, and the avowed and real goals – in an attempt to draw a clear and accurate picture of economic sanctions as an instrument of foreign policy and to arrive at conclusions regarding their usefulness and limitations.

3 Methods of Applying Economic Sanctions

The principal task of this chapter is to identify and describe the various methods of applying economic sanctions. One should here recall the comprehensive descriptions of the types of economic sanctions found in the Covenant of the League of Nations and the Charter of the United Nations. Article XVI, paragraph 1, of the Covenant states:

> All the Members of the League . . . undertake immediately to subject it [the member resorting to war in disregard of the Covenant] to the severance of all trade or financial relations, the prohibition of all intercourse between their nationals and the nationals of the Covenant-breaking state, and the prevention of all financial, commercial or personal intercourse between the nationals of the Covenant-breaking state and the nationals of any other state, whether a Member of the League or not.

The Charter of the United Nations also lists types of economic sanctions, stating in Article 41:

> Measures not involving the use of armed force . . . include complete or partial interruption of economic relations and of rail, sea, air, postal, telegraphic, radio, and other means of communication. . . .

All economic sanctions involve attempts to impose controls. These can be broadly categorized as (a) restrictions on the flow of goods, (b) restrictions on the flow of services, (c) restrictions on the flow of money and (d) control of markets themselves in order to reduce or nullify the target's chances of gaining access to them. In the remainder of this chapter we shall attempt to describe what these different types of controls involve and give examples of how they have been applied.

RESTRICTIONS ON THE FLOW OF GOODS

There being two directions for the flow of goods, restriction of the flow of goods is necessarily of two kinds: export and import restriction. The export-restriction type of economic sanction is represented by the imposition of export embargoes, selective or total. The purpose is to deprive the target of its ability to import certain goods essential for its civil population, raw materials necessary for industrial production, or military *matériel*, etc.

The most essential requirement, without which life cannot be sustained, is, of course, food. A classic case of a food embargo occurred during the Napoleonic Wars, that imposed by France against Britain, which was then suffering from poor harvests. Very recently, similar steps have been taken by two American administrations. When the Soviet Union intervened in Afghanistan's internal political conflict and sent its forces into that country, President Carter imposed a grain export embargo on the Soviet Union in early 1980. Two years later, the Reagan Administration again applied a grain embargo on Moscow after martial law was declared in Poland. At that time, the United States also banned Polish fishing vessels from entering the 200-mile fishing zone off the American coast.

A similar essential requirement is pharmaceuticals. If supplies from external sources were suspended, for example, developing countries with populations subject to endemic diseases and lacking the capacity to manufacture medicines etc. would be hard hit, but even developed countries may be seriously affected by such sanctions.

Modern developed countries need a wide range of raw materials for their industries and the lack of vital resources could even paralyse their economies. Oil is the most typical of these. Since the modern industrial economy is highly dependent upon oil, not only as a raw material for manufactured goods but also as an energy source for electricity and transportation, a lack of oil could mean catastrophe. In 1973, when the United States resumed arms supplies to Israel during the Yom Kippur War, the Arab OPEC countries employed an oil export embargo against the United States, the Western European states and Japan. The economies of the target states, except possibly that of the United States, were thus put under great pressure.

Moreover, in the military area, oil has been of major importance in war ever since the advent of the internal combustion engine. Oil is now an absolutely essential requirement for a war effort. It has given economic sanctions an increasingly effective dimension since World War I. An oil embargo can prevent a target from embarking on military operations or prevent its further use of force. In 1941, when the Japanese forces advanced into Indo-China, such considerations were behind the United States' imposition of a full-scale oil-export ban on Japan.

Besides oil, many kinds of raw materials are essential for modern warfare. Britain's embargoes on the export of Malayan rubber and Indian chrome to Japan and the areas under Japanese control were derived from the same idea.

More recently, embargoes on 'strategic goods' and advanced technology have had the same purpose. Without them no advanced industrial development is possible, and the development of strategic armaments is rendered impossible. The US-led embargo on the export of strategic goods and advanced technology to the Communist bloc was designed to ensure a shortage or lack of such materials and know-how so as to weaken the East's strategic position *vis-à-vis* the West.

More directly, the prohibition of the export of arms, munitions and other implements of war impairs the target's ability to engage in military operations. Economic sanctions applied collectively by the League of Nations against Italy included such arms embargoes. The United Nations' mandatory sanctions against South Africa, agreed in 1977, also included a boycott on arms and munitions, to prevent South Africa from using them to suppress domestic anti-apartheid movements or give military support to South Africa-supported factions in the frontline states.

With respect to the efficacy of export controls, the more essential it is for the target to obtain the embargoed goods, whether to maintain the well-being of its economy or to attain the objective which those imposing the controls deem impermissible, the more substantial the effect may be expected to be. The wider the range of commodities subject to embargo, the more effective the sanctions should be. Sanctions on luxury or non-essential goods, say Yves Saint Laurent perfume or Fortnum and Mason tea, can never compel a country to desist from a war, though they may possibly have a slight psychological deterrent effect.

The other way of controlling the flow of goods is to restrict the import of goods from the target. Whereas export embargoes have a direct impact upon the target, import embargoes hit the target's economy in a less direct manner. They reduce the target's foreign exchange earnings, damaging its ability to purchase in international markets, so leading to economic hardship similar to that caused by export embargoes. Whereas the purpose of export embargoes is to deprive the target of the possibility of importing certain goods which it needs, the key purpose of import embargo measures is to deprive the target of its ability to finance imports of such goods. As long as the target of sanctions still retains the necessary purchasing capability, it can obtain the goods it needs.

Total import embargoes should, obviously, be the most effective. With selective import embargoes, the more the embargoed goods contribute to the target's income, the more effective the sanctions will be. In July 1960, when the Castro regime became openly hostile to the United States and moved closer to the Soviet Union, the United States applied import controls on sugar from Cuba. (Three months later the United States expanded its sanctions into a total trade embargo.) Cuba's entire economy was geared to this one product, which accounted for nearly 80 per cent of its export earnings. The UN mandatory sanctions against Rhodesia agreed in December 1966 were selective import embargoes on several kinds of goods, among them tobacco. (In May 1968, these sanctions were upgraded into a comprehensive trade boycott.) Tobacco was then Rhodesia's principal product, yielding about a third of its export earnings.

Finally, to these two ways of controlling the flow of goods should be added the suspension of material economic aid, technically termed 'aid in kind' (the suspension of financial aid is discussed later). This obviously causes shortages of the goods concerned, and, therefore, has an effect similar to that of export embargoes. In 1948, when the Netherlands refused to grant independence to the Dutch East Indies, the United States threatened to withhold aid in kind under the Marshall Plan, and some aid shipments were actually suspended.

RESTRICTIONS ON THE FLOW OF SERVICES

The flow of services among countries includes sea, land and air transportation, telecommunications via submarine cables and satellites, and postal services to and from the target. Cutting such links will certainly mean severe inconvenience for traders in the target country (and perhaps also in the country imposing such sanctions).

During the 1981 Polish crisis, the United States issued a statement, on 29 December 1981, to the effect that it would ban the landing of all Aeroflot aircraft at American airports and that Russian shipping would not be permitted to enter US ports. Similar sanctions were mutually imposed by Britain and Argentina after the beginning of the Falklands crisis in April 1982.

In 1983, after a Korean airliner was shot down by a Russian jet fighter, a special meeting of NATO ambassadors was held on 9 September 1983 to discuss a ban for a fixed period on all commercial flights from the Alliance countries to the Soviet Union. Although they failed to agree on concerted action, most of the NATO members, and also Japan, Switzerland and New Zealand, announced the suspension of all flights to and from the Soviet Union for 14–60 days. Some of those countries, for instance Switzerland and Britain, also suspended Aeroflot's right to overfly their airspace.

Sanctions prohibiting transport services have been resorted to relatively frequently, but to date there has been no case of the severance of tele-communications lines for traders, bankers and other businessmen, who to a great extent depend on international telex and telephone systems for their day-to-day business transactions. In the case of Rhodesia, a ban on telecommunication links with Rhodesia was actually urged by African states in the United Nations. However, such a ban did not materialize, as Britain and the United States opposed it in the Security Council.

RESTRICTIONS ON THE FLOW OF MONEY

A country's imports are paid for by exports, visible or invisible, by capital transactions or with gold. If any country or group of countries imposes sanctions rendering the first two methods of payment impossible, the target's ability to purchase must be seriously reduced. A target in such a position can still continue to make purchases, as long as its reserves of gold and foreign exchange permit this, but its reserves will be steadily depleted, and in due course its ability to purchase exhausted.

The aim of money controls, therefore, is clearly analogous to that behind import embargoes on goods from the target, in that it is directed against the target's purchasing power. The difference between the two lies in the fact that, while the prohibiting of imports from the target restricts its supply of foreign exchange derived from exports, the inter-ruption of financial movements into the target precludes any possibility of compensating for those losses by, for example, borrowing.

Among the numerous steps that can be taken to prevent the flow of money may be mentioned measures to prevent:

(a) loans to or on behalf of the target's government, or any person or corporation in the target;

(b) subscriptions to loans issued in the target or elsewhere by or for the target's government, or any person or corporation in the target;

(c) banking or other credits, and any further execution by advance, over-draft or otherwise of existing contracts to lend for or to the target's government, or any person or corporation in the target;

(d) issue of shares or other capital fictations for any person or corporation in the target;

(e) subscriptions to such issues of shares or capital flotations in the target or elsewhere;

(f) transfer of assets belonging to the target's government or any person or corporation in the target;

(g) the acceptance of any new deposit of the target's currency into its clearing account in payment for exports to the target.

As far as the effectiveness of these measures is concerned, it is in general likely that financially powerful exporting states are unlikely to suffer unduly, whereas financially weak countries will be extremely vulnerable. This principle partly applies also to the import boycott measures previously mentioned.

In the case of the League of Nations sanctions against Italy in 1935, most of the financial measures listed above, except the freezing of the target's assets (i.e. measure (f)), were imposed under Proposal II–IIa.[1] The case of the American sanctions against Cuba is one of the important examples of the freezing of assets. The United States froze about $33 million worth in Cuban assets deposited in American banks. The US Administration went further, and denied the Cuban government banking facilities. Freezing of the target's assets was also employed by Britain against Rhodesia, with nearly £10 million of the Rhodesian Reserve Bank's holdings being frozen.[2] After the Argentine invasion of the Falklands, Britain froze all Argentine assets.

The relevant statutory instrument, The Control of Gold, Securities, Payments and Credits (Argentine Republic) Directions 1982, was implemented on 3 April 1982 by the Treasury in the exercise of powers conferred upon it by section 2 of the Emergency Laws Act 1964, stating:

> Except with permission granted by or on behalf of the Treasury no order given by or on behalf of the Government of or any person resident in the Argentine Republic . . . shall be carried out, insofar as the order:
> (i) requires the person to whom the order is given to make any payment or to part with any gold or securities; or
> (ii) requires any change to be made in the persons to whose credit any sum is to stand or to whose order any gold or securities is to be held.[3]

In one example of restrictions on loans, banking and other credits, the West agreed not to grant any new credits or to reschedule the accumulated debts of Poland, when its government imposed martial law in December 1981. Since loans can also be obtained from international financial organizations such as the IMF, efforts were made by states imposing sanctions to block such loans to the target. During the Suez crisis, the United States blocked approval of IMF loans to Britain and France in order to frustrate the Anglo-French attempt to reoccupy the Suez Canal Zone in collaboration with Israel.[4] After the Falklands War began, the British delegation to the IMF opposed the rescheduling of the Argentine debt, and eventually succeeded in blocking it.

CONTROL OF MARKETS

Where markets of specific commodities or goods are concerned, control is aimed at creating an artificial scarcity and higher prices in markets for commodities essential to the target. A good example of this type of 'sanction' is the action taken by the Allies against Germany during World War II. John Maynard Keynes was one advocate of this measure. The Allies made purchases far in excess of their needs of Portuguese and Spanish wolframite, a substance used in anti-tank ammunition and other military hardware. This measure was very effective, in that it kept the wolframite out of the hands of the Germans, at the same time forging closer political links between the two selling countries and the Allies.

One could envisage the United States attempting to buy up all the wheat in the world market to put the Soviet Union in the position of being unable to import wheat. Similar action was, in fact, taken by Britain in World War I, when Britain bought up Balkan grain in order to prevent her enemies from acquiring it.

Next, money market controls must be considered. A classic case of this kind of control is provided by the sanctions against Rhodesia. Britain expelled Rhodesia from the sterling area and closed the London capital market to Rhodesian dealing. Rhodesian sterling was blocked and could no longer be converted into other currencies in Britain. Since the London market was one of the world's two largest, the measure seriously damaged the credit standing of Rhodesian sterling. In the case of Cuba, the United States prohibited most Cuban dollar transactions in all banks in the United States.

SUMMARY

In this chapter a variety of means available as economic sanctions have been looked at. In some cases the imposer employs all possible means in an attempt to inflict the greatest possible economic damage upon the target, whereas in other cases the imposer chooses the means considered most effective or, as the case may be, least damaging. Naturally, all means are not always available to all imposers. Clearly a country that does not produce, refine or trade in oil cannot impose an oil export embargo. If the would-be imposer's economy is small, earning little hard currency and depending for those earnings exclusively on its sales of, say, fishery products, a fishery products export embargo is unlikely to be really feasible. Thus, the effectiveness of economic sanctions depends to a certain extent upon the means and methods practically available to the imposer. The purpose of Chapter 4 shall be to determine the circumstances in which economic sanctions work and the situations in which they do not.

4 The Efficacy of Economic Sanctions

When, in 1935, the League of Nations, as the principal instrument for the maintenance of peace, was discussing the unprecedented imposition of comprehensive economic sanctions on Italy, some members argued that collective security could be assured only by the employment of force, or rather, only if it were understood that force would be used to assure it.

Do economic sanctions work? The purpose of this chapter is to investigate whether they do, in what circumstances they work and in what circumstances they do not, and, further, what kind of steps can be taken by the imposer to increase their efficacy.

CIRCUMSTANCES CONDUCIVE OR OTHERWISE TO THE EFFICACY OF SANCTIONS

First, what circumstances are conducive, or otherwise, to the effectiveness of economic sanctions? The following seven conditions seem in general to be so conducive.

(a) Dependence on trade

The greater the importance of foreign trade in the target's domestic economy, the greater the probable economic impact. A completely self-sufficient economy, if such exists, will be completely immune to any kind of influence exerted by coercive economic measures, while a country totally dependent upon trade cannot fail to suffer a great deal. Poor countries virtually self-sufficient in food and clothing are to that extent less vulnerable than rich countries which import vital raw materials and fuel.

(b) Size of economy

The smaller the target's GNP, the more effective the sanctions may be. This hypothesis derives from the probability that a small economic surplus must limit the target's flexibility in the allocation of resources aimed at resisting the sanctions.

(c) Trade partners

The more closely interwoven the target's trade has been with specific partners, the more vulnerable it is should those partners join in the sanctions. After World War II, the Soviet Union forced its satellite states to make their economies largely dependent upon its own. This seems in great part to have been intended to create a situation which would enable the Soviet Union to keep them under its control.

(d) Availability of substitutes

The more difficult it is for the target to find alternative foreign sources of supply, alternative foreign markets or substitutes (domestic or foreign) for the goods covered by the sanctions, the more effective the sanctions will be. At the time of the Arab oil sanctions against Western Europe and Japan, most of those advanced nations had to meet the demands of the oil exporters to a greater or lesser extent, in great part because the Arab OPEC countries accounted for the vast bulk of world oil exports, but also because of the lack of any viable substitute for oil. In 1954, the Soviet Union switched from Australian to South African wool. Thereupon, Australia simply sent her wool to customers previously supplied by South Africa. The effect of sanctions against Italy in 1935 was to increase Italian trade with, and dependence on, Germany, an adverse effect from the point of view of the imposers. When the USSR suspended economic links with Yugoslavia in 1948, the latter expanded her trade with, and received economic aid from, the West.

(e) Foreign exchange reserves

The smaller the target's foreign exchange reserves, the harder it is likely to find it to resist economic sanctions. Countries with very scanty foreign exchange reserves must necessarily find themselves strangled by the lack of any capacity to buy what they need, particularly in an emergency, such as natural disaster or war.

(f) Monitoring

From the point of view of the monitoring of a boycott, the more easily monitored, or even controlled, the target's trade relations with other countries are – for instance, by means of naval or land blockades – the more effectively the sanctions should work. Such blockades have, of course, often been resorted to in time of war, as in the Royal Navy's blockade of the German coast during World War I, and even in peacetime, as in Britain's interception of ships bound for Beira to prevent oil from being carried to Rhodesia through a pipeline (this action was in fact authorized by the Security Council). At the time of writing (late December 1990), a UN-authorized sea and air blockade of Iraq is in effect.

If the target state is an island lacking substantial sea and air power, or is land-locked and surrounded either by countries taking part in the sanctions or by impenetrable terrain such as high mountains or desert, then the imposers can monitor the target's external trade without difficulty. In the case of the Arab states and the Palestinian Jews in 1946 (from 1948, the State of Israel), the latter would have been hard hit, had the Arabs been able to enforce the embargo by a naval blockade.

(g) Economic system

As far as institutional factors within the target are concerned, state-trading countries are less vulnerable to economic sanctions than those in which foreign trade is carried on by the private sector. In countries with a free enterprise system, since the costs of economic sanctions fall directly upon private enterprises, they are usually reluctant to support, may even oppose, the policy of resistance advocated by their government. The government of a state-trading country is not subject to such pressure. There, the impact of economic sanctions is not felt directly by the population but by the government, though the population may eventually suffer because of commodity shortages. Moreover, in most cases state-trading states are also able to exercise firm control of public opinion, and this, too, reduces their vulnerability to economic sanctions.

Similarly, taking into account the cost of imposing economic sanctions, where what might be termed the 'reverse' of the above conditions pertains in the imposer's favour, the chances of sanctions being effective must, in general, be enhanced. (Notwithstanding the likelihood that in many cases an imposer will be in a better position than the target to find alternative sources of supply or markets, a trade embargo, clearly, reduces not only the target's total trade but also that of the imposer.)

(i) Dependence on trade

The smaller the importance of foreign trade in the imposer's domestic economy, the less will it suffer by imposing sanctions, the longer will it be able to maintain them, and, hence, the more effective are the sanctions likely to be.

(ii) Size of economy

The greater the imposer's GNP, the less likely is it to suffer by imposing sanctions.

(iii) Trade partners

The more closely interwoven the imposer's trade has been with a specific country, the more difficult its position, should that trade partner be a wrong-doer it makes the target of economic sanctions.

(iv) Availability of substitutes

The easier it is for the imposer to find alternative foreign sources of supply, alternative foreign markets or substitutes (domestic or foreign) for goods covered by the sanctions, the less the damage to its economy is likely to be, and, thus, the greater the likelihood of sanctions that will do serious damage to the target being imposed, and continued.

(v) Foreign exchange reserves

The greater the imposer's foreign exchange reserves, the more successful are sanctions likely to be.

(vi) Monitoring

The less easily monitored and controlled are the imposer's trade relations (the target at times adopts counter-measures against the imposer), the more successful the sanctions should be.

(vii) Economic system

The greater the extent to which the government of the country imposing sanctions controls that country's foreign trade, the more effective the sanctions should be.

SANCTIONS SUCCESSFUL IN FAVOURABLE CIRCUMSTANCES

The five cases of successful imposition of sanctions discussed below demonstrate the fundamental importance of the above conditions in ensuring the efficacy of economic sanctions.

1933: UK against the USSR

On 12 March 1933, four British engineers were suddenly arrested in Moscow by the Soviet secret police, the Ogpu, and charged with 'sabotage aiming at the destruction of electrical stations'. Two days later, two more engineers were imprisoned. The company's offices were raided by the police, and papers seized.

The engineers were working in Moscow, on the basis of a technical aid agreement between Britain and the Soviet Union, for the Metropolitan-Vickers Electrical Company, an English firm which had sold power plant extensively to Russia. Sir Esmond Ovey, British Ambassador to the USSR, repeatedly requested the Soviet Foreign Commissariat for information, but no satisfactory reply was received to his questions regarding what charges had been brought against the arrested engineers and as to the nature of the facilities accorded them. He was later informed that a representative of the British Embassy would be allowed to visit the prisoners, but only in the presence of a Soviet official and on condition that no reference be made to the matter during those interviews.

Considerable anxiety was felt in Britain, particularly when a report was received from Moscow that on 15 March the Soviet Central Executive Committee had proclaimed the whole Soviet Union under a state of emergency, depriving the courts of their normal functions and endowing the Secret Police with extended powers to inflict without trial 'all forms of punishment with especial rigour'. News reports from Moscow stated that a number of Russian employees of the company had also been arrested and that arrests were expected to continue. The Soviet press explained that the electrical 'plot' was closely connected with agricultural sabotage, for which about 35 officials had already been shot without trial.

A public trial, however, began on 12 April. It was revealed that the charges against the six British engineers were based upon alleged attempts to damage various pumps and motors and to destroy generators in certain electric power stations, and also to induce Russian engineers to wreck furnaces and blades and to order greater quantities of foreign equipment than were necessary so as to deplete Soviet foreign currency reserves, thereby helping to undermine the stability of the Soviet regime.

Nevertheless, the prisoners' being cut off from any meaningful communication with their friends or Embassy staff and the Ogpu's methods of interrogation, during which all legal assistance was denied, caused serious anxiety in Britain as to the fate of the six engineers. Also, in view of notorious precedents of travesties of justice in the Soviet courts, it was extremely doubtful whether the courts would do justice in this case. These concerns, then, aroused strong indignation among the British public, which called upon the government to protest to the Soviet Union.

Although the British government was, clearly, unable to deny the right of any sovereign state to arrest suspected criminals, it had no hope that the prisoners would be given a fair and impartial trial before the Soviet courts, and, therefore, began to consider the suspension of imports from the Soviet Union in the event of no satisfactory settlement of the dispute being reached. The British government, however, carefully refrained from doing anything which might prejudice the position of the British engineers. On 18 April the courts passed sentence on the six British engineers, two being sentenced to two to three years' imprisonment, the other four to expulsion. The British government immediately suspended commercial negotiations in progress with the Soviet Union, and on the following day banned imports of Russian goods. The Soviet government declared a counter-embargo on British goods. However, negotiations to settle the dispute began on 26 June. The two imprisoned engineers were eventually released on 1 July and the embargoes were lifted.[1]

As Table 4.1 indicates, there was a marked upward trend in Soviet exports until 1930, when they reached a peak. They declined sharply thereafter, mainly as a result of the world depression.[2] What made the situation worse for the Soviet Union was the fact that Britain had been the largest importer of Russian goods since 1930 (see Table 4.2), taking 24 per cent of Russian exports, amounting to about £20 million. Moreover, since the Soviet Union was unable freely to use favourable balances in one country to pay for imports from another (the Soviet Union was not unique in this), it could not have brought British goods (imports of which had totalled roughly £11 million in 1932) with foreign currency earned by selling to other countries goods covered by the British import embargo.

Given these circumstances, the import embargo imposed by Britain must have been severely felt by the Soviet Union.

Table 4.1   Russia's foreign trade (millions of dollars)

Year	Exports	Imports	Balance
1913	775	700	+ 75
1925	326	424	− 98
1926	364	346	+ 18
1927	411	367	+ 44
1928	404	490	− 86
1929	482	453	+ 29
1930	533	545	− 12
1931	417	569	−152
1932	295	362	− 67
1933	254	179	+ 75
1934	215	119	+ 96
1935	189	124	+ 65
1936	159	158	+ 1
1937	193	151	+ 42
1938	148	158	− 10

Source: Beloff, *The Foreign Policy of Soviet Russia 1929–1941*, Vol. 1, p. 40.

Table 4.2   Destinations of Russian exports during the First Five-Year Plan
(percentages)

	USA	UK	Germany	France
1913	0.9	17.6	29.8	6.6
1929	4.6	22.0	23.3	4.5
1930	4.0	27.0	19.0	4.2
1931	3.0	32.0	16.0	3.5
1932	3.0	24.0	17.0	4.9

Source: Beloff, *The Foreign Policy of Soviet Russia 1929–1941*, Vol. 1, p. 41.

1951: UK against Iran[3]

The Iranian people had long complained about the arrangements whereby the royalties paid by the Anglo-Iranian Oil Company were out of all proportion to the sums it paid to the British government in taxation. Furthermore, they were dissatisfied with the fact that the Company was not subject to Iranian taxation, and also with the fact that the Company was selling oil to the British Admiralty at an undisclosed price, while giving only a small discount to Iranian citizens. This provided a groundswell of support for Dr Mossadeq, who had launched a nationwide campaign for the nationalization of the Company. He also gained the support of many traditionalist religious groups, which disliked all foreign influence. On 30 April 1951, Dr Mossadeq became Prime Minister. On 2 May, the law nationalizing the Company came into effect. On 27 September, the Abadan refinery was taken over by the Iranian government, and early in October British staff were expelled from the oil fields.

Throughout this period, a number of conciliatory proposals were made by the British government, under pressure from the United States, which felt the need to strengthen Iran against Communist penetration and, therefore, desired an early settlement of the dispute. However, all the British proposals were turned down by Iran. Shortly after the takeover of the Abadan refinery, Britain appealed to the UN Security Council, calling on the Council to urge Iran to continue negotiations. This attempt ended in failure, as the Soviet Union supported Iran. The British government then filed suit with the International Court of Justice, which eventually dismissed the application on the grounds that Iran did not accept the Court's jurisdicion.

Economic action was then taken against Iran. Britain progressively restricted exports to, and reduced imports from, Iran. Up until 1950 the UK had been by far the largest supplier of goods to Iran, and the UK and the USA the largest importers of goods from Iran. In 1948 and 1950, respectively, Britain imported 39.8 per cent and 26.0 per cent of Iran's total exports, with Iran importing 27.4 per cent and 28.0 per cent of its total imports from Britain. Thus, Iran's dependence upon Britain was pronounced.

Moreover, the Company asserted that title to Iranian oil produced in the Anglo-Iranian Oil Company concession area had not passed to Iran, and its threat to take legal action against any concern or individual purporting to buy the oil deterred almost all oil importers, Czechoslovakia and some Italian firms being the only exceptions. Imports of oil by Italian interests became the subject of litigation brought by the Company in Italy. The major oil companies would not be likely to risk a dispute with the Company, despite the Iranian government's offering low prices in an attempt to find buyers. Also, the glut in the world oil market that developed in 1953 made it even more difficult for Iran to sell its oil.

Iran's income from oil (most of it exported by the Anglo-Iranian Oil Company) accounted for no less than 90.9 per cent and 86.4 per cent of the total value of its exports in 1948 and 1950. Britain's successful mobilization of a purchasing boycott resulted in an enormous loss of the principal source of the foreign exchange with which Iran normally paid for its imports, in value far in excess of its non-oil exports. In addition, owing to the expulsion of the Company, Iran no longer received the millions of pounds sterling which the Company had previously converted into rials for expenditures in Iran (conversions of sterling into rials in March 1950 to March 1951 amounted to roughly £21.5 million[4]).

What made things worse was that Britain suspended conversion into dollars on behalf of the Iranian government of a large quantity of sterling, dollars needed to cover its imports from the dollar area. In 1948 such imports had amounted to 42 per cent of Iran's total imports. In November 1951, Iran withdrew $8.75 million from its deposits with the IMF as a stop-gap, and applied to the United States for a $120 million loan. In March 1952, however, the US Senate refused to approve it, though the United States continued military aid. In these circumstances, non-barter imports by Iran were, for all practical purposes, halted.

Up until the end of 1951, Iran's economic position was not critical. Because of the exceptionally high level of imports in 1950 and early 1951, warehouses were well stocked. In order to cover the budgetary deficit, the Iranian government withdrew special funds amounting to £14 million from its sterling account in London for the purpose of financing essential imports.[5] Barter trade with Germany had been restored to its prewar level, and a new barter agreement had been concluded with the Soviet Union. Also, the majority of Iranians were small farmers, giving an economy much less easily disrupted by the growing financial strain than a more complex economic structure would have been.

However, unemployment was gradually worsening, particularly in the oil province of Khuzestan. The unemployed oil workers had continued to be paid by the government, but their numbers grew so large that by the end of 1951 the government was unable to afford to do this. Iran's budget deficit for the period March 1951 to March 1952 was approximately 4,000 million rials. As economic collapse came nearer, social unrest grew, in part incited by the Communist Tudeh Party, and opposition to Mossadeq's National Front Party gained momentum. The financial difficulties continued, and July 1952 found Iran on the verge of bankruptcy and chaos.

The Iranian people's dissatisfaction with the economic situation increased. So did resentment at Mossadeq's attempt to seek dictatorial powers after a sharp conflict with the Shah in August 1952. Following a prolonged power struggle, the Shah dismissed Mossadeq in August 1953, and, with the assistance of the British and American intelligence services, took complete control of the country.

This led to the resumption of talks between Britain and Iran, and the final agreement was concluded in August 1954. The terms of this agreement were that a consortium was to be formed of the Anglo-Iranian Oil Company (a 40 per cent share), Royal Dutch Shell (14 per cent), and the Compagnie Française des Pétroles (6 per cent). The remaining 40 per cent was to be held by five major American companies: the Gulf Oil Cooperation, New Jersey, Socony-Mobil, Standard of California and the Texas Company (8 per cent each).

The success of sanctions in this case also derived from the fact that Iranian oil was not vital to the West. After the July 1951 shutdown at Abadan, production at oil fields and refineries in other countries was increased. Similarly, the Anglo-Iranian Oil Company was able to obtain supplies of crude oil from its interests in Kuwait, Iraq and Qatar sufficient to offset the deficiencies caused by the shutdown in Iran. Further, the Company's construction of new refineries in the UK, France, Italy, Germany, Belgium and Australia, as well as the increased capacity of existing refineries, made up for the capacity lost at Abadan and Khurramshahr. By July 1952, both the West in general and the Anglo-Iranian Oil Company in particular had secured adequate non-Iranian supplies of oil.

In conclusion, economic sanctions proved effective in this case, mainly for the reasons outlined earlier under conditions (a) dependence on trade, (c) trade partners, (d) availability of substitutes and (e) foreign exchange reserves favouring the imposer, and (iii) trade partners, (iv) availability of substitutes and (v) foreign exchange reserves with regard to the target.

1958: USSR against Finland[6]

Towards the end of the 1950s, the domestic political situation in Finland was one of strong polarization into two opposing camps. In one camp were the People's Democrats and the Independent Social Democrats, who were pro-communist. In the other camp were the Conservatives and the Social Democrats, who were anti-communist. Though the Agrarians were in some respects a mediating force, they had traditional links with the Independent Social Democrats.

In May 1957, Dr Vieno Sukselainen, leader of the Agrarian Party, formed a cabinet consisting principally of Agrarians and Social Democrats. However, partly owing to a recession in the world economy originating in the United States, Finland was experiencing falling exports and production, together with rising unemployment and a crisis in state finances. This led to differences between the Agrarians and the Social Democrats over economic policy, and eventually Sukselainen resigned on 18 October.

After a period of political infighting, President Kekkonen decided on 29 November to appoint a 'business' cabinet headed by Berndt Fieandt, President of the Bank of Finland.

Fieandt's basic economic policy was to liberalize trade relations with the West by abolishing compulsory licensing for imports from Western countries. In fact, imports from the West increased by nearly 29 per cent from 1957 to 1958, so much so that a devaluation of the finnmark against Western currencies became necessary to compensate for the trade imbalance. Despite the existence of such economic reasons for the partial realignment of the Finnish economy towards the West, there were signs which indicated that the Soviet Union regarded the development as a deliberate change in Finland's political stance, a change unfavourable to the Soviet Union.

Soviet criticism became open when a new Finnish cabinet was formed on 29 August 1958, following a general election in July. The new cabinet was led by Karl-August Fagerholm, leader of the Social Democrats, although the People's Democrats were the party with the largest number of seats, having gained seven seats in the election, the largest increase in seats by any political party. (The distribution of seats in the Parliament is given in Table 4.3.) Soviet newspapers and periodicals began to attack the new government and the political programme adopted by it.

Diplomatic relations with the Soviet Union became strained. The personnel of the Soviet Embassy in Finland was halved. Finnish diplomats in Moscow encountered difficulties in meeting officials of the Soviet Foreign Ministry. The Soviet Ambassador to Finland, Lebedev, was recalled to Moscow in September, ceasing to be ambassador to Finland in October, but no successor was appointed. China took similar action.

Further, the Soviet Union suspended trade relations with Finland. These were based on yearly trade contracts. Negotiation of the yearly

Table 4.3   Distribution of seats in the Finnish Parliament

	1954 election	1958 election
People's Democrats	43	50
Independent Social Democrats	—	3
Agrarians	53	48
Conservatives	24	29
Social Democrats	54	48
Others	26	22
Total	200	200

contracts usually took place in October and November, with the contracts being signed early in December. In 1958, however, the Soviet Union was unwilling to receive the Finnish delegation. The existing trade contracts expired at the end of November. When President Kekkonen visited Moscow in May 1958, the Soviets had offered a loan worth some 400–500 million roubles. In the summer of 1958 a fishing agreement that would have allowed Finnish fishermen to fish inside Soviet territorial waters had been discussed. Conclusion of both agreements was postponed. Finland's trade relations with China, which were arranged in a similar manner, followed a similar course, China also suspending negotiations for a new trade agreement.

Table 4.4   Distribution of exports and imports by currency area in 1957 and 1958 (values in thousand million finnmarks)

Currency area	Entire year 1957		January–July 1957		January–July 1958	
Export		%		%		%
US and Canada	10.9	5.1	5.9	5.8	5.9	4.5
Sterling Area	50.0	23.5	24.9	24.2	31.9	24.3
Other EPU countries						
Multilateral	53.5	25.2	26.2	25.5	24.9	26.6
Bilateral	17.1	8.1	6.6	6.4	11.7	8.9
Eastern Bloc	62.4	29.4	29.3	28.5	36.3	27.7
	(42.4)	(19.9)	(20.1)	(19.6)	(24.5)	(18.4)
Others	18.5	8.7	9.8	9.6	10.4	8.0
Total	212.4	100.0	102.7	100.0	131.1	100.0
Import						
US and Canada	13.0	5.7	8.6	7.1	8.0	6.1
Sterling Area	40.8	17.9	19.4	16.0	24.3	18.4
Other EPU countries						
Multilateral	72.3	31.7	34.2	28.3	50.9	38.6
Bilateral	14.1	8.2	8.2	6.8	7.6	5.7
Eastern Bloc	70.2	30.8	40.2	33.2	32.5	24.6
	(40.3)	(19.7)	(21.9)	(18.1)	(22.4)	(17.0)
Others	17.5	10.4	10.4	8.6	8.7	6.6
Total	227.9	100.0	121.0	100.0	132.0	100.0

EPU = European Payments Union.
Source: R. Väyrynen, 'A Case Study of Sanctions: Finland – the Soviet Union in 1958–59', *Co-operation and Conflict* (March 1969), p. 212. The figures in parentheses refer to the Soviet Union.

Table 4.4 shows the importance of the different currency areas in Finland's foreign trade. Finland depended on the Soviet Union for about 20 per cent of its foreign trade, and on the Eastern bloc as a whole for almost 30 per cent. In Finnish–Soviet bilateral trade, Finland supplied ships, machinery, other metal products, timber products, consumer goods, petroleum, sugar, iron, coal, etc. The industries worst hit by the Soviet measures were the timber industry and shipyards. In addition, three-quarters of the production of the metals industry went to the USSR. The Finnish metals industry experienced financial difficulties during the summer and autumn of 1958, and from the autumn of 1958 to early 1959 Finland experienced its most serious period of unemployment since World War II, particularly in mining, engineering and shipbuilding.

Despite these effects, the economic situation in Finland was under control. Nevertheless, the Fagerholm Cabinet resigned on 4 December and Sukselainen again formed a government, this time consisting only of Agrarians, with the exception of Ralf Torngren, an independent member, as Foreign Minister. Shortly afterwards, the Soviet Union normalized its diplomatic and trade relations with Finland.

In this case, sanctions satisfying the conditions listed earlier concerning (b) size of economy and (c) trade partners with regard to the target, and (i) dependence on trade, (ii) size of economy and (iii) trade partners with regard to the imposer were successful.

1973: The Arab members of OPEC against the USA, Western European countries, Japan, etc.[7]

After the Six-Day Middle East War in 1967, the Arab states had considered imposing oil embargoes against the United States, Britain and West Germany in retaliation for their support for Israel. Shortly after the outbreak of the Yom Kippur War on 6 October 1973, the United States began an airlift of equipment to Israel. On 16–17 October, the oil ministers of the ten Arab countries met in Kuwait and decided to raise oil prices by 70 per cent. They also agreed on a 5 per cent production cutback from the September level and on a like cutback in each succeeding month until all Israeli forces had been withdrawn from the territory Israel had occupied in the 1967 war. The communiqué issued added that:

The conferees took care to ensure that reductions in output should not affect any friendly state which has extended or may in the future extend effective concrete assistance to the Arabs. Oil supplies to any such state will be maintained in the same quantities as it was receiving before the reduction. The same exceptional treatment will be extended to any state which takes a significant measure against Israel with a view to obligating it to end its occupation of usurped Arab territories.[8]

The communiqué also called on Arab countries to halt all oil supplies to the United States. Between 18 October and 2 November all the Arab OPEC members except Iraq announced a complete embargo on oil exports to the United States, the Netherlands and Canada. On 4 November, the Arab oil ministers met again to coordinate the embargo and cutback, and agreed to increase the cutback to 25 per cent. In addition, the embargo against the United States was expanded to include all indirect shipments to the American oil market.

In 1973 the United States imported 27 per cent of the oil it consumed, with 28 per cent of its imports coming from the Arab OPEC countries.[9] In the same year, 62 per cent of the European OECD members' energy requirement came from outside, nearly all of it in the form of oil, 74.8 per cent of their oil imports coming from the Middle East. (Britain's dependence on OAPEC countries' oil was 63.0 per cent, West Germany's 71.7 per cent, France's 73.5 per cent, the Netherlands' 71.2 per cent and Italy's 77.9 per cent.) Ninety per cent of Japan's energy requirements had to be imported, with oil accounting for 79 per cent, while 78.1 per cent of the oil imported by Japan came from the Middle East.[10]

These figures demonstrate the extreme vulnerability of the countries of Western Europe and Japan, and the relative self-sufficiency of the United States. Owing to this vulnerability, the European NATO members did not cooperate with the American airlift of equipment to Israel. They also pledged friendship and 'offered bilateral trade agreements, technology, arms deals and general economic assistance'[11] to the Arab nations. The extent of the pledges and offers varied from country to country.

Britain, France and Spain were regarded as 'friendly' nations, who were to receive 100 per cent of their September 1973 levels, notwithstanding the production cutbacks. At their meeting on 18 November 1973, the Arab oil ministers agreed to exempt, on a one-for-all basis, all EEC members (except the Netherlands) from the scheduled 5 per cent December cutback. At the Arab summit meeting in Algiers on 26–28 November it was agreed to compensate non-embargoed European nations for the loss of supplies normally trans-shipped via the Netherlands. At the oil ministers' meeting on 24–25 December, it was decided to resume supplies to Belgium via Rotterdam at the September 1973 level. The Arab oil ministers convened in Vienna in March 1974 and decided to classify West Germany and Italy as 'friendly' nations. The embargo imposed against the Netherlands remained intact, despite earlier statements by the Dutch government on 4 December to the effect that it regarded the Israeli presence in the occupied territories as illegal.

The Japanese Chief Cabinet Secretary issued a statement on 6 November 1973 that Japan 'categorically opposes any acquisition of territory by force, . . . has supported the Security Council Resolution 242, [and] has a full understanding of the desire of the Arab countries to recover their territories.' Japan also sent the Deputy Prime Minister to eight Arab states and offered to assist development projects in those countries. The Arab summit endorsed a decision to exempt Japan from the December cutbacks. At their December meeting, the oil ministers agreed on special treatment for Japan which would not subject it to the full range of cutback measures.

When the Arab measures were first announced, the United States responded angrily, considered a food embargo as a retaliatory measure, and even hinted a military action. But it did not adopt any retaliatory action. Instead, it continued to attempt to promote dialogue between the contending sides. Early in November 1973, Secretary of State Kissinger held talks with both the Egyptian Foreign Minister and the Israeli Premier, and later sought to mediate an Israeli–Arab peace conference. Although Kissinger said on 21 November that the United States would not change its Middle East policies because of the Arab oil embargo, the Arab oil ministers saw the American efforts as a concession, and made a conciliatory gesture, expressing the hope that:

The desire of the US Government to participate in the search for a just and peaceful settlement of the problems will be fruitful and will lead to results beneficial to the peoples of the world and in particular to bilateral relations between the Arab and the American peoples.[12]

The Arabs' positive assessment of Kissinger's intensive shuttle diplomacy led, on 18 March 1974, to the lifting of the oil embargo against the United States by all the Arab states except Iraq and Libya.

In conclusion, as far as Western Europe and Japan are concerned, the Arab oil embargo was effective because of conditions concerning (d) availability of substitutes and (g) monitoring with regard to the target, and (vii) monitoring with regard to the imposer. These industrial countries' dependence upon oil was enormous. There was no ready substitute for it as a raw material. Since the Arabs were the world's largest producers, it was extremely difficult to find alternative suppliers. Moreover, their production cutback caused the soaring oil prices which had a devastating impact upon the industrially advanced countries.

Though the impact on the United States was less serious, the result of the embargo was a moderate US response to the Arab countries and American efforts to promote a settlement between the Arab countries and Israel.

1990: Soviet Union against Lithuania

In the process of the easing, or loss, of the previously tight central government control over the republics, a radically secessionist movement developed in the small Baltic republic of Lithuania. On 11 March 1990, Lithuania's Supreme Council unilaterally declared independence, on the grounds that they had been independent until 1940, when they were annexed by Stalin on the basis of a secret deal with Nazi Germany (the so-called Molotov-Ribbentrop Pact of 1939). It made it clear that the declaration was non-negotiable, and attempted to accumulate *faits accomplis* evidencing Lithuania's status as an independent country. The Soviet government, for its part, insisted that Lithuania was part of the Soviet Union and could leave only in accordance with the Soviet rules on the matter. On 13 April, it delivered an ultimatum, giving the Lithuanians two days to rescind the measures they had introduced since 11 March, i.e. three laws challenging Soviet authority, including one rejecting the Soviet army's spring call-up and one providing for new identity cards.

In the end, threats gave way to action on 18 April. The Soviet government suspended all oil supplies to Lithuania and reduced supplies of natural gas by 80 per cent. The Lithuanian government announced on 21 April that Soviet exports to Lithuania of other goods, such as metal products, woods and chemicals, had already been suspended. Lithuania is almost totally dependent for its supplies of oil, natural gas and coal on the other republics. Lithuania had been purchasing Soviet oil at the subsidized price of 30 roubles per 1,000 cubic metres, about $7.8 per barrel. Given the fact that Lithuania's average daily oil consumption amounted to approximately half a million barrels, it would have cost $3.3 billion in hard currency to buy oil in world markets at the world market price (at that time about $18 per barrel). To do this would have been absolutely impossible, as Lithuania was said to be then earning only $200 million a year in hard currency. Owing to this oil ban, the large oil refinery at Mazeikiai had to shut down, further exacerbating Lithuania's financial predicament. In addition, not only was Lithuania more heavily dependent on natural gas than any other Soviet republic, stocks in the republic were at that time very small. Without this source of energy, Lithuania's chemical industry also had to shut down. Lithuania had a nuclear power station at Ignalina, but most of the key engineering staff were Russians. Even if this station's output were only halved because of lack of personnel, Lithuania's economy could easily be crippled.

Lithuania is more than self-sufficient in foodstuffs, exporting to other republics of the Soviet Union. As an anti-blockade measure, it introduced food rationing and on 22 April halted shipments of food, construction materials and other products to the rest of the Soviet Union. However, the fact was that the economically small Lithuanian Republic clearly needed the neighbouring superpower far more than the latter needed it. Lithuania's Prime Minister, Mrs Prunskiene, travelled to Norway and Finland in the hope of securing alternative supplies of raw materials. But there was uncertainty whether the Soviet port authorities would allow them to enter Lithuania.

The West could have helped even more effectively by exerting pressure upon the Soviet Union than they could have by selling oil to Lithuania. They could have denied the Soviet Union credits from the proposed European development bank. But in view of possible negative effects the West's measures might have, such as postponement of the Bush–Gorbachev summit meeting early in June and delay in German unification, President Bush said in Bermuda, where he met the British Prime Minister, 'Now is no time for escalation.' 'Keep Gorbachev in power' was the prevailing note in western capitals. The Lithuanian Supreme Council may have counted on the West's assistance to prevent the Soviet blockade when it first proclaimed independence. In the event, it received no such assistance, merely warm good wishes.

In the end, on 29 June, Lithuania decided to freeze its unilateral declaration of independence of 11 March for 100 days, during which time Lithuania and Moscow agreed to negotiate.

SANCTIONS UNSUCCESSFUL DESPITE FAVOURABLE CIRCUMSTANCES

We have examined five cases in which sanctions were successful largely because of the conditions existing at the time. However, there is no difficulty in finding examples of failure despite favourable circumstances. In fact, there are a number of cases of economic sanctions ending in failure where most of the favourable conditions hypothesized earlier by and large prevailed. The following five cases are typical examples. In the last two cases, almost all the conditions were met.

1935: League of Nations against Italy[13]

Tension had arisen along the border between Italy's African colonies and
Ethiopia, and the first clash between Italian and Ethiopian forces occurred
in December 1934. Despite various efforts made by other powers and in
the League of Nations, Italy invaded Ethiopia on 3 October 1935. Regarding this as a breach of Italy's obligations under Article XII of the Covenant not to resort to war, the League agreed to impose comprehensive
economic sanctions comprising (a) the prohibition of exports and re-
exports to Italy of animals used for labour and of strategic raw materials,
including rubber, iron ore, nickel, chromium, etc.; (b) the prohibition of
imports of Italian origin, except printed materials, gold, silver and coins,
goods subject to existing contracts and goods of Italian origin to which
more than 25 per cent of their value had been added by processing outside Italy; (c) financial restrictions on credits, share subscriptions, etc.; and
(d) a ban on the export of arms and ammunition to Italy.[14]

The purpose of these sanctions was to bring Italy to a position where it
would be unable to continue the campaign. In the event, however, its forces
conquered Ethiopia, using all the means of modern warfare, including gas.

Raw materials export embargo

According to the figures published by the Co-ordinating Committee of the
League of Nations (see Table 4.5), the prohibition on the export to Italy of

Table 4.5   Exports of strategic raw materials to Italy and its colonies
(November 1935 – June 1936)

	Index in volume terms *(November 1934 – June 1935 = 100)*
Transport animals (such as horses, camels, and mules)	55.3
Rubber	7.2
Aluminium	28.1
Iron	40.4
Tin	15.8
Nickel	23.1

Source: Royal Institute of International Affairs, *International Sanctions*, pp. 56–7,
and others.

strategic raw materials resulted in a considerable decline in that country's imports of those materials in volume terms. Although Italy had indeed been dependent upon purchases of those materials from abroad, the ban on them might not have been very effective, as Italy had built up large reserve stocks. In addition, an oil embargo was not applied.

Moreover, as Table 4.6 shows, Italy's leading trade partners were Germany, the USA, Britain, France, Switzerland, India, Argentina, Austria, Belgium-Luxembourg, Romania and Hungary. Of these, the United States, Germany and Switzerland followed a non-participation policy and Austria and Hungary did not cooperate with the League's collective measures. Exports from those countries (except Switzerland) which did not participate in sanctions against Italy and its colonies increased after sanctions were imposed (see Table 4.6).

The import embargo

When considered from the point of view of the boycott of imports of Italian goods, Table 4.7 demonstrates that the total value of imports of commodities from Italy and its colonies declined sharply after the imposition of sanctions. But the effect was mitigated by an increase in participating countries' imports of Italian goods through non-participating countries, whose share of total Italian exports amounted to 37.9 per cent in 1934.[15] Although the import increases for those countries which did not apply sanctions were relatively small (see Table 4.8), the fact that

Table 4.6   Exports to Italy and its colonies from principal countries
(in thousand old US gold dollars)

	November 1934–June 1935	*November 1935–June 1936*
Germany	39,433.9	44,006.2
United States	28,175.6	31,024.3
United Kingdom	20,845.9	2,311.5
France	15,174.2	6,576.6
Switzerland	10,782.8	7,769.2
India	9,041.4	2,253.0
Argentina	9,024.1	3,738.4
Austria	8,468.6	11,476.9
Belgium-Luxembourg	7,249.5	4,178.6
Rumania	7,083.6	3,411.2
Hungary	6,232.2	7,945.0

Source: Royal Institute of International Affairs, *International Sanctions*, p. 58.

Table 4.7   Monthly imports of commodities from Italy and its colonies

	Index in value terms (Figures in the same months of the previous years = 100)
November 1935	117.3
December	78.2
January 1936	56.5
February	49.5
March	51.9
April	46.8
May	48.6

Source: Royal Institute of International Affairs, *International Sanctions*, p. 102, and others.

Table 4.8   Imports from Italy and its colonies by principal countries (in thousand old US gold dollars)

	November 1934–June 1935	November 1935–June 1936
Germany	31,004.1	33,243.1
United Kingdom	15,583.2	4,008.0
United States	14,306.0	17,149.5
Switzerland	12,781.9	8,321.1
France	11,876.2	3,457.1
Argentina	5,713.5	5,883.8
Austria	4,339.4	4,243.5
Hungary	3,887.1	4,279.7

Source: Royal Institute of International Affairs, *International Sanctions*, p. 102.

they did not reduce imports from Italy must also have tended to undermine the League's policy.

Financial restrictions

As mentioned in Chapter 3 in the section on restrictions on the flow of money, the financial restrictions imposed on Italy were fairly comprehensive. Circumstances were also such as to suggest that they were likely to prove reasonably effective. Partly as a result of the general world depression and partly owing to the overvaluation of the Italian lira, Italy's financial position had been steadily deteriorating even before sanctions were imposed. An overvalued lira had put a severe strain upon the balance of payments by handicapping Italian exporters. As a result, gold reserves had been falling, dropping from 7,397 million lire at the end of 1933 to 5,883 million lire at the end of 1934. During 1935, this trend had been further aggravated by the preparations for the Abyssinian campaign, and during the last ten days of July 1935 no more than 267 million lire in gold reserves remained.[16]

Thus, in the summer and autumn of 1935, Italy should have been particularly vulnerable to pressure in the form of the denial of financial facilities. However, the League's action had been anticipated well in advance. It had already affected the activities of foreign bankers, who became increasingly unwilling to grant credits or overdrafts. As early as 23 August 1935, the British clearing banks decided to limit credits to Italy. Five days later, on 28 August, French banks took similar action. On 5 October the American Export-Import Bank refused further credits to Italian businesses.[17] M.J. Bonn holds that the financial sanctions 'did not imply much more than the moral sanctification of a prudent business-like attitude'.[18]

Nevertheless, since the lira was devalued by nearly 40 per cent, the Bank of Italy must have lost considerable quantities of gold. It would have been taken for granted that this would have seriously impaired Italy's ability to buy from other countries.

Arms and ammunition export embargo

There was a marked decline in the flow of arms and ammunition to Italy. The United States, Germany and Switzerland did cooperate with this part of the League's concerted action, and forbade the export of arms and ammunition to either Italy or Ethiopia. However, Italy possessed an independent arms industry making it generally self-sufficient in that area, and exported rather than imported military products (it was the world's eighth-largest arms exporter) in 1935.[19] Therefore, this action could have done little to prevent Italy's invading Ethiopia.

1939–41: USA, UK and others against Japan[20]

Throughout the 1930s, ways of limiting the growing political and economic influence of Japan in East Asia and the West Pacific were discussed in the League of Nations. The conclusion was nearly always that US collaboration was essential to the success of economic pressure, partly because the United States continued to be by far Japan's largest supplier of commodities and goods and partly because the League could not risk war without the assurance of American military support. Therefore, in the late 1930s, Britain in particular repeatedly requested the US Administration to co-operate in putting economic pressure upon Japan.

The essential factor in any blockade calculations was Japan's enormous dependence upon overseas supplies of raw materials. To maintain its political and military standing as a great power, Japan needed industrial strength, which resources from within her main islands alone could not give. She lacked the essential ingredients of a massive steel industry, such as high-quality coking coal, iron ore, scrap iron and ferro-alloy ores. Her deficiencies in other essential commodities, such as rubber, tin and, above all, oil, were well known.

Japan's industrial position had been considerably improved by its earlier acquisitions of territory and more recent occupation of parts of China. The so-called 'Inner Zone', which included Korea, Southern Sakhalin, Taiwan, Manchuria and the occupied parts of China, increased her 'domestic' production of chromium, manganese, molybdenum and tungsten ores. But she was still dangerously dependent on sources far beyond this area for oil and a variety of other products indispensable for her industry. Japan was particularly dependent upon the United States, but also on the British and Dutch colonial areas, and Australia and Canada. The most important of the materials which she obtained from these sources were petroleum, iron ore, non-ferrous metal ores and rubber.

President Roosevelt's response to Britain's pleas for collaboration against Japan was relatively cool. However, fears that the Europeans and perhaps the United States might resort to economic encirclement grew within Japan, and her economic vulnerability was seriously discussed within the Japanese government.

Despite the President's reluctance, the United States made a low-key attempt to undermine Japan's economy. In June 1938, the Department of Commerce made it known that its position was that US exporters should hold a confirmatory forward letter of credit before accepting orders from Japan. On 1 July, the State Department sent a letter to manufacturers and exporters of aircraft requesting them not to send Japan aircraft armament, parts or accessories. This certainly worried the Konoye government. The urgent need to safeguard economic independence was pointed out, particularly by the Japanese army and navy, because of the possibility that the growing United States antagonism might eventually end in armed conflict. The 'Marco Polo Bridge Incident', which occurred in the latter half of July, marked both the outbreak of the Sino-Japanese War and the beginning of Japan's southward campaign.

The ensuing fighting stretched from Peking to Shanghai and Nanking, with Nanking falling in December 1938. With a view to bolstering Chinese resistance, the United States announced on 15 December a credit of roughly $25 million to Chiang Kai-shek, followed by Britain's announcement of £500,000 in credits to facilitate British exports via the Burma Road. In March 1939, Britain provided China with additional credit to establish a currency stabilization fund to assist China's foreign trade (mainly by way of the Burma Road).

Economic pressure was stepped up on 26 July, at the height of the Tientsin Crisis. The United States announced that the Japanese–US Trade Agreement of 1911 would cease to have effect from 26 January 1940. On 30 March, the State Department made it known that $20 million in additional credits would be available to Chiang Kai-shek. On 2 July the President signed the Defense Act, which established a licensing system for the export of military goods. A presidential order of 25 July extended the application of the Defense Act so that licences would be required for the export of petroleum and its by-products and of scrap, and a week later the President restricted the export of aviation spirit to countries outside the western hemisphere. But as far as oil exports to Britain were concerned, Mr Wells told Lord Lothian on 29 July that the Americans intended to grant licences for all British requirements.

This action was taken about a week after the Japanese Procurement Department had placed orders with the Japanese subsidiary of Shell for the early delivery of 17 million gallons of aviation spirit from the United States. Since Japan was very short of this commodity, the training of Japanese pilots would have been retarded had Japan not been able to obtain supplies from the Anglo-Iranian Oil Company and had it not been for technical difficulties in the United States impeding implementation of the measure.

Because of these technical difficulties, according to a report sent by the British Embassy in Washington to London on 19 September, the total supply of 86 octane fuel shipped or about to be shipped to Japan from the United States in August and September had already exceeded one million barrels, almost equal to the total volume of aircraft fuel shipped to Japan in the whole of 1939. The reason was that technically 86 octane petrol did not come within the scope of the US export licensing system, which gave aviation spirit an 87 octane rating. As to supplies of aviation fuel from the Anglo-Iranian Oil Company, Britain could not risk precipitating a war by refusing Japanese demands so long as the then critical phase of the war in Europe lasted and so long as the United States was unable to assure Britain of military support.

On 26 September 1940, President Roosevelt further tightened the economic pressure by declaring an embargo on exports of iron and steel scrap as from 16 October, except to countries of the western hemisphere and Britain. This measure was announced four days after the Vichy Government had agreed to the military occupation of Tonkin by Japan. Negotiations between Japan and the Netherlands for a similar agreement on crude oil supplies were due to commence on 16 October. Since domestic coal suitable for coke production was limited in Japan and her domestic production of iron ore small, she was already finding it necessary to rely more on domestic scrap than on pig iron in the production of steel. Imports from the United States during 1940 accounted for 32 per cent of her total consumption of iron and steel scrap, and 82 per cent of her supplies of iron ore.

On 27 September 1940, the Tripartite Pact was signed in Berlin. Economic pressure was stepped up by the United States on 31 December, with the export of iron ore, pig iron and a number of ferro-alloys and semi-finished products being made subject to licence. From 6 January 1941, the licensing system was extended to cover cobalt, strontium, metals and ores, abrasives and tools incorporating industrial diamonds. Britain, which had re-opened the Burma Road from October 1940, also restricted exports of key materials to Japan.

On 25 July 1941, economic pressure against Japan reached its height. President Roosevelt announced the freezing of Japanese and Chinese assets in the United States. Again, similar measures were adopted by Britain. A week later the United States banned all exports to Japan except low-grade oil, cotton and food. By mid-September, Britain and the Empire had, for all practical purposes, brought trade with Japan to a virtual standstill. The Dutch had held up all oil shipments from the Dutch East Indies. India was holding exports of cotton to 1940 figures. Some iron ore and manganese from Japanese-owned mines in Malaya was still being exported, but the quantity was very small. Ships already sailing from the Atlantic coast of South America to the Far East were carrying to Japan from South America a wide variety of key materials, including castor oil from Brazil, which was particularly useful for aircraft lubricants. But on 31 July 1941, the US Department of Commerce announced that the Panama Canal would be closed to Japanese shipping. The Japanese made a number of attempts to circumvent efforts to encircle them. They tried to export goods through non-participating countries, particularly Portugal and Portuguese Macao, but a blockade was mounted.

By October the Japanese were getting increasingly short of foreign exchange reserves. They had already made gold transfers to cover the cost of the Indo-China operation and for their purchases of raw materials there and in Thailand. They were next forced to use gold for purchases in South America. There were reports of $9,250,000 worth of gold arriving there in the second half of October. It was known that the quantity of gold available to Japan to supplement its limited foreign exchange reserves was not large; estimates for the end of September varied between $117 million and $150 million. Exports of raw silk were extremely important to Japan as a source of foreign exchange. Raw silk accounted for no more than 18.6 per cent of the total value of her exports, but it was particularly important because no imports of raw materials were required for its production. Of Japanese raw silk 83 per cent (in value terms) was exported to the United States.

Nevertheless, these coercive economic measures failed to dissuade Japan from resorting to force. Rather, they caused it to do so in order to secure sources of supply of raw materials, particularly oil. What enabled Japan to opt for the use of force was the stocks she had accumulated before commencing war in 1941. The British Ministry of Economic Warfare estimated these stocks at the levels shown in Table 4.9.

The Ministry also estimated Japanese oil stocks at between 5,400,000 and 6,700,000 tons in November 1941.[21] The US Navy Department estimated Japanese reserves of oil at 69 million barrels, enough to sustain naval operations for more than a year.[22]

Table 4.9   Japanese stocks

Commodity	Metric tons		Months' supply
Nickel	2,000–3,000		3
Zinc	80,000–100,000		12
Lead	100,000		12
Antimony	2,000–3,000		6
Wolfram	5,000–6,000		12
Mercury	2,000,000	lb	24
Tin	4,500		8
Copper	200,000		12
Aluminium	25,000	plus	
	300,000	of bauxite	18
Cobalt	700		30
Chrome	120,000		24

Source: William A. Medlicott, *The Economic Blockade*, vol. 1, pp. 122–3.

1948–53: USSR and other Cominform countries against Yugoslavia[23]

No sooner had the zone of Russian domination in Eastern Europe been established than in March 1948 a breach began to open between Yugoslavia and the rest of the bloc. Tito and his associates, who had attained power on their own without the aid of the Red Army, had a substantial power-base in Yugoslavia. This enabled them to pursue a nationalist policy for the future of Yugoslavia. Stalin, however, was annoyed by what he saw as the disloyalty of the Yugoslav Communists led by Tito.

On 28 June 1948, the Cominform finally expelled the Yugoslav Communist Party for its independent attitude. It severed diplomatic relations with Yugoslavia, plotted internal subversion, incited public international denunciation and even threatened military action. It then employed a trade boycott and ended the aid programme.

Marshall Tito's government had been faced with a pressing need to demonstrate tangible successes for the new Communist regime in the economic field by meeting the urgent need for reconstruction following the devastation of World War II. To this end, he had an ambitious programme of economic development, industrialization and business reorganization. The need for industrial development meant the burden of a large foreign debt to the West for Yugoslavia.

Until the Soviet-imposed sanctions, Yugoslavia had been largely dependent on trade with other Communist bloc countries. In 1948, 57 per cent of her imports came from them, while they took 52 per cent of her exports. Yugolavia was in the process of recovering from the wartime devastation, and the first five-year plan for economic development had started only a year before. Under the plan, Yugoslavia had been importing a considerable volume of processed goods and industrial products from the USSR and Eastern Europe in return for raw materials and foodstuffs. Moreover, it needed financial aid and technical assistance for its development programme.

The economic sanctions brought all this to an end, and from early 1949 to mid-1953 neither trade nor aid was forthcoming from the Cominform countries. The trade boycott was, therefore, certainly a severe blow to the Yugoslav economy, and undoubtedly also to the Tito government, given the importance of economic factors in the country's politics and foreign relations. Moreover, Yugoslavia could hardly go it alone, surrounded as it was by four Cominform states in which mobilization was proceeding daily, an unfriendly Greece, Austria, part of which was then occupied by the Soviet armed forces, and Italy, still intransigent over Trieste.

Nevertheless, the Cominform sanctions were not effective enough to force Yugoslavia to accept the policy dictated by Moscow. Yugoslavia did not alter its independent stance following the introduction of sanctions, and even accelerated the pace of its economic development. This was largely owing to the fact that the United States and Western Europe jumped in to help, as is shown by Table 4.10, and with their assistance Yugoslavia steadily pursued industrialization. This point will be discussed further in the next main section of this chapter.

1960: USA (and from 1964 the OAS) against Cuba[24]

After a long internal armed and political struggle lasting throughout the 1950s, Castro and his followers gained power in Cuba. Under the Agrarian

Table 4.10   Changes in the geographical distribution of Yugoslav trade, indicated by sample patterns in the years 1939, 1948, 1952 and 1965 (percentages)

	1939		1948		1952		1965	
	I	E	I	E	I	E	I	E
Western Europe[a]	72	66	33	39	63	77	37	43
Eastern Europe and USSR	15	23	57	52	—	—	33	35
Asia	2	1.5	2	1	10	3	7	9
Africa	2	3	2	4	1	3	4	5
North America	5	5	4	3	25	15	14	6
Latin America	4	1.5	2	1	1	2	3	2
Oceania	0	0	0	0	0	0	2	0
Total value (thousand million dinars)	10.3		181.0		185.9		663.8	

I = imports; E = exports

[a] This includes all countries of Europe not belonging to Cominform; it excludes Albania.

Source: *Jugoslavija 1945–64: Statisticki Pregled* (Belgrade, 1965), pp. 202–5; information reproduced in F.E.I. Hamilton, *Yugoslavia: Patterns of Economic Activity* (London, 1968), p. 311.

Reform Law promulgated on 17 May 1959, the maximum landholding permitted was limited to around 1,000 acres. This seriously affected the position of foreign landowners, most of whom were Americans. The United States, though admitting Cuba's right to expropriate, insisted in a note of 11 June that it should be accompanied by prompt, adequate and effective compensation. The Cuban government replied that it did not have the resources to pay compensaton earlier or in larger amounts, and on 2 November certain American cattle, iron ore and petroleum landholdings were taken over, and on 6 January 1960 the first US sugar plantations.

Angered by the expropriations and also threatened with the rise of Communism in Cuba, the US Administration began to consider obtaining powers to cut the sugar quota. On 13 February, the Cuban government signed an agreement with the Soviet Union to barter sugar for Soviet goods, accompanied by a loan worth $100 million. Measures and countermeasures escalated. On 3 July, the US Administration obtained powers from Congress to alter the sugar quota, and on 6 July, when Cuba took over US banking, industrial and trading concerns, rescinded the whole Cuban quota. On 13 October the Cuban government nationalized banks and major industrial companies, and on 19 October the United States embargoed exports to Cuba other than medical goods and foodstuffs. By early 1962 sea and air links were severed.

The United States also denied the Cuban government banking facilities. In July 1963 most dollar transactions by the Cuban government were banned in all banks under United States jurisdiction. Licences were required if persons subject to US jurisdiction wished to undertake property transactions in Cuba. Altogether, $33 million in Cuban assets in banks under US jurisdiction were frozen.

Despite repeated attempts to mobilize a collective economic embargo by the Organization of American States (OAS), the United States did not succeed in this objective until July 1964. The discovery of an arms cache in Venezuela triggered mandatory sanctions against Cuba, as members of the OAS saw it as pointing to the possibility of future penetration by Communism into the rest of the Western hemisphere. At the ninth meeting of the OAS, in July 1964, it was decided to sever all diplomatic relations with Cuba. All trade except food, medicine and medical equipment transactions was banned, as was all transportation by sea except for humanitarian reasons.

In this example of economic sanctions, nearly all the conditions which are thought to increase their efficacy were satisfied. Throughout the 1950s Cuba's imports were equivalent to roughly a third of her national income. The scale of her economy was undoubtedly far smaller than that of the

United States. Trade for 50 years prior to the embargo had been concentrated with one neighbour, the United States, which took more than 60 per cent of Cuba's exports and supplied over 70 per cent of her imports.

Moreover, Cuba's entire economy had been dependent upon a single product, sugar, which accounted for approximately 80 per cent of her export earnings. In addition to the fact that the OAS countries later joined the embargo, Western Europe had its own suppliers of sugar. Therefore, alternative markets appeared very difficult to find. The Eastern bloc helped Cuba through barter trade, but this meant increased transport costs owing to the very long distances separating it from its new trading partners. Also, Cuba's entire economic structure had been dependent upon American equipment. The lack of spare parts not only impaired factories' operations but often forced them to close.

Notwithstanding the fact that the United States did not seek support from its NATO allies for the trade embargoes against Cuba, Western European trade with Cuba declined considerably, probably owing to Cuba's lack of foreign exchange. This was not helped by the freezing of Cuban assets and the prohibition of dollar transactions in the United States.

As for the United States, on the other hand, its general economy was almost unaffected. Other sugar suppliers stood ready to fill the Cuban quota – and American travel agencies had little difficulty in directing tourists elsewhere.

Nevertheless, the sanctions failed. The result was that Castro became even more Communist than he had been and his Cuba more closely tied to the Soviet bloc than before. The economic hardships inflicted upon Cuba might perhaps have been unendurable, had it not been for the assistance from Communist countries, mainly the USSR. This point will be discussed further in the next main section.

1966 and 1968: UN against Rhodesia[25]

From the day Ian Smith became Prime Minister, on 14 April 1964, speculation in the British colony of Southern Rhodesia about a unilateral declaration of independence (UDI) intensified. In early September, during talks with the British Prime Minister, Sir Alec Douglas-Home, Smith proposed a referendum to see whether the majority of the population of Southern Rhodesia supported independence on the basis of the 1961 Constitution. Douglas-Home rejected this proposal, and pointed out the economic consequences. These were underlined by his successor as Prime Minister, Harold Wilson, who warned that UDI would lead to 'disastrous economic damage'. The referendum was, nevertheless, held on 5 November, with a huge majority of the votes cast endorsing independence on the basis of the 1961 Constitution. Although Britain maintained its opposition, the Southern Rhodesian government issued a Proclamation of Independence. Britain then banned imports of Rhodesian tobacco, expelled Rhodesia from the sterling area and progressively boycotted other imports and exports. Britain also called for the cooperation of the major international oil companies in stopping sales of oil to Rhodesia.

Two years passed, with Rhodesia unsubdued. In December 1966, Britain at last appealed to the UN Security Council, which resolved on 16 December that, as the situation in Rhodesia was a threat to peace, all members should suspend trade with Rhodesia in selected key commodities, including oil. In May 1968 the Security Council adopted a British proposal upgrading the sanctions, and decided on the severing of all communications and diplomatic relations, as well as a total trade embargo.

Rhodesia appeared highly vulnerable to economic sanctions of this kind. Its exports in 1965 accounted for no less than two-fifths of the national income, of which one third was spent on imports. Its GNP was relatively small. Britain, which initiated the trade boycott, had been its major trading partner, supplying some 30 per cent of Rhodesia's imports and taking roughly 25 per cent of its exports. Following the UN's approval of mandatory economic sanctions, Rhodesia was faced with even greater difficulty in finding alternative sources of supply and substitute buyers for its products.

In fact, as is well known, the economic sanctions were most effective with regard to tobacco exports, partly because Rhodesian tobacco was relatively easy to identify, and also because other sources of supply of tobacco were available round the world. In 1966, because of the drop in tobacco sales, the value of Rhodesia's exports fell by nearly 37 per cent. Moreover, Britain's action in freezing Rhodesian assets held in Britain and expelling Rhodesia from the sterling area precipitated a crisis in the country's foreign exchange position. Transport costs must inevitably have increased owing to the more circuitous routing of both exports and imports.

As a result of these economic sanctions, spare parts ran short, which caused problems in the transport and communications fields. The sanctions included an oil embargo. Admittedly, Rhodesia was mainly dependent upon solid fuel, oil having supplied little more than a quarter of its power needs. However, the oil embargo was disruptive and meant higher domestic prices and increased foreign exchange costs.

Nonetheless, the sanctions were not effective enough to topple the Smith regime, or even change its policy. A combination of Rhodesian efforts to mitigate the effect of sanctions and outside assistance saved it from complete collapse. This point will be dealt with in the next main section.

A CASE SATISFYING ALL THE CONDITIONS

At dawn on 2 August 1990, Iraqi President Saddam Hussein sent his army into the small neighbouring state of Kuwait. To punish Iraq for this illegal act violating Kuwait's sovereignty, independence and territorial integrity, the international community virtually unanimously decided on the imposition of economic sanctions.

The crisis began on 17 July, when President Hussein vehemently condemned Kuwait for lowering oil prices by violating the OPEC agreement on production quotas. However, after intensive high-level diplomatic efforts by the major oil-producing Arab countries, including visits by Saudi Arabia's Foreign Minister to both Iraq and Kuwait, the tension appeared to have lessened, since an OPEC meeting in Geneva on 27 July reached agreement on raising the price of oil to $21 a barrel. This was, however, illusory. Indeed, tension did not subside but intensified when Iraqi and Kuwaiti officials met in Jeddah on 31 July to discuss the two countries' border issue. As it had repeatedly done before, the Iraqi side asserted Iraq's claim to two Kuwaiti islands, Bubiyan and Warba. The talks were broken off, and an irate Iraq suddenly launched its vastly superior forces against Kuwait, quickly capturing all of that country.

Alarmed by this invasion, the United Nations Security Council responded with unprecedented swiftness and decided on full-scale economic sanctions against Iraq. On the very day of the invasion, the Security Council determined the existence of a breach of international peace under Article 39 of the UN Charter.[26] Only four days later (6 August), it invoked Article 41 of the Charter, deciding that all UN member states should prevent (a) the import of all commodities and products from Iraq or Iraqi-occupied Kuwait, (b) the sale or supply to Iraq or Kuwait of any commodities or products other than 'supplies intended strictly for medical purposes and, in humanitarian circumstances, foodstuffs', (c) the transshipment of all commodities and products to Iraq or Kuwait, and (d) the provision of any loans or any other financial assistance, again except for payments for medicine and food.[27] The Security Council, further, called upon non-member states to act strictly in accordance with the above decision.[28] Major industrialized countries, such as the United States, the EC countries and Japan, had already initiated their own economic sanctions.

The 1989 GNP for Iraq and Kuwait was only about $74 billion and $24 billion, respectively, making total production available to President Hussein some $98 billion at most, whereas the GNP of the United States alone was $5,201 billion. The imposers' combined GNPs were, thus, vastly larger than that of the target. Moreover, because of the Security Council's decision, which is binding on all UN member states, economic encirclement was bound to be virtually complete. Iraq had depended on imports for 80 per cent of its food supplies, its industry also relying heavily upon imported spare parts and raw materials (other than oil). The major suppliers of those materials had been the USA, the EC countries, Japan, Australia and Canada, all of which backed the embargo. So, sooner or later, factories in Iraq could have been expected to suffer from shortages and eventually have to halt operations.

Ninety-five per cent of Iraq's foreign exchange had been earned by its exports of oil. Major importers of oil from Iraq and Kuwait (under Iraqi control following the invasion) are shown in Table 4.11.

Table 4.11   Major importers of Iraqi and Kuwaiti oil (10,000 barrels per day)

Importers	Iraqi exports		Kuwaiti exports			
	Crude oil (b/d)	(%)	Crude oil (b/d)	Oil products (b/d)	Sum (b/d)	(%)
USA	34.8	16.6	8.5	—	8.5	6.4
Japan	17.2	8.2	21.1	13.4	34.5	25.9
Italy	15.3	7.3	5.0	12.0	17.0	12.8
France	12.1	5.8	0.3	—	0.3	0.2
Spain	9.0	4.3	1.2	—	1.2	0.9
Netherlands	3.7	1.8	10.4	6.3	16.7	11.5
Britain	6.8	3.2	0.4	1.6	2.0	1.5
Australia	—	—	—	0.8	0.8	0.6
West Germany	2.9	0.3	0.3	—	0.3	0.2

Source: OPEC, *Annual Statistical Bulletin 1988*.

Table 4.11 would suggest that, with almost all its oil exports blocked, Iraq could have hoped to earn virtually no foreign exchange. Ninety per cent of Iraqi oil had been shipped either by pipeline across Turkey to the Mediterranean or through Saudi Arabia to the Red Sea. Both routes were now closed, with both those neighbours participating in the sanctions. Moreover, Syria did not intend to reopen an old Iraqi pipeline to the Mediterranean.

On 25 September, the Security Council further determined measures to restrict flow of services. It called upon all UN member states 'to detain any ships of Iraqi registry which enter their ports and which are being or having been used in violation of' the UN resolution calling for collective economic sanctions 'or to deny such ships entrance to their ports except in circumstances recognized under international law as necessary to safeguard human life'. The Council also decided that all member States should 'deny permission to any aircraft to take off from their territory if the aircraft would carry any cargo to or from Iraq or Kuwait other than food in humanitarian circumstances', and that 'all States [should] deny permission to any aircraft destined to land in Iraq or Kuwait, whatever its State of registration, to overfly its territory'.

Iraq's foreign exchange reserves were fairly small. This was quite natural, in view of the fact that its foreign debt is estimated to have amounted to over $80 billion during the eight-year Gulf war with Iran and that even more recently its defence spending had been amounting to as much as some $15 billion a year. As of December 1990, its total gold and foreign exchange reserves amounted to less than $9.5 billion (including $1 billion in gold and $2 billion in hard currency looted by Iraq from the Kuwaiti Central Bank). Although Iraq and Kuwait had overseas assets amounting to $4 billion and $100 billion, respectively, all of those assets were frozen. Iraq was, naturally, no longer able to rely on generous aid from the Gulf states or on trade credits from the West.

Iraq has land borders with five countries, without whose cooperation no sanctions would work effectively. Syria, to the north-west, had long been Iraq's enemy. President Assad had felt personal animosity towards Iraq's Saddam Hussein for many years. Iran, to the east, had also been Iraq's bitter military rival. On 15 August Iraq made peace with Iran, accepting Iran's condition of abandoning Iraq's claim to the whole of the Shatt-al-Arab. However, although Iran must have hesitated to take sides with America, it needed western credits and technology to rebuild its economy. Moreover, Iran still feared that an increase in Iraq's power might enable it to dominate the region. So, it was unlikely that Iran would help Iraq. Turkey, in the north, imported 60 per cent of its oil from Iraq, also earning $400 million a year from the pipeline. But President Ozal made it clear when US Secretary of State Baker visited Turkey that Turkey would stop the piping of Iraqi oil through its territory.

Saudi Arabia, to the south, would normally have been in considerable danger stopping Iraqi oil being shipped from its Red Sea terminal. However, with US forces providing defensive cover for Saudi territory, Saudi Arabia decided to join in the embargo. Jordan, to the west, traditionally regarded Iraq as its protector against Israel and has maintained close ties with Iraq. So, Jordan was seen as the only route into or out of Iraq. However, western navies were soon patrolling off the coast of Jordan to close possible loopholes.

The Persian Gulf, the Red Sea and the Mediterranean Sea had already been full of western naval vessels patrolling to prevent any leakage, when, on 25 August, the UN Security Council called upon member states to use measures necessary under the authority of the Council 'to halt all inward and outward maritime shipping in order to inspect and verify their cargoes and destinations and to ensure strict implementation' of the UN resolution calling for economic sanctions against Iraq.[29]

One serious blow the sanctions could have dealt the imposers was an oil shortage. With President Hussein controlling 20 per cent of the world's oil reserves, blockading Iraq could have led to shortages and very much higher oil prices. The imposers successfully sought to avoid such damage by four means: (a) providing security protection to Saudi Arabia so as to prevent another 20 per cent of the world's oil reserves from being controlled by the Iraqi invader; (b) prevailing upon oil-producing nations to expand output; (c) reducing oil consumption to the greatest extent possible; and (d) initiating discussions on the release of security reserves of oil by imposer goverments in the near future.

So, at the time of writing in early November 1990, with most of the conditions hypothesized above in this chapter satisfied, a successful outcome appeared very probable, though not certain.

OTHER FACTORS AFFECTING THE OUTCOME OF SANCTIONS

We have thus far outlined a number of cases, some apparently successful, some not. In interpreting the outcome in these cases, however, three problems must be taken into consideration. The first is whether it was economic sanctions, other means employed in conjunction with them or extraneous factors which brought about the outcome desired. With regard to the Soviet economic sanctions against Finland, it is still debatable which proved decisive, the economic sanctions in the form of the suspension of trade relations and postponement of selected payments or the fear of possible military action by the Soviet Union.

As far as Soviet military action is concerned, Väyrynen argues:

> From the summer of 1957 onwards relations between the party and the military began to deteriorate. Later the party intensified political control over the military. In October 1957, Minister of Defence Zhukov Malinovski took his post. In the spring of 1956 the grip of the party was further tightened . . . in the fall of 1958 party–military relations were again almost normal. . . . It is not likely that the military would have to urge the leaders to take military action against Finland.[30]

Knorr, however, maintains that 'there is no relevant evidence, and the presence and effect of military fear remains a matter of speculation.'[31] Nevertheless, bearing in mind the Soviet intervention in Hungary in 1956, together with the Berlin crisis in 1958, one may assume that there were reasonable grounds for the Finnish government's fearing Soviet military action.

In connection with Britain's boycott of oil imports from Mossadeq's Iran, it has already been pointed out that the US Central Intelligence Agency's activities in Iran were a crucial factor leading to the collapse of the Mossadeq regime. The growth of internal opposition to the Mossadeq regime was certainly a direct result of Iran's economic problems, which, in turn, derived from the impossibility of selling oil, but the Mossadeq regime was overthrown by a coup engineered by the British and American intelligence services. The success of the coup was, however, partly attributable to internal opposition to Mossadeq, especially in the army, with which the outside agencies could work. As Roy Parviz Mottahedeh explains, 'The Central Intelligence Agency had orchestrated the coup against Mussadegh's [Mossadeq's] National Front in 1953, which restored the Shah.'[32] To attempt to assess how significant the CIA's contribution was would be beyond the scope of this study.

The second problem concerns the time-frame used in evaluating success or failure. Some countries subjected to economic sanctions may be able to calculate the losses and gains so quickly and admit them so openly that they will act, for example, in conformity with economic rationality. Others will at first stubbornly resist any kind of humiliating measure, but in time be compelled to view the situation more objectively, then move slowly and reluctantly towards an economically rational attitude. Success or failure has to be determined in the light of the appropriate time-frame.

No typical cases have been isolated where economic sanctions ended in success after the lapse of some considerable time. However, the case of the USSR sanctions against Yugoslavia exhibits some significant features. In the autumn of 1954, Yugoslavia modified its foreign policy towards the Eastern bloc, from one of antagonism to one of conciliation. On 25 October 1954, Marshal Tito delivered a speech in which he referred to the ending of the hostility between Yugoslavia and neighbouring Cominform countries and the Soviet Union. When Khrushchev and Bulganin visited Belgrade on 26 May 1955, the joint Yugoslav-Soviet communiqué indicated that both sides would foster *rapprochement* in the political, economic and cultural areas. During 1955, trade with East European countries was resumed and a substantial reorientation of Yugoslavia's trade towards the Soviet Union and other Communist countries began.

One could argue that this change in policy was determined by Yugoslavia's accumulating debt to the West, chiefly the United States. In December 1954, that debt reached approximately $400 million, of which 39 per cent was tied up in long-term loans, with most of the short-term debt requiring full or substantial repayment in 1955–6. Moreover, the interest on these loans was high.

The principal reason for Yugoslavia's large western foreign debt was the scale of industrialization from 1948 onwards, which necessitated massive purchases of capital goods from abroad. The other major reason for the accumulation of those debts was that Yugoslavia had radically to increase military expenditure after the deterioration of its relations with the Eastern bloc. From 1949 to 1954 such expenditure constituted a higher percentage of GNP than in any non-Communist country in Europe. In 1952, for instance, the percentage was 22.3. Yugoslavia's debts to the West for defence assistance were substantial.

Yugoslavia's leaders were well aware that economic assistance could be converted into a means of control. In this context, the only means of preventing a continuing accumulation of debt without retarding the pace of industrialization was to normalize relations with the Eastern bloc. From this viewpoint, the economic sanctions are to be seen as having been successful. Nonetheless, given, for example, the changes in Soviet foreign policy after Stalin's death, concluding that the change desired by the Soviet Union was not the result of the sanctions would not be self-evidently perverse. Ulam writes:

> It is evident that the new leadership as a team believed in the need of improving at least the tone of relations between the USSR and the outside world. The tyrant's foreign policy had created an air of tension

which, apart from being a source of danger to Russia, was largely unnecessary. The policy toward Tito had not brought down the Yugoslav regime, but it was having unfortunate effects on various left-wing elements elsewhere that might otherwise sympathize with the USSR.[33]

What is certain is that over time any number of vital factors in international relations may change. To prove direct cause-and-effect linkage becomes increasingly difficult the longer the sanctions have been in operation.

The last problem we must consider here concerns whether or not the objectives which the imposers seek to achieve by economic sanctions are in truth those which they state openly. If the true objective lies elsewhere, the effectiveness of sanctions ought, naturally, to be assessed in the light of that objective.

For instance, if the real objective of the economic encirclement of Japan in 1941 was not to dissuade Japan from resorting to war but, by creating economic difficulties, merely to undermine her military strength so as to ensure her strategic inferiority, then the sanctions should be interpreted as having achieved their aim. They were even more successful if the true goal was to drive Japan into a corner and to make it so aggressive that popular opinion in the United States would shift sufficiently to allow Roosevelt to go to war (which may be considered to have suited his political ambition). If the aim of the UN collective economic sanctions against Rhodesia was in fact to declare and signify international refusal to grant recognition to the Smith government rather than to topple it, one may conclude that the sanctions were successful.

Further examination of this question will be undertaken in Chapter 6, which looks at the aims of economic sanctions.

SUMMARY

The chapter began with hypotheses regarding the circumstances in which economic sanctions should work and the circumstances in which they will not. Then attempts were made to prove that those hypotheses were valid by investigating several actual cases of economic sanctions. It was found that those hypotheses were largely correct, but that they did not explain everything about economic sanctions. In particular, it was found that in some cases economic sanctions failed despite the existence of favourable conditions. The next chapter will seek to establish which factors have prevented, and will prevent, sanctions from working.

5 Factors Limiting the Effectiveness of Economic Sanctions

In Chapters 3 and 4 not only were a number of cases identified where economic sanctions were successful, largely owing to the existence of favourable conditions, but also some cases where they proved unsuccessful despite the existence of such conditions. This suggests that in situations where such conditions are satisfied there may, nevertheless, be other factors which can limit the efficacy of sanctions. These factors are investigated in this chapter.

TEMPTATION TO OTHER COUNTRIES AND COMMERCIAL CONCERNS TO HELP THE TARGET

First, the effectiveness of economic sanctions will be greatly vitiated if assistance is extended to the target, either by non-participating states or a state among those imposing sanctions which is tempted to gain an advantage over the others. Incentives which may induce countries to seek, as it were, to steal a march on the serious imposer of sanctions are of two kinds, one economic, the other political.

While a trade embargo is in operation, a country can seek to take advantage of the opportunity to profit by commercial relations with the target. Since it has fewer suppliers, the target is likely to accept trading conditions favourable to those willing to help it. The fewer the countries willing to assist, the greater will be the profit. Countries may easily succumb to such a temptation.

For instance, when, in the aftermath of the Soviet invasion of Afghanistan, the United States imposed an embargo on grain exports to the USSR, it sought to persuade other countries, in particular, grain-exporting allies, to cooperate. However, Canada and Argentina did not discontinue their exports of grain to the Soviet Union. The Canadian government decided on 23 July 1980 not to participate in the embargo, although it promised that Canada would not sell the Soviet Union more grain than usual. Argentina, however, actually increased its grain sales, asserting that the situation was not serious enough to justify collective economic sanctions. Probably these countries desired to gain a commercial advantage or, at least, to safeguard their current and future trading positions.

When Cuba was the target of US economic sanctions, Spanish trade with Cuba increased from $10 million in 1962 to $24 million in 1963. In 1965, Spain concluded a five-year trade agreement with Cuba, under which it agreed to supply Cuba with a variety of ships, principally cargo vessels, and other items. Spain also established a regular air service to Cuba.[1] Canada, too, increased trade with Cuba, from $13 million in 1960 to $31 million in 1961,[2] and diverted to Cuba wheat originally destined for the Soviet Union.[3] Australia and New Zealand helped to restock Cuba's badly neglected livestock herds by selling 700 head of breeding cattle.[4]

Besides economic incentives to help the target, there have been political incentives which have induced countries to undermine the effectiveness of sanctions. Where a group of states applies sanctions against a member of their own bloc, a state that is their political or military rival may seek to exploit the opportunity to weaken the bloc and reduce its opponents' international influence by assisting the victim. When the Soviet Union and other East European states suspended all commercial relations with Yugoslavia, the United States and Western Europe, particularly Britain, West Germany and Italy, immediately expanded their trade with, and economic and military aid to, Yugoslavia. Once the embargo had been instituted, these Western countries became new markets for Yugoslavian raw materials and semi-manufactured goods and new suppliers of vital fuel and capital goods.[5]

An excellent example in which the East–West roles were reversed is the case of the USA against Cuba. The Soviet Union began to import Cuban sugar in exchange for Soviet goods, also granting Cuba a $100 million loan. The Cuban government concluded a trade agreement with Poland. China also announced that it would purchase Cuban sugar.

In cases where the countries of Bloc A attempt to use economic coercive measures to punish a country belonging to Bloc B, the result will very naturally be that the effectiveness of the measures will be undermined by an increase in economic transactions between the victim and the countries of Bloc B. Thirteen months after the West imposed sanctions against Poland, the Polish Communist Party, on 5 February 1983, acknowledged that its GNP had declined by around 25 per cent, but its trade with Comecon countries had increased from 48 per cent to 66 per cent of its total trade.

Difficulties arise too with respect to 'neutrality'. If one side in a military conflict is stronger than the other, countries standing outside the conflict, if they know that they are unable to maintain the balance of power by supporting the weaker side, are in general inclined either to remain neutral or to side with the stronger, there being little possibility of gaining an advantage by any other course. In economic conflicts, there is no such snowball effect; if anything, the opposite is true. Neutral countries can assist the target state by exporting goods in short supply and importing commodities of which it has a surplus. They may do so by encouraging private concerns in their countries to increase trade with the target, or by acquiescing in dealings between their nationals and the target. Also, and less conspicuously, they can stand between imposer and target, serving as loopholes for the transit of embargoed goods.

An indirect export trade may develop, with the target exporting goods to non-participating countries and those countries re-exporting them as their own goods, possibly even to the countries imposing sanctions, or, alternatively, with non-participating countries importing goods from the target and exporting to sanctions-imposing countries similar domestic goods which would otherwise have been consumed internally. The reverse process, whereby goods from countries operating sanctions find their way to the target, may also occur.

In this connection, mention should be made of the different role played by non-participating countries relative to different types of sanctions. First, import embargoes are more easily monitored and enforced than export embargoes. It is easier for the imposer to determine the origin of goods than their destination. One of the means normally used by an imposer to prevent indirect trade through non-participating countries is to require certificates of origin for imports from non-participating countries.

Yet another point is illustrated by the case of the League of Nations sanctions against Italy, where the Co-ordinating Committee decided that goods grown or produced in Italy which were subjected to some process in a non-participating country or goods manufactured partly in Italy and partly in another country would be considered as falling within the scope of the prohibition, unless 25 per cent or more of the value of the goods at the time they left the place from which they were last consigned was attributable to processing undergone since the goods left Italy.

As lemons imported into the Netherlands were found to be of Italian origin, the Committee suggested that certificates of origin should be necessary where goods were imported from non-participating countries. (However, it was later found that a considerable illegal trade was carried on through Germany, Italian goods being described as of 'German origin'.)

Similar steps were taken by the United States to prevent indirect trade with Cuba. For instance, the United States today still requires countries (such as France and Italy) which export stainless steel to issue certificates proving that Cuban nickel was not used in the manufacture of stainless steel to be exported to the United States.

To avoid such loopholes, therefore, states imposing sanctions attempt to persuade other countries to join in. As in the cases of the League of Nations sanctions against Italy and the UN sanctions against Rhodesia, states initiating sanctions may appeal to international organizations to agree on joint sanctions. If the target is a member of the same international organization as the imposer, the latter may take the matter before the organization and attempt to obtain a decision to punish the target. The OAS sanctions against Cuba and the Dominican Republic and the Cominform sanctions against Yugoslavia and Albania are good examples of this.

In the case of the Dominican Republic, the United States tried to persuade the OAS to decide on collective economic sanctions, and successfully obtained the member countries' cooperation, not only in stopping arms sales but also at a later stage in extending 'the suspension of their trade with the Dominican Republic to the exportation of petroleum products, trucks and spare parts'.[6] Likewise, the Kennedy Administration made strenuous efforts to persuade the OAS to apply a virtually comprehensive collective trade embargo against Cuba. It was, however, 1964 before the OAS agreed to extend the range of goods embargoed from arms only to all commodities other than food and medicine.

Such attempts to mobilize support can fail despite all the imposer's efforts, as a number of cases demonstrate. Even when an international organization has decided on mandatory economic sanctions, not all countries have acted upon the decision. In the case of the 1935 Italian sanctions, the League's decision to forbid trade with Italy was ignored by Stalin. In the case of Rhodesia, South Africa and Portugal did not follow the UN decision.

If such mobilization using international organizations is unattainable, the imposer may still seek to persuade as many other countries as possible, particularly allies or other friendly nations, to take part in the sanctions. In the case of the prohibition of all sales of 'strategic' goods to the Soviet bloc, the United States requested its allies in Europe and to Japan to take similar action. Likewise, Britain asked EEC members to adopt joint economic coercive measures against Argentina during the Falklands War.

Even where its allies or other friendly nations reject the imposer's request, or are at least reluctant to follow suit, the imposer can sometimes force them to do so by bringing political or economic pressure to bear. In 1947, the Cold War became a reality and the United States began to introduce an embargo policy aimed at denying the Communist bloc 'strategic' goods. The Communist bloc then attempted to import most of the embargoed goods from West European countries, which desired to expand trade with any country in order to rebuild their war-devastated economies. The United States, therefore, sought to compel its reluctant allies in Western Europe to join in the embargo by threatening to suspend economic and military aid to them.

Likewise, in the case of the United States against Cuba, the United States pressured friendly nations to stop shipments to Cuba. When a British firm sold buses to Cuba and a French concern locomotives, the US Administration invoked the Foreign Aid Act and discontinued aid to those countries. Similarly, when a number of firms in Britain, Italy, France, West Germany and the Netherlands were about to export equipment for natural-gas pipelines to the Soviet Union, the United States warned that it would stop further transfers of technology relating to such equipment to those firms, should they fulfil the contracts with Moscow. In the first two cases the pressure succeeded; in the last it failed.

Loopholes are exploited not only by states, but also by commercial concerns. In the case of Cuba, the Castro government continued to obtain spare parts originating from the United States because black markets were operated by international racketeers who bought the parts in Canada, transferred them to Casablanca, and from there shipped them to Cuba.[7] Dummy operations were created in countries such as Mexico to import American products and then ship them to Cuba.[8]

When the League of Nations imposed collective sanctions against Italy, American oil companies helped Italy. As indicated in Chapter 4, some American oil companies exported oil to Japan even when the United States decided to ban oil to Japan. The 'Bingham Report' demonstrated the futility of the oil sanctions against Rhodesia.[9] Indeed, after 1966, when the United Nations agreed to apply sanctions against Rhodesia, British oil companies continued to supply Rhodesia with oil.

COST OF SANCTIONS TO IMPOSERS

If the target is a small island, supervising sanctions can be easy and cheap. In most cases, however, the target has extensive borders with friendly nations. Then the imposers may find it very difficult and costly to prevent smuggling and close loopholes. The closing of frontiers presents few administrative difficulties so far as road and rail communications are concerned. It is merely a matter of frontier posts. Greater vigilance is necessary along stretches of frontier not crossed by roads or railways, because of the greater opportunities afforded to smugglers. With regard to sea blockades, it is necessary to have naval forces (or at least ships of some kind) constantly patrolling near all the relevant ports and coastline.

The cost to imposers is not limited to those of supervising the sanctions. The second factor which impairs the efficacy of sanctions is related to the fact that, as a result of the interwoven character of international trade, economic sanctions have a twofold effect: upon the target's economy and upon the imposer's economy. Export markets may be lost and vital imports and interest and dividend payments on investments abroad cut off. Established and mutually beneficial economic links can be permanently severed. Thus, the imposer must be prepared to pay a price in order to inflict damage upon the target. At times, the imposer has to pay a higher price than the target, as when, for instance, the imposer finds it harder than the target to obtain substitutes for the products it used to purchase from the target or alternative markets for the goods it used to sell to it. Ironically, the closer the economic links with the target, the better economic sanctions will work; but, at the same time, the higher will be the cost for the imposer.

During the Napoleonic Wars, Britain was suffering from a shortage of grain and needed to purchase supplies from France. Napoleon introduced a total trade embargo against Britain. This measure, however, resulted in a glut on the French domestic grain market and the French crops became unsaleable. Napoleon was then obliged to permit the export of grain to Britain. Moreover, following imposition of the embargo, France began to suffer because of her self-imposed exclusion of British industrial goods.

This classic example is from the rather distant past, but there are many modern instances. In most, countries whose economies would probably have been harder hit than those of the targets, felt they could not afford to, and therefore in the event did not, participate in collective economic sanctions. Had Yugoslavia joined the League of Nations' economic sanctions against Italy, the damage to its economy would probably have been enormous, owing to its considerable dependence on trade with Italy. Yugoslavia, therefore, opted out. Austria, Hungary and Albania, which also had strong trading links with Italy, also declined to take part.[10]

In the case of Rhodesia, Botswana and Malawi were too vulnerable to risk full involvement in the economic sanctions. Also, Zambia had such long-standing links with Rhodesia that, despite its strong opposition to the Smith regime, it was unable to sever all trade relations with Rhodesia. The decline in world copper prices and a poor harvest, in fact, aggravated

Zambia's economic plight and made it even more dependent on its traditional ties with Rhodesia. As a result, those three countries did not take part in the sanctions. South Africa and Portugal – Rhodesia's ideological allies – could hardly afford to 'have Rhodesia lose, since this might encourage similar processes directed against themselves'.[11] Four Western powers – the United Kingdom, France, West Germany and the United States – were, in differing degrees, reluctant to make sanctions complete, because of their enormous vested interests.[12] Galtung refers to the information made public by the Commonwealth Office on 31 January 1966:

(a) Zambia: export sanctions 30% effective.
(b) South Africa: export sanctions 0% effective.
(c) West Germany: export sanctions 70% effective.
(d) Malawi: export sanctions 0% effective.
(e) United States: export sanctions 45% effective.
(f) Congo (Leopoldville): export sanctions 0% effective.
(g) Portuguese territories: export sanctions 0% effective.
(h) France: export sanctions 60% effective.

As to the cost of the economic sanctions to Britain, widely differing estimates have been made. But the cost was certainly '£100 million plus and this was one of the factors which led to the devaluation of the pound in November 1967'.[13]

With respect to the difficulty of attaining effective sanctions against South Africa, Margaret Doxey writes that 'one can cite Western reluctance to sever profitable connections with South Africa'.[14] James Barber and Michael Spicer described the issue thus:

> Too deep an involvement could create great strains within the West . . . On the economic side, while recognizing that essential ties must be retained – for example, those relating to strategic minerals – and that some Western states, notably the United Kingdom, could not afford to break all their links, a sustained effort should be made to develop alternative sources of supply and trading relationships.[15]

Some Western states, notably Britain, could not afford to sever all their links with South Africa, for both economic and security reasons. From an economic point of view, it was always argued that a lack of South African resources and the severing of trade relations could cause immense unemployment. On the security side, boycotting South African 'strategic minerals' would have been extremely dangerous, since the Soviet Union, the principal – or even the only – alternative supplier of some of those minerals, would then have had a virtual monopoly of them and thereby be able to undermine Western security.

South Africa was, however, basically extremely vulnerable to economic sanctions. Since its racist policies had made it an international pariah, almost unanimous support for sanctions against it could certainly have been obtained. Since there is no convenient route through which sanctions-breaking on a large scale could be arranged, blockades directed against South Africa could have been very effective. Industrialization had made it dependent upon overseas trade. Moreover, it has no oil resources, though it had stockpiled oil and had developed the capacity to produce oil from coal. Economic sanctions against it could, therefore, have been expected to be extremely effective. However, resolutions in the UN Security Council calling for sanctions always met with Western vetoes and the measures adopted by the United Nations have been rather cosmetic. As Barber and Spicer say, 'the Western states are the only ones which can make sanctions bite against South Africa, but . . . it is they . . . which would have to suffer the heaviest cost in imposing them.'[16]

To take another case, that of the West's economic sanctions against the USSR after the Polish government declared martial law, West Germany, nevertheless, arranged to increase its natural-gas imports from the Soviet Union. This was probably because the Soviet Union was seen as an energy source, hitherto more reliable than the Middle East, vitally important for diversification of sources of supply.

In a sense, what is involved is the problem of an unequal sharing of the burden among the participants in sanctions. The Arab OPEC countries, in their oil embargo, attempted to settle the question of distribution of burden by bearing in mind the specific situation of each participant as specified below. Their communiqué issued on 17 October 1973 stated that:

> Each Arab oil exporting country . . . cuts its oil production by a recurrent monthly rate of 5 per cent . . . until the production of every individual country reaches the point where its economy does not permit of any further reduction without detriment to its national and Arab obligations.[17]

In the economic sanctions against Poland, the West suspended all negotiations on the rescheduling of Poland's debts, which were said to be over $25,000 million,[18] and also decided to provide Poland with no new credits. According to the Polish newspaper *Rzeczpospolita* new credits extended to Poland dropped sharply from $4,500 million in 1981 to $1,500 million in 1982 (it was also forecast that the amount would fall to $500 million in 1983). Poland's production in 1982 was 87 per cent of the previous year's and in 1983 was only 80 per cent of the 1981 figure.[19] However, voices calling for an end to the ban on negotiations for rescheduling eventually grew louder and louder in the West European countries. They insisted that the West should respond positively to recent conciliatory measures taken by the Polish government, such as the ending of martial law and the release of a considerable number of political detainees. What they were in fact anxious about was (as they indeed pointed out) that not to reschedule the Polish debt would be equivalent to a *de facto* moratorium. At a series of 'Paris Club' meetings, Western bankers began to express alarm that their loans might become irrecoverable. At the same time, neutral countries, such as Switzerland and Sweden, sharpened their criticism of the sanctions on the grounds that they might well damage their interests as well as those of the imposers.

A typical instance of the problem of burden-sharing among the imposers was the pipeline issue. In December 1981, the United States, as part of action in retaliation for the declaration of martial law in Poland, imposed an embargo on supplies to the Soviet Union of equipment for the Siberian gas pipeline. It toughened the embargo on 22 June 1982 to 'include equipment produced by subsidiaries of US companies abroad as well as equipment produced abroad under licences issued by US companies'.[20]

This provision affected European contractors. Offenders could be prohibited from receiving exports of any goods or technical information relating to oil and gas equipment technology from the United States. There were even suggestions that assets of foreign companies breaking the embargo should be frozen in the United States.

Nearly $17,000 million of the Soviet Union's total hard currency earnings of $34,000 million in 1981 came from energy exports.[21] Soviet experts hoped that when the 4,500 km pipeline was completed, the Soviet Union would export to Western Europe at least 40,000 million cubic metres, or 30,000 million, should Austria take up 'its option to increase its imports by 66 per cent'.[22] This huge natural-gas export capability would be in addition to 'the 25.5 billion cubic metres now being delivered annually to Western Europe under previous long-term agreement'.[23] Bearing all these points in mind, the effect of the expanded sanctions would have been a severe economic stranglehold on the Soviet Union, since such a gas pipeline could not in practice be built without the assistance of several West European engineering companies.

But Western Europe could not afford to go along with the Americans. Energy-related trade was of crucial importance for Western Europe in protecting its commercial and strategic interests. Strategically, the Soviet Union's desperate need for hard currency militated against her political manipulation of Western Europe through energy supply. Reducing the opportunity for the Soviet Union to earn hard currency through the energy trade with Western Europe would diminish its interest in maintaining stable relations, and so leave Western Europe more vulnerable. Commercially, further curbs on Soviet energy development would reduce Soviet creditworthiness, so harming the interests of West European banks. Moreover, as elaborated on below, several major European engineering companies with pipeline equipment contracts with the Soviet Union would suffer a huge loss of earnings, if those contracts were to be cancelled, and this loss would have affected many of their subsidiaries.

In France, major companies threatened by the American decision to extend sanctions were Dresser-France (a subsidiary of Dresser Industries of the United States), Rockwell-Valves (a subsidiary of the US Rockwell group), Alsthorm-Atlantique (a French state-owned firm with a licensing agreement with General Electric) and Creusot-Loire (a French company with a licensing link with Cooper Industries of the United States). Total orders relating to the pipeline for these French companies, plus other smaller companies, were worth roughly $700 million.[24] In France, the Confédération Générale du Travail, the country's largest trade union grouping, called for a protest demonstration at the Dresser factory, claiming that jobs would be lost if the compressor contract were shelved or cancelled.

British companies involved were John Brown Engineering of Clydebank (a British company unable to complete the contract without rotors supplied by General Electric) and its subsidiaries, which in all were under contract to supply £134 million worth of goods for the pipeline.[25] According to Lord Cockfield, then Trade Secretary, the action taken by the Americans put at risk equipment contracts worth £220 million awarded to about a dozen British companies.[26] The loss of the pipeline contract was reported to threaten 1,700 jobs at John Brown Engineering.[27]

In West Germany, AEG-Telefunken, the financially troubled electrical and electronics group, was a major victim of the American action. It had won a DM650 million order (at that time equivalent to £151.1 million) to supply 47 gas turbines for compressor stations.[28] The American action threatened even the very survival of AEG-Kanis, its turbine-making subsidiary, which was dependent on licences and the supply of key components from General Electric.

Other major firms which were affected by the American action were Nuovo Pignone of Italy, a subsidiary of the state-owned ENI energy agency, and Sensor Nederland, a Dutch subsidiary of the US instruments group Geosource. The total value of commercial interests at risk in all these firms in five European countries was estimated at about £1,000 million.

For all these reasons, therefore, the American attempt to place energy-related technology under controls for foreign-policy reasons, and, what is more, to extend US domestic rules to other sovereign states in a manner which the Europeans saw as illegal, was wholly unacceptable to the West European countries. Consequently, their governments ordered the companies concerned in their countries to ignore the American instructions and to honour the terms of their contracts with the Soviet Union. Some European companies actually shipped equipment to the Soviet Union.

On 23 June 1982, the EEC Foreign Ministers Council issued a strong statement of protest describing the American action as 'unacceptable to the Community'. The Council of Europe on the 29 June endorsed this position of the Community, stressing the view that 'the maintenance of the open world trade system will be seriously jeopardized by unilateral and retroactive decisions on international trade, attempts to exercise extra-territorial legal powers and measures which prevent the fulfilment of existing trade contracts.'

Having been 'embarrassed' by the difficulties which the sanctions, originally directed at the Soviet Union because of its role in the introduction of martial law in Poland, created within the Atlantic Alliance, the United States, after long and difficult talks with its incensed allies, decided in mid-November 1982 to give up trying to pressure its friends in Europe regarding the pipeline. *The Guardian* commented on 15 November 1982:

> There are some lessons for Washington here. Don't suddenly announce a painful economic policy and expect your allies to troop into line. Don't hector for the sake of domestic effect . . . And perhaps most important, don't brush aside the imperatives of politics in other lands whilst you yourself – over grain exports to Russia – are bending desperately before your own political winds.[29]

Legal issues relating to this case will be dealt with later.

Because of the costs to the imposers, pressure to abandon embargoes tends to increase over time. Sanctions will sometimes mean the imposer losing economic competitiveness *vis-à-vis* those helping the target. In practice, an imposer will frequently hesitate to impose, or continue, sanctions for fear that its economic rivals may profit. Imposers are apt to be caught in 'the prisoners' dilemma'. This fear was seen to operate in America after the Tiananmen incident in China in 1989.

In the spring of 1989 thousands of students, teachers and workers were demonstrating in the centre of Peking, calling for more democracy and an end to corruption. The protests began on 15 April, the day Hu Yaobang, who had been sacked as Chairman of the Communist party two years before for being too liberal, died. They continued during the meeting of the Asian Development Bank in Peking in May and the official visit of the Soviet leader, Mr Gorbachev, to China on 15 May, when several hundred foreign journalists were in China. On 20 May, martial law was imposed in parts of Peking, and the situation reached a climax on the night of 3–4 June, when the People's Liberation Army shot many demonstrators in and around Tiananmen Square. A Chinese government spokesman said that the death toll was 300, of whom 23 were students, while western intelligence sources claimed that 7,000 died (6,000 civilians, the rest soldiers). The truth will probably lie somewhere in between.

Condemning 'the violent repression in China in defiance of human rights', the major western industrial countries, the United States, Britain, Japan, France and West Germany and others, suspended arms trade with China, where such trade existed, and agreed that, 'the examination of new loans by the World Bank be postponed'.[30] However, they hesitated to decide upon economic sanctions, though they eventually suspended provision of new economic aid to China. For instance, under the provisions of the Jackson-Vanik Amendment to the 1974 Trade Act, the US Administration was to cancel the most-favoured nation treatment for countries which do not permit their citizens the right and opportunity to travel freely or emigrate. However, President Bush waived the application of the provision for one year. In June 1990, when this one-year deadline was approaching, Winston Lord, US Ambassador to China from 1985 to 1989, argued in the *New York Times* in favour of the extension of most-favoured nation status for China for a further one year, saying that 'competitors in Japan, Europe, . . . and elsewhere . . . would profit, at America's expense.'[31]

PRESSURE GROUPS WITHIN THE COUNTRY IMPOSING SANCTIONS MAY OPPOSE THEIR IMPOSITION

The third factor which can reduce the efficacy of economic sanctions is also connected with the problem of burden-sharing – not among the states imposing sanctions, but among various interested groups within a participating state. The imposition of economic sanctions obviously tends to affect different domestic groups in different ways. Some may have to sacrifice enormous economic profits, while others may gain. Those groups which will suffer, though perhaps recognizing the need for sanctions, may bring heavy political pressure to bear to dissuade their government from adopting such measures.

When the Carter Administration sought to impose a grain embargo against the Soviet Union on 4 January 1980 following the invasion of Afghanistan, farmers in the mid-western United States voiced strong opposition to the idea, because it would mainly be they who had to pay the price of the embargo. The head of the American Farm Bureau Federation issued a statement that 'The President took aim at Russians with a double-barrel shotgun, but hit the American farmers instead.'[32]

This led to Administration measures to divert surplus grain to government storage, food aid for developing countries and the manufacture of alcoholic products. By these means, the Administration tried to compensate to some extent for the lost grain sales to the Soviet Union, to prevent grain prices from plummeting and to mitigate the effects of the unequal burden that would fall on those farmers. But for such adjustments, the complaints of the farmers might well have been loud enough to frustrate the introduction of a grain embargo.

Sensitivity to the farm lobby induced Ronald Reagan, then the Republican presidential candidate, to maintain in his election campaign that 'the effect of the embargo had been detrimental to US farmers and of doubtful general impact, since the Soviet Union was able to buy grain elsewhere, notably from Argentina.' In contrast to his generally tough line against the Soviet Union, President Reagan lifted the grain embargo on 24 April 1981. When doing so, however, he said that 'the final decision has been delayed lest the Soviet Union should mistakenly think it indicated a weakening of our position' and that 'the United States . . . has condemned and remains opposed to the Soviet occupation of Afghanistan and other aggressive acts around the world . . . There will never be a weakening of this resolve.'[33]

In August 1983 the US Secretary of Agriculture flew to Moscow to sign a new five-year grain sales agreement, negotiation of which had been suspended on 29 December 1981 after the imposition of martial law in Poland. *The Guardian* of 23 August 1983 commented:

> Since President Carter imposed the grain embargo on the Russians after the invasion of Afghanistan, America's share of the Soviet market has fallen from 75 per cent to about 20 per cent. The plight of American farmers (who played a large role in Mr Reagan's election to the presidency) has put tremendous political pressure on the Administration to increase this share.[34]

In the light of the figures in Table 5.1 below, and of those in the *Guardian* article just quoted, it would appear that the US grain embargo against the USSR could have been extremely effective.

In contrast is the existence within countries imposing sanctions of interest groups which welcome the benefits that will accrue to them from the imposition of sanctions. A good example is the US trade embargo against Japan before World War II. The American silk and synthetic fibre industries, which had suffered from the growing popularity of Japanese silk in the American market, welcomed the embargo, regardless of its purpose, since their share of the market was increased. Naturally, it was not in their interest that the sanctions should end quickly.

In the case of China in 1990, the American Chamber of Commerce in China wrote to members of the US Congress insisting that withdrawal of China's most-favoured-nation status would be 'catastrophic to American business interests in China and to American consumers of Chinese

Table 5.1   The Soviet grain situation, 1981–3 (million metric tonnes)

1981–2	Total consumption in USSR	210
	Total imports to USSR	46
	For animal feed	116
1982–3	Total consumption in USSR	213
	Total imports to USSR	32.5
	For animal feed	117

Source: US Department of Agriculture, *USSR Grain Situation*, 13 December 1983, p. 5. The USSR does not publish its own figures, and these are the best estimates available.

products'. It voiced the fear that denial of most-favoured-nation status would 'almost certainly result in an immediate retaliatory action by the Chinese government' and 'provide China with a legal basis for discriminating against U.S. companies', and that 'American companies would be placed at a serious disadvantage'. The letter added that 'duties on machine parts and mechanical equipment would climb from 12 per cent to 17 per cent; duties on aircraft parts and engines would rise from 6 per cent to 11 percent, and bottle- and can-production equipment would leap from 70 per cent to 90 per cent'. It further predicted that increased tariffs, 'would produce a ripple effect on American companies providing services in China, including shippers, freight forwarders, insurance companies, law firms, bankers, and trade consultants.'[35]

FEAR THAT ECONOMIC SANCTIONS MAY LEAD TO MILITARY CONFLICT

The fourth limiting factor is the fear that economic sanctions are likely to lead to military conflict. This fear has two aspects. One concerns the fear that the target state or states strangled by the sanctions may feel compelled to take military action against the imposer(s). This fear will be a particularly important factor where the price of defeating the target state in an armed conflict promises to be high, and all the more important if it appears likely that the imposer may lose a war.

In December 1935, in the midst of the League's economic sanctions against Italy, the British Foreign Secretary, Sir Samuel Hoare, and the French Foreign Minister, Pierre Laval, met in Paris and secretly agreed on an arrangement which would have meant Ethiopia's ceding territory and accepting Italian economic expansion and settlement in southern Ethiopia. However, the terms of this plan became public, the short-term result being serious public criticism (domestic and international) and a longer-term result loss of confidence in the reliability of the economic sanctions. The British Under Secretary for Foreign Affairs explained in the House of Lords that, in the light of British government policy, severer sanctions would not be imposed, because:

> We do not in the least intend to take any action which Italy, for some reason obscure to us, although the Italians may think it quite clear, can interpret as isolated action done in hostility to Italy and which may cause us to find ourselves at war.[36]

When a great power is subject to economic sanctions, less powerful states in the same region may prove reluctant to participate in coercive measures against it. One example is the reluctance of the West European countries, especially West Germany, to join in economic sanctions against the Soviet Union. When requested by the United States to intro- duce cooperative sanction measures against Iran because of its detention of American diplomats in Tehran and against the Soviet Union in re- sponse to its intervention in Afghanistan, the EEC countries, particularly West Germany, showed more sympathy for sanctions against Iran, fearing that sanctions against the Soviet Union would put an end to the *détente* which had flourished throughout the 1970s.[37] Sanctions against the Soviet Union might well have increased the military threat to Western Europe posed by the Eastern bloc.

One might, however, suspect that a key factor here was the impor- tance for West Germany of trade with the Soviet Union. In fact, West Germany was the Soviet Union's largest trade partner, exporting almost exclusively industrial goods, half being machinery and plant, and import- ing essential raw materials for its industries, such as enriched uranium, palladium, titanium, natural gas and crude oil. Nonetheless, the Soviet Union accounted for only 2.1 per cent (DM6,600 million) of West Germany's total exports; its dependence upon imports from the Soviet Union also being very small.[38] West Germany's reluctance to impose sanctions against the Soviets is, therefore, to be attributed more to security considerations, given West Germany's proximity to the USSR, than to economic dependence.

The other fear concerns public opinion pressure within the countries imposing sanctions for military punitive measures against the target. When economic sanctions have little effect, or when they work very slowly, public opinion is apt to grow impatient and demand that the government take more effective steps, or may criticize it for being unable to punish the target. The government is then in a grave dilemma.

It is here necessary to recall the third limitation (dealt with in the previous section) regarding pressure groups within the country imposing sanctions which may oppose their imposition. The government of a country initiating sanctions has to make a great effort to convince both its own nationals (particularly those groups which sanctions are likely to effect adversely) and also other countries whose cooperation is sought of the need for sanctions (the latter may well be tempted to seek to profit from trade with the target). By so doing, the initiating state seeks to consolidate the unity of the side imposing sanctions. Without such unity, the sanctions will soon prove ineffective. In order to obtain cooperation, however, the initiating state sometimes has to hint that, if economic sanctions are ineffective, then more direct methods (i.e. military action) will be necessary. On the other hand, however, by such brinkmanship aimed at driving the target into a corner the initiating state may often 'paint *itself* into a corner'. If economic sanctions are protracted without noticeable effect, the initiating country will be brought to a point where the only alternative to admitting failure is military action.

Until December 1966 when the UN Security Council decided to apply selective economic sanctions against Rhodesia, Article 41 of Chapter VII of the UN Charter[39] had never been invoked. The principal reason is that a decision in accordance with the article is legally binding on all parties. The Cold War and the power of the veto may have prevented it from being used as intended. It has, however, also been suggested that it was avoided owing to the fear that any economic or other diplomatic sanctions recommended or decided upon under Chapter VII might easily lead to military action, if the sanctions were to prove ineffective.[40]

Given these two opposite fears regarding military conflict, imposers have to seek to ensure the efficacy of the economic sanctions while minimizing the risk of escalation into military conflict. The force of coercive economic measures should be kept within certain limits so as not to make the target take up arms. Similarly, the incitement to sanctions in imposing countries should also be kept within certain limits in order to avoid later escalation because of domestic pressure for military sanctions.

LEGAL LIMITATIONS

The fifth limitation on the efficacy of economic sanctions relates to international law. One school of thought argues that the international legal system does not permit any economic coercive measures. Let us first examine this argument with respect to the general international rules agreed by the United Nations. Article 2(4) of the UN Charter requires that member states 'shall refrain in their international relations from the threat or use of force against the territorial integrity or political independence of any state.' Thus (except when the use of force is based on the right of self-defence, individual or collective, or authorized by the UN Security Council) this article forbids the use of measures involving force. The question of whether economic force is included in 'the threat or use of force' seems to have been more or less settled in the course of debates in the UN Committee on Friendly Relations. The consensus reached in this Committee was that Article 2(4) should not be extended to cover the use of economic force, but that the use of economic force should, rather, be regulated by the duty of non-intervention.

Both the Declaration on Non-Intervention of 1965[41] and the Declaration on Principles of International Law Concerning Friendly Relations and Co-operation among States of 1970,[42] both adopted in the afore-mentioned Committee, expressly state:

> No State may use or encourage the use of economic, political or any other type of measures to coerce another State in order to obtain from it the subordination of the exercise of its sovereign rights and to secure from it advantages of any kind.

Moreover, the Resolution on Permanent Sovereignty over National Resources of 1973[43] supported the position of the two declarations just quoted, deploring 'acts of State which involve force, armed aggression, economic coercion or other illegal or improper means in resolving disputes' and emphasizing 'the duty of all states to refrain in their international relations from military, political, economic or any other form of coercion'. Furthermore, the purport of provisions of the 'Charter of Economic Rights and Duties of States' of 1974[44] is the same as that of the quoted paragraph of the 1970 Declaration.

With respect to the legal limitations imposed by the general international rules agreed by the United Nations, two points should be noted. The first concerns the binding force of those declarations and resolutions. One could argue that they lack the legally binding force of treaty provisions. Against this, it could be argued that they have gradually been accepted in the international community, and so cannot be ignored. The second point concerns the interpretation of Article 2(4) of the UN Charter. As noted by the UK representative on the UN Committee on Friendly Relations, to interpret the article as applying only to military coercion 'was not to say that all forms of economic and political pressure which threatened the territorial integrity and political independence of another State were permissible; they might well constitute illegal intervention.'[45]

A second source of legal limitation on economic coercive measures is a group of international agreements, both multilateral and bilateral, concerning international trade relations and monetary policy coordination. These international agreements normally contain provisions, such as most-favoured-nation clauses, aimed at, or having the effect of, prohibiting coercive economic measures. For instance, the General Agreement on Tariffs and Trade (GATT), concluded at Geneva in 1947, declares the illegality of certain economic activities. Article 1 incorporates a most-favoured-nation clause in order to eliminate discriminatory export prohibitions or restrictions. Article 13 prohibits discriminatory quantitative restrictions.

Given these two categories of legal limitation, those relating to UN rules and definitions and those deriving from international trade agreements, in what circumstances can economic sanctions legally be imposed? The following four possible areas affording sanctuary to such economic measures are next considered.

(a) Article 103 of the UN Charter states:

> In the event of a conflict between the obligations of the Members of the United Nations under the present Charter and their obligations under any other international agreement, their obligation under the present Charter shall prevail.

If, for instance, the Security Council makes the decision provided for in Article 41 of the Charter, any economic sanctions applied in accordance with this decision become legal (more precisely, assuming that, or in so far as, one accepts the UN's rights to legislate). Here, the imposers must first be members of the United Nations, and secondly, decisions under Article 41 have very often not been taken because of the veto. The first is not a serious problem, as most states are members of the United Nations, but the second is a clear obstacle.

(b) Certain treaties, such as GATT, contain provisions under which the parties to the agreement accept the possibility of institutionalized sanctions being ordered or authorized against them in certain circumstances. Article 23 of GATT provides for authorization of retaliatory action by the contracting parties whether by one or more or all, but the institutionalization of such arrangements within treaties, bilateral or multilateral, is in fact very rare.

(c) A state can claim that unilateral economic measures, even though coming within the ambit of use of force, are still justified if used in self-defence. The state in question then has to prove that such measures are an unavoidable response to wrong-doing by another state posing as imminent and irreparable danger to its security and independence in a situation allowing no alternative means of defence.

(d) A state may seek to justify the imposition of sanctions by invoking its right to take reprisals. In the field of general international law, reprisals have traditionally been accepted (and, in general, continue to be accepted) as a means of settling international disputes. Although armed reprisals are clearly normally illegal under the UN Charter, whether economic reprisals are normally legal or not is still a matter of controversy. It is not possible to categorize economic reprisals as unlawful *per se*. On the contrary, the category is one which must be accepted as an exception to the general prohibition of economic coercion. Derek W. Bowett proposed criteria for judging the legality of economic reprisals, saying:

A state's resort to economic reprisals must still be subject to the accepted, traditional pre-conditions for armed reprisals. Those require:
(1) a prior international delinquency against the claimant state
(2) redress by other means must be either exhausted or unavailable
(3) the economic measures taken must be limited to the necessities of the case and be proportionate to the wrong-doing.[46]

To what has been said thus far should be added two further points. The first concerns trade embargoes on food and pharmaceuticals. An export embargo on food is generally considered to be a highly effective type of sanction, since food is an essential daily requirement and a sudden increase in internal production is extremely difficult to achieve. Also, the degree to which imports of pharmaceuticals are essential, even in a developed country, gives an embargo on them greater efficacy than one on other products. However, embargoes on such necessities are questionable on humanitarian grounds, and it is still debated whether international law forbids them.

It has, for instance, been argued that UN approval is required before a food embargo can be applied. As previously mentioned, Argentina advanced this argument in the case of the US-led embargo against the Soviet Union in 1980. The United States retorted that the grain concerned was not for human consumption but for animal fodder. These facts seem to suggest that an embargo on the export of food for human consumption has come to be recognized as of doubtful legality, or at least as improper from a humanitarian point of view. The same may be true of pharmaceuticals, though perhaps to a lesser extent, and the same principle could be extended to cover essential energy supplies, particularly to those countries, for example Japan, which lack adequate domestic sources of energy. Although it is still arguable whether such humanitarian considerations have already been recognized as part of the established international law or not, humanitarian considerations have often been given as a reason for not imposing or supporting such embargoes, as has been seen. A certain amount of effectiveness may have to be sacrificed because of humanitarian considerations.

The second point concerns the extra-territorial application of domestic rules and regulations. This issue has arisen both in the case of the Siberian gas pipeline and that of the American Embassy staff held hostage in Iran. The first case will be looked at here, the second in Part Two.

In order to penalize the Soviet Union for its role in the introduction of martial law in Poland, the United States instituted a series of export controls. From 30 December 1981, these were applied in accordance with the Export Administration Act of 1979 and the Export Administration Regulations of the US Department of Commerce. On 22 June 1982, the Department amended the Export Administration Regulations so as to extend controls on the export of oil- and gas-related equipment and technology to the Soviet Union to 'include exports of non-US origin goods and technical data by US-owned or -controlled companies, wherever organized or doing business, as well as certain foreign products of US technical data not previously subject to controls'.[47] Under Section 11 of the Act, it was provided that violations, wilful or unwilful, of any provision of the Act or the Regulations should be punishable by fine or imprisonment. Section 385.2(c)(1) of the Regulations was revised to read:

As authorized by Section 6 of the Export Administration Act of 1979, prior written authorization is required for foreign policy reasons for the export or re-export to the USSR of oil and gas exploration, production, transmission or refinement goods of US origin . . . Also included in the scope of this control are technical data of US origin related to oil and gas exploration, production, transmission and refinement . . . The foreign product of such data is also controlled.

The Western European countries denied the legality of this American action. For instance, Lord Cockfield, then British Trade Secretary, described it as an 'unacceptable extension of American extra-territorial sovereignty'.[48] The EEC Foreign Ministers Council issued the following statement on 23 June:

This action taken without any consultation with the Community implies an extra-territorial extension of US jurisdiction which in the circumstances is contrary to the principles of international law, . . . and unlikely to be recognized in courts in the EEC.

The EEC sent a note to the United States on 12 August in which it advanced a more detailed argument claiming that the American action ran counter to generally accepted international law. It argued that the amendments to the US Export Administration Regulations 'purport to subject to US jurisdiction companies, wherever organized or doing business, which are subsidiaries of US companies or under the control of US citizens, US residents, or even persons actually within the US', but that such a claim was not in conformity with a recognized principle of international law, i.e. the territoriality principle. The note went on to argue that 'the subjection to US jurisdiction of companies with no tie to the US whatsoever, except for a technological link to a US company, or through possession of US-origin goods' could not be justified under another recognized principle of international law, i.e. the nationality principle. It, therefore, concluded that such direct extension of US jurisdiction was '*a fortiori* objectionable' to the Community.[49]

Britain, for instance, invoked its Protection of Trading Interests Act to circumvent the US demand and on 2 August ordered the British companies concerned to comply with existing contracts. A French Minister, Jean-Pierre Chevènement, a member of the five-man policy-making inner cabinet, said in his letter to the French companies concerned that if Dresser continued to comply with orders from its American management, 'the decision has been taken to requisition' it to ensure that 'the contracts concluded with the Soviet Union are carried out'.[50]

American plans early in 1983 to renew and reinforce the extra-territorial provisions of the Export Administration Act of 1979 were the object of EEC criticism. A memorandum delivered to the US Administration on 28 April 1983 by Sir Roy Denman, Head of the EEC Delegation in Washington, stated that such an approach 'runs counter to the basic international law'.

The legal argument on this issue has not yet been finally concluded, but, if arguments such as those put forward by the Europeans prevail, the illegality of the extra-territorial application of domestic rules and regulations will clearly function as a limitation on the efficacy of economic sanctions.

FEAR THAT THE TARGET MAY BE EMBRACED BY THE OTHER BLOC

The sixth limitation relates to fear on the part of the countries imposing sanctions that by taking such measures against one of their partners, they may cause it to seek help from the other side. To lose a political partner may well be seen as even less acceptable than tolerating its 'wrong-doing'. To reduce that risk, the countries concerned may be willing to reduce the probability of success for their sanctions.

The principle may be illustrated by reference to a prewar example. In the case of the League of Nations sanctions against Italy, Britain and France were reluctant to alienate Italy, because of their growing apprehension regarding German expansionism. Therefore, neither country wished to carry sanctions to the point where there was a serious likelihood of Italy's siding with Hitler's Germany.

France may have had even more solid grounds for avoiding alienating Italy than Britain, since France was more vulnerable than Britain to a direct attack by Germany, and was, indeed, haunted by the spectre of a resurgent militant Germany. Even when sanctions were being imposed by the League, Laval, the French Foreign Minister, 'kept in regular contact with the Italian Government, assuring it that any action France might take would only be nominal.'[51]

For its part, the British government argued, Barber comments, 'that they could go no further than the French.' In fact, Sir Samuel Hoare, the British Foreign Secretary, discussed the proposed sanctions with Laval, and agreed on a double approach:

On the one hand, a most patient and cautious negotiation that would keep him [Mussolini] on the Allied side; on the other the creation of a united front at Geneva [the League of Nations] as a necessary deterrent against German aggression.[52]

Winston Churchill said in the House of Commons that 'we must do our duty . . . We are not strong enough to be the law-giver and the spokesman of the world.' He also wrote in a letter to Neville Chamberlain that 'it would be a terrible deed to smash up Italy, and it will cost us dear.'[53]

When Hitler reoccupied the Rhineland on 7 March 1936, Britain and France needed Italian solidarity for the preservation of the Locarno Treaties and the Treaty of Versailles. In such circumstances, although experts consulted by the various governments agreed that oil sanctions against Italy were technically feasible, they were not in the end applied. Doxey describes the final stage of the sanctions thus:

No extension of sanctions was proposed . . . Events moved swiftly in Ethiopia and on 2nd May the Emperor was forced to flee the country. Mussolini . . . announced the annexation of Ethiopia on 9th May . . .

much depended on Britain. In a speech to Conservative MPs on 10th June, . . . Neville Chamberlain declared that the continuation of sanctions would be the 'very midsummer of madness'. . . . A week later the Cabinet endorsed this position. . . . On 15th July the Sanctions Committee met to recommend the lifting of measures . . . [54]

The case of the US sanctions against Cuba is proof that such a fear can be realized: sanctions which do not succeed may result in a worsening of the original situation. Sanctions against Cuba helped to make the Communist revolution there even more radical, pushed Cuba into the arms of the Russians, and gave the Soviet Union a strategic foothold on the United States' doorstep. Castro became very much more of a Communist than he had been before. What was worse, the situation developed into a direct confrontation between the two superpowers. Of 'the missile crisis of October 1962', Schreiber notes that: 'It is possible that the extension of the Soviet influence in Cuba . . . might have occurred even in the absence of a policy of economic coercion, but the policy clearly hastened these developments.'[55]

HARDENING THE POSITION OF THE TARGET

Under the seventh set of circumstances, there is the possibility that economic sanctions may harden the attitude of the target state. The political leader of the target state can excite the nationalistic sentiment of the entire population by stigmatizing the sanctions as a humiliating affront to the nation, and thereby promote national unity in the face of outside pressure. When hit and hurt, the target state will tend to react like any self-protecting organism, seeking to reduce the damage and to restore the status quo ante.

In Cuba, economic sanctions were depicted as an attack by a rich imperialist regime upon the poor Cuban people and gave 'Castro a scapegoat to divert attention from internal problems and the errors of the regime'.[56] 'Standing up to the North American giant helps make Castro look like a hero',[57] and this made it easier 'for Castro to justify a large army and totalitarian controls'.[58]

Exercising complete control of mass communications and the media, while at the same time permitting (albeit in an on-and-off way) the emigration of those citizens most discontented with his regime, Castro successfully increased popular identification with his government and created solidarity within the country. This fact not only saved Castro from either having to change his policy or fall, but actually strengthened his position in Cuba, which enabled him to adopt a harder line *vis-à-vis* the United States.

In the case of Italy, the British and French governments were apprehensive that Mussolini might use the opportunity to unite the Italian people against them and against the League of Nations.

In Rhodesia the enforcement of sanctions tended to create internal cohesion, particularly among the European minority. It reduced the influence of racial moderates and those most loyal to the Crown in the white population and encouraged consolidation of opinion against the externally imposed economic coercion. Posters displayed in Salisbury after UDI said 'We would rather suffer at your hands than give in.'[59] It was similarly argued, when the imposition of economic sanctions against South Africa was considered, that white South Africans would 'see themselves fighting for their own survival, and in this struggle they would be prepared to endure severe economic hardship',[60] and that the political will of the white South Africans was 'a steel which would be tempered by adversity'.[61] The greater the degree of solidarity within the target, the less likely will any group even hard hit by sanctions be to seek to persuade their government to reach an agreement with the imposer.

The ultimate objective of the sanctions against Rhodesia was to force the white regime to abandon the discriminatory constitution and to save black Rhodesians from poverty. Sanctions against South Africa would have had similar goals. The sanctions imposed against Rhodesia, however, inflicted economic suffering not only upon whites, but upon blacks also, with, ironically, the latter suffering more than the former. Sanctions affected Rhodesia's tobacco industry much more than any other. As the tobacco industry was the main employer of black Rhodesians, they were the principal victims.

Economic sanctions that do not discriminate between the 'guilty' and 'innocent' in the target may encourage the formation of a unified front to the imposers in the target. This was the case even with South Africa. Sanctions hurt those they were meant to help – black South Africans. Sanctions against South Africa certainly increased 'the siege mentality of whites' and drove 'liberals to support the government'.[62] It was, therefore, repeatedly argued that for all these reasons the West should use contact and communication as a means of influencing the Republic.

The choice between stick and carrot is important in such cases. Should the imposer promise the target rewards or threaten it with punishment? David Baldwin assumes that promised rewards are more likely to have the desired results, as people are more open to influence by those friendly to them.[63] In Knorr's words:

Nationalism has made societies keenly sensitive to international affront. Rather than promoting political disintegration in the target state, coercive trade sanctions tend to foster political integration.[64]

Galtung describes the situation thus:

Sanctions may give the leaders pretexts to demonstrate their ability to share the plight of the people . . . in general the thesis that economic sanctions, at least to start with, will have a tendency to create social and political integration rather than disintegration seems to be a relatively strong one.[65]

Economic sanctions may thus, where this limitation operates, even exacerbate the situation and make the target more intractable.

DEFENSIVE MEASURES BY THE TARGET

The eighth limitation stems from the fact that, when economic sanctions are proposed and imposed, the target will naturally not be passive, but will take all possible defensive action. The efficacy of sanctions will be diminished where the target is able to accumulate stocks of goods during the period between the time sanctions are first canvassed and the date they come into force. A similar result will occur if the target realigns its economy so as to bring about a rapid decrease in export–import trade with the imposer and a shift towards trade with non-imposers and increases domestic production.

Moreover, the target may also resort to retaliatory counter-measures, such as nationalizing the property of the imposer or its citizens, freezing funds deposited within the target state or cancelling its debts to the imposer. Though it may take time, the target will seek to adjust its economy so as to reduce dependence upon that of the imposer. It will try to find new trade partners – new markets for its exports and new suppliers of imports. Such a response was seen in most of the cases discussed. Several years after the imposition of sanctions against Cuba, her capital goods stocks had gradually been replenished by new equipment from the Soviet Union and Western Europe, thus alleviating the spare-parts crisis.

Also, the target may seek to increase its self-sufficiency by, for example, stockpiling commodities expected to be in short supply, diversifying its production, diverting resources from export industries to import substitution. Italy, for instance, faced with the League of Nations' sanctions, adopted this approach, drastically reducing imports of non-essential goods, particularly those not essential for the conduct of the campaign in Abyssinia and the maintenance of the Italian war machine. Japan, having anticipated the imposition of sanctions, took preventive action well in advance.

In Rhodesia, the Smith regime stockpiled vital foreign goods, also trading through South Africa and other adjacent countries, and introduced exchange controls, domestic rationing and a strict monetary and fiscal policy. It also withheld debt-servicing and dividend payments abroad, and encouraged import-substitution industries. In 1971, exports were close to pre-sanctions levels. National income in real terms was at its lowest level in 1966, but in 1967 began to turn upward. Imports also increased in 1967, reached pre-sanctions levels in 1968 and even exceeded them in 1971.

If sanctions fail to attain quick, clear-cut success, their effectiveness tends to diminish with time, with the possibility of success becoming increasingly remote. Once the target has made itself independent of the imposer, sanctions continued or newly applied by that imposer can hardly again damage the target's economy. Before the imposition of the grain ban against the Soviet Union, the United States' share of Soviet grain imports was nearly 60 per cent, but it fell to about 20 per cent after the ban.[66] Only if the Soviets resumed the pre-sanctions level of grain purchases from the United States could the same kind of sanction against the Soviet Union ever again have the same impact.

Ironically enough, sanctions sometimes have a desirable effect on the target's economy. For example, sanctions against Rhodesia even helped its economy at that time, since it responded by withholding debt-servicing and dividend payments abroad and mitigated the shortages in its foreign exchange reserves which had existed before the sanctions. Sanctions may also serve as a form of involuntary protection which, where an 'embryo' industry exists, may well have beneficial effects for the target's economy in the long term. As Grieve puts it: 'The stimulus to restructure the country's economy away from the weakness of the colonial phase is, in the long term, beneficial rather than harmful.'[67]

All such defensive measures adopted by the target must, clearly, be counted as limiting the efficacy of economic sanctions.

SUMMARY

It can thus be seen that in most cases there are factors which limit the efficacy of economic sanctions. Imposers have sought ways and means to evade or overcome them, or to keep their impact to a minimum. However, these factors mean that in any given case the effectiveness of economic sanctions will almost always be in doubt. Notwithstanding this fact, states seem today to be more inclined than ever to resort to economic sanctions, rather than to military sanctions. In the following chapter the reasons for this will be considered and also what other goals economic sanctions may have.

6 The Aims of Economic Sanctions

Thus far the usefulness of economic sanctions as an instrument of foreign policy has been examined and the types and efficacy of such sanctions and the factors limiting their effectiveness have been looked at. In this chapter what kinds of objectives and goals states have when they choose economic sanctions from among the various means available, and why they choose them, will be considered.

The study of particular cases of sanctions reveals that the imposers have almost always set out and proclaimed their objectives. It is also clear that the objectives in pursuit of which sanctions are imposed are far from simple or straightforward.

The limitations elaborated on in Chapter 5 are such that the effectiveness of the sanctions contemplated must always remain in doubt. Certainly, failure to attain the goals proclaimed is likely to reflect badly on the imposers and undermine their prestige at home and internationally. So far, however, there have been no signs that states are becoming any more reluctant to resort to economic sanctions – quite the contrary. The question, therefore, arises why states are so disposed to use them. This question, in fact, suggests that there might be other, hidden goals, distinct from those proclaimed.

PROCLAIMED AND HIDDEN GOALS

Before attempting to discover what those hidden goals may be, it should first be established what aims have been proclaimed in the various cases of economic sanctions. As defined in Chapter 2, economic sanctions are designed to punish the target because of its breach of certain rules and/or to prevent the target from infringing rules which the imposer deems important. Here, the expression 'certain rules' is not narrowly limited to legal rules, but includes political principles etc.

In the case of the League of Nations sanctions against Italy, the rule which the imposers attempted to make the target observe was a legal one expressly stipulated in the Covenant of the League of Nations. The League decided that Italy's invasion of Abyssinia constituted a use of military force against a fellow member of the League in contravention of the obligation under Article XII of the Covenant not to resort to war until three months after the award by the arbitrators or the official decision, etc. In the case of Rhodesia, the UN Security Council decided that the illegal nature of Rhodesia's Unilateral Declaration of Independence and its repressive domestic policies with regard to its black population were in contravention of the Charter of the United Nations.

Similarly, in the cases of Britain and Iran in 1951, the USA and Cuba in 1960 and France and Algeria in 1971, the rule the imposers invoked was a legal one, i.e. appropriate compensation should be paid when states nationalize foreign concerns within their territories. In the case of the USA against the Dominican Republic, the rule once more had a legal character. The United States, and later the OAS, insisted that the Dominican plot to assassinate the President of Venezuela violated the legal principle of non-intervention.

In the case of the Arab oil embargo against the United States, the EEC and Japan, the Arab states insisted that the target states should support Arab demands that Israel should surrender all the Arab lands which it had occupied in the war of 1967. Here, too, the rule in question had, to some extent, a legal character, in that Israel's occupation of those lands was asserted to be illegal, though, as the targets may be said to have had no clear legal obligation to support the Arab states, it could also be seen as a political rule. Likewise, when the United States, the EEC member states and Japan adopted economic sanctions against Poland, the imposers argued that 'imposition of martial law . . . , the massive violation of human rights and the suppression of fundamental civil liberties [were] in contravention of the United Nations Charter, the Universal Declaration on Human Rights and the Final Act of Helsinki'.[1]

On the other hand, the rule involved can be a political principle (for example, the 'rule of friendship'). In such cases acceptance is, of course, often less general, in some cases only the imposer seeing the principle as a rule. In the cases of the USSR against Yugoslavia in 1948, against China in 1960 and against Albania in 1961, the rule which the Soviet Union invoked was a mere political principle which she alone (with perhaps some of her satellite states) held to be a rule. In these cases the Soviet Union regarded the targets as disloyal allies and clearly announced that Moscow expected them to return to the fold.

Some might be tempted to claim that most economic sanctions ended in failure, considering that they were unable to attain their proclaimed goals. However, if there are other objectives, or if the true aim lies elsewhere, the effectiveness of economic sanctions ought to be evaluated with respect to those other objectives, or that true aim, also. In what follows an attempt will be made to categorize and exemplify other objectives (or considerations) that have played a part in economic sanctions.

The rule-making effect

By imposing economic sanctions and announcing publicly the reason why the target deserves to be punished, the imposer can let the world (not just the target) know what principles it considers to be rules which members of a particular grouping should observe, and that it is prepared to punish any member offending against those principles. A good example is provided by the case of the USA against Cuba. Soon after seizing power in Cuba in 1959, Fidel Castro increased the power of the Cuban Communist Party and became more radical in his policy. From early 1960, Cuba's economic ties with the Soviet Union were progressively strengthened. Although the direct reason for the USA's initiating economic sanctions was Cuba's nationalization of oil refineries owned by the American companies Texaco and Esso, which had refused to process Soviet crude oil, the real goals of the sanctions lay elsewhere. This was made clear by the then Secretary of State, Dean Rusk, who explained that the objectives were: 'To reduce Castro's will and ability to export subversion and violence to other American states: . . . to demonstrate to the peoples of the American Republics that communism has no future in the Western hemisphere.'[2]

Similarly, in the case of the USA against the Dominican Republic, the United States wished to be able to frustrate by means of economic sanctions the emergence of another revolutionary regime in the Caribbean on the model of Castro's Cuba, though the immediate reason for imposing economic sanctions was Trujillo's attempted assassination of the President of Venezuela.

In the case of the Soviet economic sanctions against Yugoslavia, which were well supported by the other Cominform countries, the main, declared objective was to bring Yugoslavia, which had become a 'disloyal' ally of the Soviet Union, back into the fold. However, it is easy to see the sanctions as to some extent being also a warning to other Eastern bloc states, implying that similar punishment would be meted out at them should they fail to toe the line.

Tito's attempt to base Yugoslavia's economic development upon the concept of Yugoslavia's national interest involving ambitious plans for industrialization ran counter to Russia's economic strategy, under which the Soviet Union was to supply heavy industry products while Yugoslavia concentrated on developing its rich mineral resources. Yugoslavia also declined to establish a range of cooperative joint ventures similar to those initiated in other Eastern bloc countries, obviously to the advantage of the Soviet Union.

For the Russians, Tito's independent stance was a challenge to Stalin's expectations of disciplined subordination to the Soviet Union. To have overlooked Tito's lack of respect would have been a dangerous precedent threatening the unity of the whole bloc. The Soviet Union must have thought that punitive measures against this 'satellite' state would serve as a lesson to the other members of the bloc, nipping in the bud any tendency to deviate. In taking such action, the Soviet Union presumably was also concerned to perpetuate the existing pattern of economic relations with her satellite states.

In these cases, the imposers, the USA and the USSR, showed not only every member of their spheres of influence, Latin America and the Eastern bloc respectively, but also their political opponents, that the target's activities were disapproved of, and that they were determined to mobilize collective measures to suppress similar activities by any other member. Even where economic sanctions cannot attain the proclaimed goal, they still have the value of doing something, since doing nothing can be seen as tantamount to acquiescence. The imposer uses sanctions with a view to declaring what it deems to be the norms of the grouping it belongs to (be it a universal or regional international organization). By so doing, it seeks to let each member know that any rule-breaking activity will be met resolutely with sanctions.

One of the objectives of Mr Gorbachev's economic blockade of Lithuania in 1990 was to make other republics slow their rush to independence. Movements for self-determination were gaining momentum in several Soviet republics. In Moldavia a new association had been set up which sought closer ties with Romania. In Kiev, the capital of the Ukraine, former dissidents were in control of the republic's government and refusing to obey the Communist party's leaders. Moreover, in one Baltic republic, Latvia, the Supreme Council adopted a declaration that the annexation of Latvia into the Soviet Union was illegal, and that a transitional system should be allowed pending its attainment of complete independence. A very similar declaration was issued by the Supreme Council of the third Baltic republic, Estonia. The councils of these two Baltic republics declared the illegality of their annexation by the Soviet Union, but without explicitly making unilateral declarations of independence from the Soviet Union. In fact, Gorbachev did not specifically call upon the Lithuanians to abandon their claim to independence. He simply demanded that they restore the republic's position to that of 10 March 1990. One could assume that Mr Gorbachev may have intended to imply that he might be prepared to concede the right to independence, but not by virtue of a unilateral declaration of independence. He may have meant this although, or because, he was faced with tremendous difficulty in pursuing *perestroika*, and had to tread carefully.

Such a function of economic sanctions may be described as the 'rule-making effect', 'rule-declaring effect' or 'rule-implying effect'. This is certainly one of the goals with which they are imposed.

To this should be added the 'rule-maintaining effect'. One of the reasons why France and Britain participated in the League's economic sanctions against Italy, though haunted by the resurgence of a militant Germany and, therefore, reluctant to offend one of their most important allies in Europe, was that failure to punish a violator of the Covenant would undermine the status quo established after World War I.

The demonstration effect

In many cases, imposers have invoked international law or referred to the common interests of a certain group of nations in the attempt to establish that they have justice on their side in imposing sanctions. However, conversely, as it were, economic sanctions may be imposed in order to demonstrate to the world, by the taking of decisive *public* action, the imposer's firm conviction of the justice of its position or cause. In such cases, by so doing, the imposers have sought to mobilize world opinion to put pressure on the target.

Following the institution of the Arab oil embargo against the Western industrial powers in 1973, the Arab oil ministers issued a communiqué on 22 March 1974, stating that the 'basic objective' of their measures was 'to draw world attention to the Arab question in order to create an atmosphere conducive to the implementation of UN Security Council Resolution 242 calling for total withdrawal from occupied Arab territories and the restoration of the legitimate rights of the Palestinian people'.[3]

Immediately after the Korean airliner was shot down by Soviet fighters, the United States on 7 September 1983 ordered the closure of all Soviet airline offices in the USA, and banned American airlines from arranging any connecting flights with Aeroflot. President Reagan then issued a statement on television in which he referred to:

The attack by the Soviet Union against 269 innocent men, women and children aboard an unarmed Korean passenger plane . . . This crime against humanity must never be forgotten . . . throughout the world . . .

This was the Soviet Union against the world and the moral precepts which guide human relations among people everywhere . . .[4]

Such 'sanctions' could not be expected to, and did not in fact, change the attitude of the Soviet Union, but were effective in galvanizing criticism of her around the world.

When the West announced sanctions against China after the Tiananmen incident, the principal emphasis was on the effect of condemning the violent repression of demonstrations, holding up to the world's gaze the brutal, anti-democratic act of the Chinese government and discrediting that government, rather than on the possibility of stopping the forcible suppression by inflicting economic hardship. As previously described, the Western economic sanctions against China were far from full-scale, so much so that no one could suppose that the imposers aimed at damaging the Chinese economy enough to compel the Chinese government to change its policy. The imposition of sanctions was, in fact, effective in drawing world attention to what was happening in China and, it seems clear, in affecting other governments' evaluation of this incident.

Such goals may be termed the 'demonstration effect'. The imposer attempts to achieve these effects by trumpeting the illegality of the target's activities and discrediting the target, for the purpose of securing the concerted pressure of international public opinion on the target. It is not always necessary to impose economic sanctions to obtain such an effect. Simply to voice strong criticism of the wrong-doer may, on occasion, be enough to attain this effect. But, since economic sanctions normally attract far more world attention, they are often considered necessary.

Satisfying (or placating) domestic public opinion

No government, particularly not a democratic government, can really ignore calls by public opinion for it to take resolute action against transgressors of rules of the international community etc. In such cases, the government may be compelled, especially when elections are approaching, not merely to denounce the transgression, which may not be enough to satisfy public opinion, but to resort to concrete measures, most typically to economic sanctions.

We should here look at what happened in Britain when it was imposing economic sanctions against Italy. In the 1935 election campaign the government supported the League of Nations and took a firm stand against Italy's invasion of Abyssinia. Four days after the elections (in which the National Government was returned), however, Britain imposed only limited sanctions. Referring to criticism that failure to introduce the oil embargo would be letting down the League and that public opinion would not stand for it, Sir Maurice Hankey, then Cabinet Secretary, wrote quite candidly, in his diary: 'The Government had won the election decisively. They no longer had to angle for votes from the left wing and could do what they liked.'[5]

When relations between the United States and Cuba deteriorated early in 1960, the American public demanded that the Administration take decisive action against Castro, who was loudly defying the United States.[6] George Sokolsky commented:

> Many were angered by what they considered a failure to appreciate the importance of US trade. Most did not understand Eisenhower's 'policy of patience' and wanted to hit back at the 'speck of a country' which was spitting in our face.[7]

Before the Administration took any concrete action, Congress amended existing laws which laid down the import quota for Cuban sugar. Both Democrats and Republicans had to take account of the presidential election in November. The Democrats, who had a majority in Congress, hesitated to give the powers asked for to a Republican President, but in the end they gave way, since anti-Cuban feeling grew stronger.[8]

Only two weeks before election day in November 1960, President Eisenhower announced the US export embargo against Cuba, probably in an effort to help the Republican candidate, Richard Nixon. Kennedy also promised the electorate to 'do something' about Castro.[9] Regardless of its real impact upon the target, the government of the imposer state may consider economic sanctions useful because they serve to deflect domestic public criticism or demands, appearing to constitute decisive action. When military action is, for one reason or another, impossible, and when doing nothing would be seen as an admission of incompetence or powerlessness, something has to be done. Economic sanctions meet this need.

To take another example, when Britain decided to penalize Rhodesia, Prime Minister Harold Wilson did not forget the party-political situation. According to Richard Crossman, Wilson was determined 'not to leave his flank open to Heath' and to make sure that the Labour government 'can't be blamed'.[10] In the Korean airliner case, President Reagan was faced with enormous pressure from enraged public opinion and Congressmen, particularly right-wingers. On the other hand, since the Intermediate Nuclear Force reduction talks were then at a critical stage, the US Administration may have considered it inadvisable to jeopardize the talks by full-scale economic and political sanctions, not to mention military action. So Reagan attempted to placate public opinion by taking the steps already mentioned. Congressional leaders of both parties generally agreed that 'he hit the right note'.[11] Nevertheless, right-wing conservatives, such as Richard Viguerie, criticized Reagan's measures as 'namby pamby'.[12] Other conservative leaders commented that 'he [Reagan] had lost a great opportunity for decisive leadership and let down the American public.'[13]

Finally, reference should be made to the mounting domestic pressure upon President Reagan that followed the declaration of martial law by the Polish government on 13 December 1981. On 22 December 1981, the Chairman of the Polish American Council urged the President to adopt sanctions against Poland and the Soviet Union. The same day, the International Longshoremen's Association decided to refuse to handle any ship bound for Poland. The President of the AFL-CIO (American Federation of Labor – Congress of Industrial Organizations) also made a strong appeal to President Reagan. These pressures were followed by the President's decision to announce comprehensive sanctions against the Soviet Union on 22 December.

Thus, placating domestic public opinion can be one of the objectives of economic sanctions.

Satisfying international public opinion

Failure to satisfy the demands of domestic public opinion can shift public support from the governing political party to the opposition in the domestic political arena. This fear, as we saw in the previous section, often causes the government to opt for economic sanctions. Likewise, failure to satisfy international public opinion calling for the punishment of wrong-doers may mean a shift in international public opinion support to the other bloc.

With respect to economic sanctions against Rhodesia, there was undoubtedly strong pressure from Organization of African Unity members, both within the Commonwealth and at the United Nations. After Rhodesia's declaration of independence in November 1964, Britain initiated negotiations with the Smith regime. The negotiations were protracted and there was enormous and continuous pressure on Britain at the United Nations, in meetings of Commonwealth prime ministers and through the Organization of African States, not only to frustrate the Smith regime's assertion of independence but to take more direct responsibility for African political advancement in Rhodesia.

Ignoring the OAU's calls for sanctions might have resulted in its being tempted to look elsewhere for assistance. President Nyerere of Zambia enlarged on the point thus:

> If the West fails to bring down Smith or, having defeated him, fails to establish conditions which will lead to majority rule before independence, then Africa will have to take up the challenge . . . Africa's economic and military weakness means that she would have to find allies. It is worth considering whether . . . it will then still be true to say that the Cold War does not enter into the situation and that the 'Communist bogey' is a non-sensical red-herring . . . Free Africa is not waiting . . . to see whether the West really intends to stand on the side of human equality and human freedom.[14]

Such opinions can be assumed to have influenced the final decision to impose sanctions, first by Britain and later by other Western industrial countries, especially the United States.

Britain then promised the African member states of the Commonwealth that, if the talks between Prime Ministers Wilson and Smith on board *HMS Tiger* 'got nowhere', Britain would apply to the UN Security Council for mandatory economic sanctions. The talks failed, and Britain abided by that undertaking. On 16 December 1966, the Security Council decided, acting in accordance with Articles 39 and 41 of the Charter, that 'the present situation in Southern Rhodesia constitutes a threat to international peace and security' and that economic sanctions were to be put into force by all members of the United Nations.[15] It should be noted that the Soviet Union did not cast a veto vote on that occasion. Obviously, she had to bear in mind her future relations with African countries.

Harold Wilson told the House of Commons on 11 November 1965 that, if the problem were not solved, the Commonwealth would disintegrate, that if Britain did not take the initiative others would, and that in a struggle for the soul of Africa he did not wish to see a 'Red Army in blue berets' entering Rhodesia.[16] Also, the US Administration publicly endorsed the sanctions policy on 5 January 1967. President Johnson issued an executive order making the provisions of the Security Council resolutions binding on citizens of the United States.

This goal of economic sanctions was maintained in arguments which called for comprehensive economic sanctions by the West against South Africa. It was argued that the sanctions would 'greatly help the West's relations with the Third World generally and Black Africa in particular' and would 'counter the steady spread of Communist influence' by the Eastern bloc countries, which were often seen 'as the main supporters of Black Liberation'.[17] Otherwise, it was maintained, relations between the black African states and the West would be strained to breaking point. To fail to exert pressure upon South Africa would not be in the West's interests.[18] It was even argued that the West should support the revolutionary forces, which, when they came to power, would 'turn to those who have supported them through the struggle'.[19]

So far we have in this section discussed the influence of relatively minor countries' demands for action upon a major country initiator of economic sanctions. Conversely, major country initiators have also demanded that less powerful states participate in sanctions. Since such demands have tended to come from just one or two major countries, it is arguable whether they could be said to constitute, or even represent, 'international public opinion'. Nonetheless, the desire to comply with their bloc leader's request or demand that they join in sanctions has on occasion been in itself one of the goals for less powerful nations.

West European countries and Japan have, at the request of the United States, taken part in several American-led economic sanctions campaigns, such as the three against the Soviet Union in 1980, 1981 and 1983, and that against Iran in 1980. Clearly, one of the objectives of their participation in those sanctions was to prevent the alliance with the United States from being undermined by opposition, or at least the appearance of indifference, to US policy.

In the case of the West against Poland and the Soviet Union, for instance, the US Administration exerted strong pressure upon its NATO allies and Japan. Walter Stoessel, then US Under Secretary of State for Political Affairs, said that the United States requested 'the widest possible degree of support', but that it 'wouldn't be restrained by the lowest common denominator' of the allies' opinion.[20] There was growing concern within NATO about the divergence of opinion between the USA and Western Europe. But finally, on 11 January 1982, all the European NATO members agreed to join in the US-led sanctions at a lower level of participation.

It took the United States a long time to persuade Latin American countries to cooperate in regional economic sanctions against the Dominican Republic. In August 1960 the Organization of American States urged its member states to stop selling weapons to the Dominican Republic, and in January 1961 to extend the suspension of trade to include the export of petroleum products, trucks and spare parts. These measures, however, were cosmetic, since the USA had been the only state in the Western hemisphere selling any significant volume of arms to the Dominican Republic, and the

USA and Venezuela had been the major regional suppliers of the other goods. Nevertheless, these actions went some way towards satisfying the United States' desire for joint coercive measures.

In the case of Cuba, the OAS stepped up economic sanctions and in July 1964 finally agreed to urge all members to suspend trade with the regime. However, United States attempts to secure collective sanctions against Cuba had created serious tension with those Latin American countries which were opposed to taking action against Castro.[21] The action was more a symbolic form of cooperation with the United States than an effective way of damaging Cuba.

Thus, economic sanctions have often been imposed for the purpose of meeting the demands and requests of friendly nations for participation, so as not to harm relations with them.

The lifting of sanctions as a bargaining counter

The imposition of economic sanctions does not necessarily mean the severing of diplomatic relations. Still less does it always mean war. Even after the US Administration froze Japanese and Chinese assets in the USA so as to bring mutual trade virtually to a complete standstill, negotiations between the United States and Japan continued for half a year. A few days before this measure was announced, Assistant Secretary of State Dean Acheson explained to Noel Hall, with regard to the objectives of this measure, that 'after this, the United States would be "prepared to contemplate" specific licenses for particular transactions.'[22] Medlicott comments:

> Thus it seemed that the intention was to use the freezing order as a flexible weapon, bargaining with the Japanese as to the terms upon which licenses for the release of assets should be issued. There was clearly grave disputation among the American officials as to how far the government should go and it does not appear that there was any settled intention at this stage of completely severing economic contacts.[23]

This goal was also seen in the economic sanctions against Poland imposed by the United States in late December 1981 and, to a lesser extent, by its NATO allies and Japan early in January 1982. On that occasion, three conditions were set for the lifting of sanctions: (a) an end to martial law; (b) the release of political detainees; and (c) restoration of dialogue with the Church and Solidarity. By reducing the severity of the sanctions whenever any relaxation of repressive control had occurred in Poland, the West attempted to induce Poland to abandon its repressive policy.

Britain and France seem to have had a similar objective in imposing sanctions against Italy, though this is less clear than in the above two cases. When the British and French foreign ministers drew up their terms for a settlement of this crisis, the so-called Hoare-Laval Pact, they agreed that Britain and France must continue 'a most patient and cautious negotiation' in order to keep Mussolini on the Allied side.[24] It appears that, in exchange for the lifting of economic sanctions plus recognition of Italian annexation of northern Ethiopia and the placing of the southern part of the country under its economic influence, Britain sought to guarantee its own Mediterranean route to the Middle and Far East and to safeguard British interests in the Upper Nile area, while France hoped to obviate the need to keep its army on the Italian border.

It may not be correct to assume that Britain and France already intended to use sanctions as a bargaining counter when the sanctions were imposed. They probably embraced this objective at a later stage, when the need to provide a deterrent against Germany, and, therefore, not to drive Italy into Hitler's arms, became apparent.

Thus, a country initiating sanctions first imposes economic coercive measures which can inflict economic damage upon the target and then offers to lift those measures if the target will refrain from behaving unacceptably. The term 'bargaining counter' may cause some to mistakenly see this use as 'second-best', a means of getting at least some compromise benefit, where success, victory, is impossible. In fact, trading sanctions (more precisely their discontinuance, the lifting of sanctions) in exchange for the redress the sanctions were imposed to obtain is to be seen as no less a victory for the imposer and no less a defeat for the target than where the target's economy and resolution are shattered by devastating economic blows or attrition.

This policy might reduce the level of hostility on the target's side more effectively than an uncompromisingly rigid imposition, which might well be interpreted as a declaration of economic warfare. This approach, therefore, may avoid too harsh a confrontation between imposer and target, and so smooth the way to a peaceful settlement. Naturally, whether this approach succeeds or not depends upon the circumstances, but it can certainly be counted as one of the considerations involved in economic sanctions.

Undermining the target's strategic position

In wartime, belligerent states overtly attempt to undermine their opponents' economic base in order to reduce their military strength and their ability to prosecute the war generally. Napoleon's 'Continental Blockade' was an attempt to destroy Britain's economic base by cutting off all trade with the European continent. During World War I Britain tried to strangle the Central Powers by cutting off German imports of food and raw materials, while Germany in turn sought to encircle Britain by means of its submarine forces. The principal objective of such economic measures is to reduce or terminate the enemy's imports of vital materials, to bring about various bottlenecks in the enemy's war-effort production and lower the level of economic activity in the hope of causing serious damage to its strategic position.

In peacetime, however, such economic measures cannot be adopted as easily as in wartime, particularly by advanced democratic countries, unless the initiator has adequate grounds to justify their imposition and can obtain sufficient domestic and international support or, at least, acquiescence. The mere fact that State A has increased its military strength seems to be insufficient grounds for State B's imposing economic sanctions against it, unless and until it becomes obvious that State A has the clear intention to use these forces.

But, once State A's military build-up leads to a wrong-doing which gives State B a reason sufficient to justify sanctions, then State B may resort to economic sanctions. The aim of sanctions here may be termed the 'strategic effect'. The term is all the more appropriate where, as is quite probable, State B takes advantage of the opportunity to impose sanctions as a means of removing the broader threat posed by State A by damaging State A's economic ability to maintain its military build-up. In the following four cases the imposers clearly had a 'strategic effect' as a goal.

The United States adopted an embargo policy against the Soviet Union after the Cold War became a reality in 1947. It secured the cooperation of its West European allies and Japan. Some of them showed reluctance, and the United States on occasion resorted to intimidation, hinting at the suspension of economic or military aid. The Battle Act, which was enacted in 1951, authorized the President to cut aid to any uncooperative aid recipient if he deemed this step to be in the national interest.

The Co-ordinating Committee (Cocom) established for the purpose of coordinating Western embargo policy included representatives of all the NATO states (except Iceland) and Japan. The objectives of this embargo policy appear to have been mixed, ranging from, at one extreme, a desire to express antagonism to Soviet Communism, at the other, the initiation of comprehensive economic warfare. But the main objective was to ensure continued Soviet military inferiority by suspending the export of military equipment and civilian goods which would serve to increase the Soviet Union's economic potential and so allow her to build up military strength. Huntington explains the policy thus:

> This denial approach assumed that war was highly probable, and that consequently Western nations should engage in no economic relations with the Soviet Union that might strengthen its economic, techno-logical, and military war-making capacity.[25]

Similarly, the declared goal of later Western economic sanctions against the Soviet Union was to encourage the Soviet leaders to behave better towards Poles or Afghans – though the possibility of attaining this objective was extremely remote – but the imposing countries may well also have welcomed any contribution the sanctions might make to pre-venting the target state from becoming militarily or economically stronger *vis-à-vis* the West.

With regard to the case of the USA, Britain, the Netherlands and others against Japan, the imposers continued the policy of gradually tightening the economic screw without going so far as to provoke an explosion until Japan occupied southern French Indo-China on 26 July 1941. Early in July 1941 there was considerable uncertainty on Britain's part as to which course Britain should follow, owing mainly to the possibility that the United States would leave the British and Dutch to bear the brunt of Japanese retaliation. On 20 July, Sumner Wells told Lord Lothian, the British Ambassador to the United States, that the restricting of oil supplies to Japan should be employed 'only as a last resort after it has become clear that Japan was bent on war'.[26] Britain had similar views; Lord Lothian told Sumner Wells, on 29 July 1941, that:

> The British were in much the same position as they were over the Burma Road, and could not precipitate a war by refusing the Japanese demands for oil so long as the present acute phase of the war lasted in Europe, and so long as the United States was unable to offer military support.[27]

Such a policy of gradually tightening the economic screw did not per-suade the Japanese to turn back, but instead resulted in the decision to land in southern French Indo-China, because Japan felt it imperative to secure the energy 'life-line' in a situation where the imposition of a total trade embargo was very likely. On 1 August, the United States at last announced a full-scale economic embargo against Japan. Considering the whole pro-cess up to that point, the major goal of the full-scale embargo was pre-sumably not simply to force her to comply with what the imposers considered to be international norms, but to weaken her military strength by preventing the flow of materials indispensable for the Japanese military build-up.

An imposer's strategic position can be improved if the imposition of economic sanctions raises the cost to the target not only of attempting to strengthen its forces but also, for example, of attempting to disseminate a political ideology which the imposer deems incompatible with its own or disadvantageous to it. In the case of Cuba, George Ball, then US Secretary of State, set forth on 23 April 1964 the four official aims of economic sanctions against Cuba, two of which were:

(a) to reduce the will and ability of the present Cuban regime to export subversion and violence to the other American states;
(b) to increase the cost of maintaining a Communist outpost in the Western Hemisphere.[28]

In order to compensate for the losses caused by the US sanctions, the scale of Soviet bloc aid to Cuba had to be increased. In fact, Cuba's accumulated debt to the Soviet Union between 1961 and 1967 amounted to about $1,100 million,[29] in addition to which it had debts to the other Eastern bloc states. The dispatch of technicians to Cuba and the chartering of ships for trade were enormously expensive undertakings for the Eastern bloc. The US Administration probably anticipated such consequences before or during the imposition of sanctions and so was all the more ready to impose, and continue, sanctions.

OTHER REASONS FOR CHOOSING ECONOMIC SANCTIONS

Returning to the question asked at the beginning of this chapter, why, notwithstanding the various doubts concerning the effectiveness of economic sanctions elaborated in Chapter 5, are states so disposed to resort to economic sanctions? One obvious answer is that states perceive the possibility of using economic sanctions to attain goals additional to the goals sanctions-imposing nations declare. To this must be added, however, another reason for states' advocacy of economic sanctions: states are frequently (perhaps more often than not) not in a position, whether because of weakness or for some other reason, to undertake anything more substantial than economic sanctions.

Historically, military power has been stressed, as inflicting more direct damage upon the target state and, therefore, superior to other forms of power, as there has been no effective remedy to military force other than equal or superior military force, and it has been accepted that a state could – and, if militarily superior to the target, would – use military force to punish the target, since that would be more direct and prove more effective than economic measures. Nonetheless, for a country militarily weaker than the opponent state, economic sanctions are the only substantial means available, albeit their effectiveness is doubtful. It may be taken as certain that West Germany did not even dream of attempting to 'punish' the USSR by means of military force when East Germany constructed the Berlin Wall. Equally naturally, the Arab members of OPEC opted for oil export boycott measures in 1973, not any military punitive action against the USA, Western Europe or Japan.

Nevertheless, in the last several decades militarily stronger countries, even superpowers, have also tended to opt for economic sanctions rather than military action. In fact, in most of the cases listed in Chapter 2 economic sanctions were imposed by nations that were stronger militarily than the target nations. Why did they not employ military action? One point to be stressed here is that the choice of means depends not merely on availability but also on the expected cost and efficacy.

Because of the unprecedented destructive power of nuclear weapons, it is highly unlikely that a nuclear state will attempt to employ military punitive action against another nuclear state. The fact that any lesser conflict between them could escalate to all-out nuclear war has meant that the possible cost is unacceptable, this probably dissuading them from having recourse to military action. The idea of military punitive measures against the Soviet Union will certainly not have been thought of by the United States in the cases of Afghanistan, Poland or the Korean Airlines airliner. We should not over-hastily conclude that the use of military force by one superpower against another has vanished from the face of the earth, but we can now with considerable confidence argue that deterrence has come to be seen as the only rational posture between nuclear states.

Moreover, great powers now find it more difficult, and costly, to sub-due or conquer weaker countries than in the last century or even the early part of this century. Knorr pointed out four reasons:

(a) nuclear powers' self-restraint from using nuclear weapons against non-nuclear states;
(b) actual or potential backing by the rival superpower;
(c) the diminished legitimacy of the use of force;
(d) the rapid spread of nationalism among less-developed countries and their combined will to resist bullying by great powers.

He then gives instances of how costly it has become to conquer even weaker countries:

> The French required only thirty thousand men to subdue Algeria in 1830. In 1962 they could not subdue her with a force twenty times as large. The United States encountered similar difficulties in Vietnam; . . . Estimates of the fiscal cost of the American engagement in Vietnam ran as high as $30 billion by the end of 1971.[30]

While it is equally true that the imposition of economic sanctions also requires sacrifice on the part of the imposer, and that reasons (b) and (d) above apply to such sanctions as well as to military action, nonetheless, when compared with economic measures, military coercion entails an additional cost, in that once hostilities have begun, the target country's resistance is likely to be more determined and bitter and a settlement through negotiation or compromise be far more difficult.

Furthermore, one must not ignore the political, legal or moral price, which is, of course operative in reasons (a) and (c) above. After World War I, war as an act of state was outlawed, and the Charter of the United Nations declares the use of force illegal, with very limited exceptions, such as the use of force in self-defence. Evidently, this norm is far from having been universally observed, partly because of flaws in the functioning of the collective security scheme of the United Nations, and has, therefore, been of limited effectiveness. However, it is not wholly ineffective. The experience of the Soviet Union in connection with its occupation of Czechoslovakia and that of the United States in Vietnam demonstrates how great an effort those great powers found it necessary to make to justify their use of military force. Any country resorting to force, even in order to punish an aggressor, is compelled to pay a price, for instance having to devote time and energy to proving that the use of force was inevitable or face condemnation by other countries. With regard to the use of nuclear weapons, in particular, five nuclear states have, in almost the same manner, declared (France since 1982, the other four nuclear states since 1978) that they will not 'use nuclear weapons against any non-nuclear state party to the Non-Proliferation Treaty or any comparable internationally binding commitment.'[31]

There have, indeed, been numerous cases of attempts to coerce an opponent by means of military force in the postwar era, such as the military conflicts between Israel and the Arab nations in 1967 and 1973 and between India and Pakistan in 1971. Some of the nations using military force were great powers, for example the UK and France against Egypt in 1956, the USSR against Hungary in 1956, the USA against North Vietnam in 1965–73, the USSR against Czechoslovakia in 1968, China against

Vietnam in 1979 and the UK against Argentina in 1982. These postwar precedents clearly demonstrate that the possibility of states resorting to military sanctions still exists.

But the exercise of military power is costly, and the cost tends to act as a restraint. The consequence is that states often prefer to resort to less unacceptable coercive means when satisfactory results seem likely, or, indeed, even when they do not.

SUMMARY

A state deciding to initiate economic sanctions may have one or more of a number of objectives. It will normally proclaim a set of goals, partly because the proclamation itself can on occasion be enough to attain its ends, or some of them. But states often also have objectives which they conceal, consciously or unconsciously. Some objectives are veiled consciously, partly because proclaiming them would not attain the desired effect and is, therefore, pointless, and partly because those objectives are solely concerned with the imposers' own benefit, and revealing them would weaken the justification for the sanctions, something the imposer almost always feels the need to establish in terms of the general interest. Revealing them would reduce the number of states joining in the sanctions, since they would smack of self-interest. Moreover, imposers are not always conscious of all the possible advantageous effects when they initiate sanctions. They often notice the existence of other possible goals after doing so.

In comparison with military action, economic sanctions have been seen as lukewarm. Indeed, they may often not attain the primary goal. But as long as the imposers have other goals, and as long as military sanctions would have unacceptable adverse effects, such as criticism of the imposers' destruction of human life, states will tend to use economic sanctions. In the nineteenth century, states were virtually the only actors in international relations, but in today's world the number of actors is growing. International organizations, non-governmental organizations (NGOs), religious organizations, labour unions, human rights movements, newspapers, magazines, television – all are influential. Even the voices of individuals cannot be ignored. As the number of 'actors' grows, the objectives of states' policies and the factors that must be borne in mind in implementing them become that much more varied and complex. Economic sanctions, which can serve to attain a variety of objectives at one time, are, therefore, increasingly seen as a suitable instrument of foreign policy in the complex international relations of today's world.

Part Two

The Iranian
Hostage Crisis

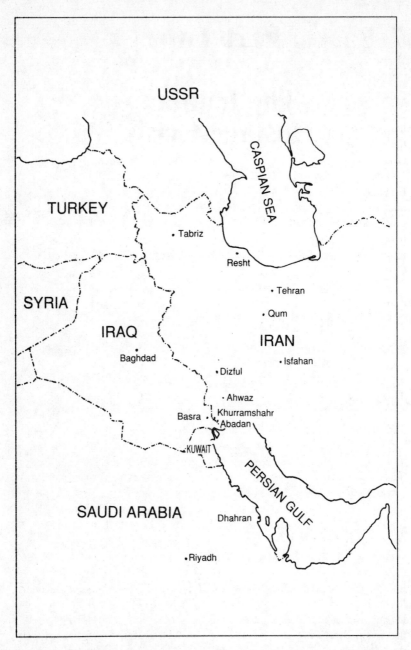

Map 7.1   Iran and neighbouring countries

7 Background to the Crisis

Part One examined a number of cases of economic sanctions from a variety of angles, drawing an overall picture. One still fairly recent case, that of the United States and Iran, will now be examined to see how the overall picture relates to this particular case and to what extent the case of the Hostage Crisis exhibits new and special features.

The US–Iran hostage crisis began when, on 4 November 1979, the US Embassy in Tehran was attacked and occupied by a group of armed Iranian students. They seized the Embassy staff and demanded that the US government extradite the deposed former Shah, then in the United States for medical treatment. This crisis lasted until 21 January 1981, when all 52 remaining hostages were released, this coinciding with the end of the Carter Administration.

Before tracing the actual process of the imposition of economic sanctions, the background to the crisis will first be briefly examined.

THE POLITICAL SITUATION IN IRAN BEFORE THE SEIZING OF THE HOSTAGES

The downfall of the Shah

The internal political situation in Iran before the seizing of the hostages had been far from stable. Persistent opposition throughout the latter half of 1978 and early 1979 to the Iranian regime headed by Mohammad Reza Shah led to the downfall of successive governments appointed by him.

Opposition to the Shah and his governments was expressed in a popular movement embracing a diversity of groups – Moslem traditionalists, liberal politicians, merchants, intellectuals, human rights advocates, students, Communists and others – many of whom had for years been suppressed and persecuted by the national intelligence and security organization, Savak. (Established in 1957 with the help of the US Central Intelligence Agency and the Israeli secret service, Mossad, Savak is said to have had 4,000 full-time members and 50,000 paid informers.) Despite having differing ideologies and different grievances against the Shah, these groups gradually became united, and were backed by the Moslem traditionalist movement. This movement was led, through his followers in Iran, from exile in Iraq from 1964 and later in France up to his return to Iran in 1979, by Ayatollah Ruhollah Khomeini, who had become increasingly influential since the disturbances in late 1977 and early 1978 and had come to be seen as the main symbol of opposition to the Shah. Inside Iran, the movement was led by the more moderate Ayatollah Seyyed Kazem Shariatmadari of Qum and also by Ayatollah Mohammad Taleghani of Tehran.

The most powerful opposition group, the Shia Moslem traditionalists, had opposed the Shah's westernizing policy, fearing that this policy would result in weakening of the authority of Islam in Iran. They also demanded full implementation of the 1906 Constitution, which provided that a council of five senior Moslem clergy should have the right of veto over all legislation. Another strong opposition group, which included politicians, students, intellectuals and human rights advocates, many of whom had joined the National Front, was categorized as liberal. In December 1977, this group set up the Iranian Committee for the Defence of Liberty and Human Rights, led by Professor Mehdi Bazarghan. Their demands included the establishment of a multi-party state, the release of all political prisoners and curtailment of the power of Savak. These groups began repeated demonstrations, frequently developing into riots, and, from late September, 'industrial action' to press for higher wages and improved benefits. The opposition movement reached its peak at the end of October 1978, when employees in the oil industry began a mass strike which seriously affected first Iran's oil exports and then its economy generally.

In an effort to appease his opponents, the Shah announced a number of conciliatory measures in the course of October 1978. These measures included the release of a large number of political detainees and the dismissal of some senior officials of Savak. The Shah also offered an amnesty to Iranian dissidents abroad, who were assured that they would not be prosecuted on their return to Iran, if they respected the Constitution, and the independence, territorial integrity and freedom of Iran. Manuchehr Azmoun, then Minister of State for Executive Affairs, made it clear that the amnesty applied mainly to students who had been manipulated by alien forces but also extended to Ayatollah Khomeini. In parallel with these appeasement measures, the Shah imposed martial law in the principal cities on 8 September and formed a predominantly military government under General Gholam Reza Azhari. By doing this he sought to restore stability to the country.

Despite these efforts by the Shah, the anti-Shah movement gradually grew, until eventually violent clashes between security forces and demonstrators took place. The Shah's last card was Dr Shapour Bakhtiar, a long-standing and high-ranking member of the National Front. On 29 December 1978, the Shah asked him to form a new government, and on 4 January 1979, after receiving the approval of Parliament, he became Prime Minister. On 11 January 1979, Dr Bakhtiar presented to Parliament a 17-point programme which included dissolution of Savak, gradual abolition of martial law, punishment of violators of human rights, release of political detainees and recognition of the constitutional rights of Moslem religious leaders in the drafting of government legislation. The programme also promised to maintain good relations with Arab countries and confirmed an earlier indication that Iran would no longer export oil to Israel and South Africa.

Nevertheless, Ayatollah Khomeini and the National Front denounced Dr Bakhtiar, expelling him from the movement. Since the beginning of January 1979, there had been visible opposition to the Bakhtiar government and by mid-January anti-government demonstrations had become even more violent. In Qazvin nearly 100 people were killed, and in Firuzabad a Savak office was attacked and prisoners freed. Ayatollah Khomeini continued to fan the flames of the anti-government movement, stating on 6 January 1979 that obedience to the new administration was tantamount to 'obedience to Satan', and called on government employees to refuse to obey the new ministers and to lock them out of their offices. The instability in Iran was so marked that on 12 January 1979, the United States dismantled its intelligence-gathering posts on Iranian territory, which had hitherto been used to track the flight of Soviet missiles and to intercept Soviet electronic communications monitoring their missiles' performance.

In these circumstances, the Shah decided to leave the country, and on 9 January ordered members of his family to surrender all their personal property to the Pahlavi Foundation (the head office of which was in the United States) 'for the use of religious, educational, social and welfare organizations organized by the people and run by them'. At last, on 16 January 1979, the Shah and Empress Farah left Iran and arrived in Aswan in Upper Egypt, where they were welcomed by President Sadat (their three youngest children had flown to the United States on the previous day). Although the Shah's absence from Iran was officially stated to be temporary (it was said that he was taking a holiday and receiving medical treatment), it was generally believed, both in Iran and abroad, that he had gone for good. On 22 January, the Shah flew to Morocco, and later left Morocco for the Bahamas.

News of the Shah's departure was greeted by the people with mass celebrations in the streets of the major towns and cities. On the same day, Ayatollah Khomeini, who on 13 January had announced the formation of a provisional 'revolutionary Islamic Council' which would replace the 'illegal government', said that his movement would not support Dr Bakhtiar, even though the Shah had left Iran. Following the Shah's departure, talks were held between the government and the opposition group, with Dr Bazargan acting as one of the main mediators. The French government suggested the possibility of a meeting between Khomeini and Bakhtiar in Paris, but Khomeini refused to meet Bakhtiar until the latter had resigned. Eventually, Khomeini announced that he would return to Iran.

Ayatollah Khomeini returned to Iran on 2 February 1979 to a rapturous welcome at Tehran airport. On the same day, Dr Bakhtiar offered to form a government of national unity embracing supporters of Khomeini's Islamic movement. Khomeini, however, rejected this offer, calling on his followers to step up their industrial action to bring down the government, and urged members of the Majlis (Parliament) to resign.

On 5 February, Ayatollah Khomeini appointed Dr Mehdi Bazargan Prime Minister of a provisional government. This was greeted by mass demonstrations in support of the Islamic revolutionary movement. Following heavy fighting in Tehran from 9 to 11 February between troops loyal to the Bakhtiar government and supporters of Ayatollah Khomeini and dissident members of the Air Force, power was finally surrendered to Khomeini's Islamic movement. On the evening of 11 February, Dr Bakhtiar officially resigned, as did the other members of the Cabinet. The Majlis and the Senate were then dissolved. On 12 and 13 February, Dr Bazargan announced a number of appointments to the new provisional government, and by 15 February a degree of calm had returned to the streets of Tehran.

Political disturbances under the new regime

As has been shown, the anti-Shah movement had been far from monolithic, including various groups with very different political goals. After this movement had attained its original objective of toppling the Shah's regime, the differences in political aims among those groups rapidly surfaced. The two principal groups were: (a) the Islamic Revolutionary Council, presided over by Ayatollah Khomeini, the principal members of which were the clergy and other Islamic fundamentalists, and (b) a group which sought to establish a democratic republic with a constitution in which human rights were guaranteed. The latter faction included the National Democratic Front, formed by Matine-Daftari (grandson of Mohammad Mossadeq). Dr Bazargan was poised between the two groups. He had, in fact, served as Under Secretary of State for Education in Dr Mossadeq's Cabinet, and also as a director of the National Iranian Oil Company under him. After the overthrow of Dr Mossadeq's regime, he had continued political opposition to the Shah, founded the National Resistance Movement, which later joined the National Front, and also the Iranian Committee for the Defence of Liberty and Human Rights in 1977. Thus, he had maintained close ties with both religious and secular opposition groups.

The Tudeh Party, which had retained a skeletal organization despite all the Shah's attempts to destroy it, also re-emerged. It described the Iranian revolution as a people's revolution with religious tendencies, and asserted that, therefore, the new regime ought to maintain the unity of the revolutionary forces. However, Dr Ibrahim Yazdi, then Deputy Prime Minister in charge of Revolutionary Affairs, emphasized on 5 March 1979 that the new Islamic regime would oppose Marxism, saying that Marxism, being based upon dialectical materialism, was fundamentally different from the Islamic creed, especially in the economic, political and social fields.

Dr Bazargan deplored this multi-sided conflict, going on to say that Iran had become a nation of 'hundreds of chiefs'. The rivalry intensified at the end of March 1979. A referendum on Iran's future constitution was held on 30 and 31 March. A draft constitution had been published on 21 February, the main provisions of which were:

(a) Shia Islam was to be the national religion;
(b) there was to be a unicameral parliament directly elected by the people;
(c) the President was to be elected for four or five years and eligible for re-election once only; and
(d) the most important sectors of industry were to remain under state control.

The question put in the referendum was 'Are you for the replacement of the monarchy by an Islamic republic, the Constitution of which will be approved – Yes or No?' Several political parties opposed the wording of this question, insisting that it did not allow a voter to choose a third political system. For instance, the National Democratic Front requested that the nature of the proposed republic ought to be left to be decided by a second referendum. As its proposal was ignored, the NDF announced its decision to take no part in the referendum. The referendum was also boycotted by other movements, such as Kurdish left-wing groups and the Kurdish Democratic Party of Iran. In the end, the result of the referendum was that most of the 20 million who did vote voted 'Yes', only 100,000 voting 'No'. On 1 April, Ayatollah Khomeini proclaimed the establishment of the Islamic Republic of Iran.

The differences between Ayatollah Khomeini and Dr Bazargan also manifested themselves in the appointment of ministers. However, the struggle over the sharing of power between the Revolutionary Council and the government was settled by agreement between the two men.

The conflict culminated at the election, held on 3 August 1979, for a Constituent Council of Experts, whose 73 members were to give definitive form to the draft Constitution. Ayatollah Khomeini seems to have influenced the election considerably by announcing that all voters should fulfil their 'Islamic duty' by voting for candidates supporting the Islamic Republic. The Islamic Revolutionary Party, the Tudeh Party and the Mujaheddin movement took part in the election, but the National Front, the National Democratic Front, the Moslem People's Republican Party and some others called for a boycott. The National Front, for instance, justified its stance by saying that it had not been allowed to broadcast its views or put up posters. The factional strife and lack of political unity was evident also in the trials and executions of officers of the Shah's regime.

On 6 November 1979, two days after Moslem students had seized the US Embassy in Tehran, Abolhassan Bani-Sadr, who, as well as being Minister for Finance and Economic Affairs with responsibility for supervision of the Foreign Ministry, was one of Khomeini's chief advisers, said that '[t]his occupation had "shown up the multiplicity of centres of decision and the Government's powerlessness to control even one of the capital's arteries"; that it had further reduced the Government's prestige both in Iran and abroad.'[1]

THE FOREIGN POLICY OF THE NEW REGIME

By 14 February 1979, the Bazargan government had been formally recognized by numerous countries, including Britain, Japan, the USSR and most of the Arab states, while other states, such as Egypt, France and the USA, accorded it *de facto* recognition. The fundamental principle of the government's foreign policy was well summarized in a statement of 11 March 1979 by Dr Sanjabi, the Foreign Minister. It said that Iran's foreign policy would be based upon independence and non-alignment, and that Iran was ready to maintain friendly relations with both Western and Eastern bloc countries.

When considering relations between the new Iranian regime and the United States, one should note the long history of antipathy towards the United States demonstrated by Ayatollah Khomeini and his followers. The main ingredient in their strong anti-American feeling was, of course,

Washington's close ties with the Shah's regime. The United States had been instrumental in the Shah's return to power in August 1953, and the Pentagon had been involved in his harsh suppression in 1963 of a national uprising directed against the US-supported socio-economic reforms for the 'modernization of Iran' (the 'White Revolution'). Because of his part in the uprising, Ayatollah Khomeini was exiled in the following year. Khomeini had condemned the Shah's agreement to grant American military personnel in Iran the right of exclusive criminal jurisdiction within their own community as a 'document of the enslavement of Iran'.[2]

In view of these factors, relations between the new regime and the United States were all but doomed to deteriorate. Soon after its formation, the Bazargan government made it clear that it would not continue the previous regime's specially close military cooperation with the United States. General Qarani, Chief of Staff of the Armed Forces, said on 21 February 1979 that the United States would be asked to close its monitoring posts on the Soviet border. Accordingly, the two American-manned electronic intelligence collection stations – one close to the Soviet border near Bandar Shah on the shores of the Caspian Sea, the other in Kabkam, a desolate spot in the mountains 80 miles south of Mashhad – were dismantled.[3] General Qarani also said on 3 March that all services rendered by US military personnel to the Iranian forces were to be terminated. In addition, Iran reduced arms purchases and withdrew from the role of policeman of the Persian Gulf.

Relations with the United States deteriorated further when the Iranian government informed the United States that Walter Cutler, the American Ambassador designate (to succeed William Sullivan), would not be welcome in Iran as he was not in a position to normalize relations between Iran and the United States. The US State Department responded by announcing that for the time being no ambassador would be sent to Tehran.

Relations with the United States plummeted when the deposed Shah was allowed to enter the United States. The Shah flew from Mexico City to New York on 22 October 1979 for medical treatment. More details of this episode will be given in the next section.

Since World War II, any blow to Washington had usually been seen as advantageous to the Kremlin. Seeing the collapse of the Shah's regime, a guardian of Western interests in the Middle East, Soviet leaders probably thought that 'no other internal upheaval and political turnabout in the Third World had brought such immediate gain and promising opportunity'.[4] In fact, the birth of the new regime in Iran did benefit Soviet interests. For instance, an attempt by the Soviet-backed People's Democratic Republic of Yemen to foment an insurrection in Yemen would not be frustrated by Iranian troops, which had been deployed to defend the pro-Western Sultan in 1973–5. Moreover, the new regime was supporting anti-American movements in the Arab countries by suspending oil exports to Israel, had sided with the Arab states opposed to the Camp David Agreement, had broken off diplomatic relations with Egypt (on 30 April 1979, though Egypt had recognized the new regime), had recognized the Palestine Liberation Organization (PLO) and supported the right of the Palestinian Arabs to establish their own state. America's abandoning of its intelligence-gathering posts inevitably strengthened the strategic position of the Soviet Union. Iran's lifting of the ban on the Tudeh (Communist) Party also benefited the Soviet Union.

Immediately after the fall of the Shah, the Soviet Union, therefore, recognized the provisional government of Dr Bazargan authorized by Ayatollah Khomeini, and on 3 March 1979 Brezhnev publicly celebrated the triumph of the Islamic revolution. He also sent a message of congratulation to Khomeini, when Khomeini proclaimed the establishment of the Islamic Republic of Iran on 1 April 1979. Dr Bazargan, meanwhile, called for the strengthening of understanding and cooperation with the Soviet Union, and in May 1979 sent Dr Mokri to Moscow as Iran's Ambassador to the USSR. Thus, there was seemingly nothing standing in the way of rapid improvement of relations between the two countries.

However, many people close to the Ayatollah Khomeini were suspicious of Soviet intentions because of their hostility to Soviet atheism and the traditional Iranian fear of Russian imperialism. Furthermore, the Communist coup in Afghanistan in April 1978 and the overthrow of the Daoud regime by the Soviet-backed Taraki caused apprehension in Iran. In particular, Moscow's reaffirmation of the Soviet–Iranian treaty of 26 February 1921, two days after Khomeini's meeting with the Soviet Ambassador, aroused Iranian uncertainty regarding Soviet intentions.[5] The USSR had always claimed that Articles 5 and 6 of this treaty gave it the right to intervene in Iranian affairs in the interests of Soviet self-defence if a third country threatened to attack the Soviet Union from Iranian territory or if Moscow considered its borders threatened.

Soviet intervention in Afghanistan proved that Iranian fears might be well founded. In September 1979 President Taraki told Prime Minister Amin to moderate his harsh measures against Moslems. On 16 September 1979, Amin took over from Taraki and pursued an even more pro-Soviet line than Taraki. Various Moslem rebel groups which then rose against the Amin government had, by 22 October 1979, gained control of vast areas of Afghanistan. On 28 October, the Amin regime, backed by Soviet troops, launched a major offensive against the Moslem rebels.

The first Iranian protest was made by Ayatollah Khomeini on 12 June 1979 to Ambassador Vinogradov. Khomeini warned the Soviets against 'interfering in Afghanistan or fomenting unrest in the Kurdish and Baluchi areas of Iran'.[6] After the overthrow of the Taraki regime, the Iranian government openly expressed sympathy for the rebel cause, and on 19 September 1979 it announced that if the Amin government continued to fight against 'Islam' and 'Islamic revolution', it would be overthrown, because it had not been formed with the consent of the Afghan people. In early September, the Soviet Union criticized the concept of an Islamic state and attacked Khomeini by name for the first time. Relations with the Soviet Union were, thus, clearly deteriorating.

Iran's foreign policy towards its neighbouring Arab states is well described in the statement of 25 February 1979 by Dr Yazdi, then Deputy Prime Minister in Charge of Revolutionary Affairs:

The success of the Islamic revolution in Iran has shown Arab neighbours that Islam provides the ideological basis for change within Moslem countries and can also replace Arab nationalism as a rallying point of Arab people . . . From now on all Islamic movements which were dormant or apologetic in their approach to change or action will come out into the open in the Arab world and in the Moslem world.[7]

The Bazargan government desired to be a model for the Islamic revolutionary movement everywhere, and sought to encourage Arab nations to follow Iran. From this standpoint too (in addition to that of its anti-American posture), Iran supported the Arab states' opposition to the Camp David Agreement, and recognized the PLO, severing diplomatic relations with Israel on 18 February 1979, and later with Egypt on 30 April of the same year. On 18 February 1979, Yasser Arafat, the leader of the PLO, was welcomed in Tehran and on the following day opened a PLO office in the premises of the former Israeli trade mission, the staff of which had been expelled. In March, the Iranian contingent of the UN Interim Force in south Lebanon (UNIFIL) was withdrawn. In the same month, the military high command in Tehran ordered the 5,000-strong Iranian expeditionary force in Oman to return home.

In an approach to the Non-Aligned Movement in the Third World, relations with Cuba improved apace. On 8 August 1979, Dr Yazdi, the Iranian Foreign Minister, and Antonio Esquivel Yebra, the Cuban Chemical Industry Minister, announced in Tehran that their governments had decided to restore diplomatic relations, which had been severed by the Shah's regime in 1976. Subsequently, Iran was admitted to membership of the

Non-Aligned Movement and was invited to attend the Havana conference held in August and September 1979.

THE SHAH'S ADMISSION TO THE UNITED STATES

Having travelled via Egypt, Morocco and the Bahamas, the deposed Shah arrived in Mexico on 10 June 1979. Regarding his admission to the United States, the Carter Administration had said on 19 April that it 'had during March 1979 indicated to the Shah that he was not welcome in the United States at that time because of the delicacy of US–Iranian relations.'[8]

Since May 1979, condemnation of the Shah had become so fierce that it even looked as though the Iranian leaders were using him to cover up their own differences. On 13 May, Ayatollah Khomeini called for the Shah's execution. Dr Yazdi said on 3 July that the government would try to bring the Shah back for trial. A radical clergyman, Ayatollah Khalkhali, was reported on 19 June to have promised a reward of $140 million to any person killing the Shah. As far as the Shah's property was concerned, the Iranian government announced on 2 May 1979 that it had asked the US government to freeze the assets of the Pahlavi Foundation and to transfer all of them back to Iran, and not to allow the Shah to enter the United States. (According to a statement issued in Geneva on 23 February, on behalf of Dr Assadollah Mobasheri, then Iran's Justice Minister, the Shah had sent £7,500 milliion abroad before his departure from Iran, and Princess Ashraf (the Shah's twin sister) had sent out another £1,500 million. On 3 March, it was officially announced that the Revolutionary Council had decided to nationalize the Shah's property, amounting to between $15,000 and $23,000 million.)

However, Dr Henry Kissinger and David Rockefeller, President of the Chase Manhattan Bank, sought to help the Shah. Dr Kissinger said on 9 April that 'A man who for 37 years was a friend of the United States should not be treated like a flying Dutchman who cannot find a port of call.'[9] Later, at Rockefeller's request, an American specialist in tropical diseases examined the Shah in Mexico and found that the lymphatic cancer from which the Shah was suffering needed expert diagnosis. This report was sent to the State Department on 16 October.

Repeated warnings had been given to the Carter Administration by the US Embassy in Tehran and by the CIA that admitting the Shah to the United States would exacerbate anti-American feeling and probably invite action against the US Embassy, which had already been temporarily occupied by left-wing gunmen on 14 February 1979. Despite these warnings, on

19 October President Carter decided to admit the Shah for medical treatment. On 22 October, the Shah arrived in New York and by 24 October the operation to remove his gall bladder and a stone in his bile duct had been successfully performed. As had been expected, the Iranian government protested to the United States.

THE SEIZURE OF THE US EMBASSY

On 4 November 1979, in the course of a demonstration by nearly 3,000 people, the US Embassy in Tehran was attacked by a heavily armed group of several hundred calling themselves 'Moslem Student Followers of the Iman's Policy'. They seized the Embassy staff, whom they accused of espionage and held as hostages, demanding the Shah's extradition from the United States. On the same day, they claimed that their action had been approved by Ayatollah Khomeini himself.

Requests for help were repeatedly made to the Iranian authorities by the American Chargé d'Affaires in Tehran. Despite those requests, no Iranian security forces were sent in time to enforce the immediate release of the hostages or to provide future protection for the Embassy.

On the following day the US consulates in Tabriz and Shiraz were also seized, with the Iranian government taking no steps to protect them. Non-Americans were released shortly afterwards, and, in accordance with Ayatollah Khomeini's order on 17 November to release blacks and women, the students released eight men and five women. Ayatollah Khomeini said, 'In the name of God, the Merciful, death to your plots, USA. The blood of our martyrs is dripping from your claws. The United States is the main enemy of mankind and of the Iranian people.'[10]

8 Action Taken by the United States

On the day of the seizure of the US Embassy and its staff, requests for help were repeatedly made by the US Chargé d'Affaires, who was then at the Iranian Foreign Ministry, and also by the US government to the Iranian Chargé d'Affaires in Washington. However, no Iranian police or soldiers were sent in time to release the Embassy staff or afford protection to them and the Embassy. On 7 November, a former Attorney-General of the United States, Ramsey Clark, was instructed to go to Iran to deliver to Ayatollah Khomeini a message of protest from President Carter. In response, Tehran radio broadcast on the same day a message from Ayatollah Khomeini forbidding members of the Revolutionary Council and government officials to meet the American representatives. In this message Khomeini asserted that 'the US Embassy in Tehran is our enemies' centre of espionage against our sacred Islamic movement'. He then made the first official demand to the United States: 'Should the United States hand over to Iran the deposed Shah . . . and give up espionage against our movement, the way to talks would be opened on the issue of certain relations which are in the interest of the nation.'[1]

In the light of these facts, together with many statements made by various Iranian government authorities, the United States decided that the seizure was an act of Iran as a state, and not merely an act of its radical nationals, and, therefore, took the following punitive measures. (In addition to these economic measures, on 10 November 1979 the United States decided to expel from her territory all Iranian students who had previous convictions or were without visas or not registered as students.)

(a) *Halt to the shipment of military parts* (8 November 1979). The US decided to suspend shipment of about $300 million worth of military parts to Iran until the matter of the hostages was resolved, although Iran had already paid for them. In fact, Iran's imports of military parts had been a relatively large part of its total imports from the United States. Also, since Iran had relied on the United States for a large percentage of its military equipment, US officials calculated that, '[w]ithout US arms supplies or spare parts for much of the year, . . . the Iranian armed forces [were] in bad shape. Many aircraft [were] too dangerous to fly, and many armoured vehicles [had] broken down.'[2]

(b) *Ban on imports of Iranian oil* (12 November 1979). President Carter announced a halt to imports of Iranian oil. Since the United States had been buying 600,000 barrels a day (b/d), worth nearly $13.8 million a day,[3] this measure was expected to reduce Iran's foreign exchange reserves and make traders reluctant to sell goods and services to Iran. However, Iran's Oil Minister, Ali Akbar Moinfar, immediately hit back by announcing that the ruling Revolutionary Council had just voted to impose a ban on the sale of oil to the United States. He also said that 'There was no problem: Iran would gain . . . since it would be able to sell more oil on the spot market.' On 24 November, he gave warning that any country hostile to Iran would face an oil boycott.[4]

(c) *Blocking all Iran's official assets in the United States and in the foreign branches or subsidiaries of US banks* (14 November 1979). Because the Iranian government appeared to be trying to withdraw all Iranian funds from US banks, to be refusing to accept payment in dollars for oil, and to be repudiating debts to the US government and its nationals, President Carter issued an Executive Order freezing all Iran's official assets in the United States or under US control, including Iranian deposits either in banks in the United States or in foreign branches or subsidiaries of US banks. Calculations regarding the total amount of Iranian assets frozen vary, but according to one calculation made towards the end of the crisis, the total amount was about $12,000 million.[5] The measure was directed towards reducing Iran's purchasing power, causing difficulty in any kind of economic transaction and, eventually, shortages of necessary materials. Since oil companies normally pay in dollars through American banks, this measure might have immediately caused difficulty with payments for Iranian oil. Iran's Oil Minister, Moinfar, said that the US dollar should be abandoned as the currency for oil transactions,[6] probably in an attempt to cause a sudden depreciation of the US dollar. The Bank Markazi, the Iranian central bank, also took counter-measures. In an attempt to free official Iranian assets frozen by the branches of subsidiaries of US banks not in the United States, it initiated lawsuits against five US banks for the return of Iranian deposits worth $3,000 million not in the United States, on the grounds that they were not under US jurisdiction.

To these initial economic sanctions taken by the US government should be added the voluntary imposition of economic embargoes by some labour unions in the United States. Some days after the seizing of the hostages, the International Longshoremen's Association stopped work on ships carrying cargoes to or from Iran. The Transport Workers Union decided to boycott the servicing of Air Iran planes arriving at Kennedy International Airport. The President of the AFL-CIO, Lane Kirkland, supported these voluntary embargo movements, saying on 25 November that 'It's a perfectly normal, spontaneous reaction of workers . . . taking that action.'[7]

The other point which should be noted concerns food embargoes. Because Iran had annually imported about 30 per cent of its food, and because Iran's once self-sufficient agriculture was in disarray and the raising of food prices and occasional shortages of food were sensitive issues for Iran,[8] it was predicted that one possible option remaining could be to stop the shipment of grain and other food. The American Farm Bureau, traditionally opposed to using food as a political weapon, announced an exception in this case a few days after the seizure.[9] In fact, however, this potentially very effective measure was not employed in the early stages. However, eventually the International Longshoremen's Union boycotted food exports to Iran, for instance, at Freeport in Texas.[10]

THE US APPROACH TO ITS ALLIES FOR COOPERATIVE MEASURES

Since Iran's trade had also been greatly dependent upon the EEC countries and Japan, economic sanctions against Iran would have proved completely ineffective without the cooperation of those countries, which, fortunately for the United States, were her allies. From 10 to 13 December, the US Secretary of State, Cyrus Vance, visited Britain, France, West Germany, Italy and the NATO Council meeting in Brussels to seek support for possible economic and financial measures against Iran. Articles in contemporary newspapers, magazines and other sources indicate that the measures proposed included:

(a) export embargoes;
(b) oil import embargoes;
(c) restricting of financial dealings; and
(d) freezing of Iranian assets.

Measure (c) was understood to involve putting pressure upon private banks to insist that Iran should make the payments on her substantial loans promptly, instead of delaying several days, the normal practice. This measure was aimed at causing additional financial problems for Iran because of difficulty in servicing and repaying her large foreign debts.

In addition to seeking agreement on these four measures, the United States will also have called upon its allies to support any future proposal in the United Nations for collective economic sanctions against Iran.

The general reaction of the European allies, notwithstanding their great dependence on Iranian oil, was to express political and diplomatic support for the United States. Each agreed that the common international interest in upholding the principle of diplomatic immunity ought to be maintained. They also considered that the Atlantic Alliance, though directed against the Soviet bloc, had a global aspect, and that they should, therefore, defend American honour and credibility with regard to Iran. At the end of the meeting of all fifteen NATO foreign ministers on 13 December 1979, a communiqué was issued stating that while the NATO governments had 'no desire to intervene in Iran's internal affairs, the seizure of the US Embassy in Tehran should be opposed by the international community as a whole and calling for the immediate release of the hostages'.[11] After this NATO meeting, Vance suggested that the United States was confident that several of her allies would coordinate economic sanctions against Iran, should the UN Security Council (perhaps because of a Soviet veto) reject collective economic sanctions.[12]

However, the allies' support was diplomatic rather than practical. They did not like to contemplate the damage to their economies that might result from cooperative sanctions against Iran. One observer wrote that 'they [the allies] offer an implicit bargain to the United States, providing their full support as long as something less is sought'.[13]

Before considering the economic anxieties of the allies, one should note the fact that the action of the United States in freezing official Iranian assets created strains in the international banking fraternity. First, efforts by some American banks to extend the freeze to Iranian official deposits held at their overseas branches in European capitals (these deposits were found at the end of the crisis to total $5,000 million – nearly 40 per cent of all Iranian assets frozen) raised a legal problem as to whether the deposits were under US jurisdiction or not. The Bank Markazi initiated proceedings in those capitals for the release of such deposits. In London, more than twenty law suits were initiated, in one of which the Bank Markazi succeeded in obtaining a temporary injunction regarding its funds.[14] Also in London, the Bank Melli of Iran filed suit against the First National Bank of Chicago for the release of £511,750. Finally, the British Parliament introduced special legislation to ban further attempts by the US Administration to enforce American law in the United Kingdom.[15]

In France, the Bank Markazi took legal action to compel the Paris branch of Citibank to release $50 million of blocked deposits. It argued that Citibank could not refuse payment under French law.[16] In Bonn, it was stated that there was no legal basis for the freezing of Iran's overseas deposits.[17] These matters angered not only bankers but also the governments of the countries in question.

They were also irritated by the action of Chase Manhattan, which in 1977 had arranged a consortium loan for Iran worth $500 million, involving British and Canadian banks. After the freezing order, Chase Manhattan froze the Iranian deposits in its London branch and asked the ten other members of the consortium to decide that immediate release of the whole loan, principal and interest, should be demanded.

Since most of the lenders were American banks, Chase Manhattan soon gained a majority. Thus, the Iranian government was formally declared to be in default. With respect to this, Anthony Sampson wrote:

> Since the revolution in Cuba and the vast expansion of the international capital market no nation had ever actually defaulted. Bankers had gone to great lengths to avoid declaring a default – whether in Zaire, or in Peru or in New York. They preferred to adopt all kinds of other devices or forms of words – rescheduling, rolling-over, or at worst 'moratorium' to avoid taking a step which would not only put a country outside the pale, but would damage the whole delicate structure of confidence in world banking. Yet now a conservative international bank was declaring a default against a country which had tried to pay the due interest, but which had been prevented because their money had been frozen.[18]

Bonn was angered by moves by Morgan Guaranty Trust to freeze the Iranian quarter-share in Germany's Krupp steel concern, as a means of safeguarding its loans. The West German Finance Minister, Hans Matthoefer, protested that 'the foreign companies were interfering "in matters that affect our foreign policy"'[19] These financial frictions caused the EEC to be suspicious of the US approach for cooperative steps to punish Iran, because US attempts to block the release of Iranian deposits, said to be necessary in order to punish Iran, seemed also to be intended to protect American commercial and official assets at the sacrifice of the business interests of its allies' financial institutions.

In addition to these strains between the United States and its allies over financial and jurisdictional issues, each of the allies had its own vital interests to protect, which made it reluctant to be involved in economic sanctions against Iran. Britain, for instance, with her large economic, political and military stake in the Gulf and in oil money, would have been hard hit, if, through her cooperation with the United States, she had played a significant role in using financial weapons against an oil-producing country. Indeed, the Arab OPEC countries had already indicated to London that 'they are watching closely to see if the British Government is prepared to enlist in the Carter financial freeze strategy'.[20] Although Shell and BP had wider interests in Iranian oil, oil imports from Iran accounted for only 5 per cent of Britain's total oil intake. However, her having taken a leading part in any wider embargo could have endangered London's role in recycling oil money from OPEC countries and as an international banking centre.[21]

Moreover, trade embargoes could hit jobs, particularly in the motor industry. Chrysler's British subsidiary had a contract with Iran for the export of kits worth £150 million a year. Major consultancy and construction projects in Iran could also suffer. British Steel had a contract worth £32.7 million for a steel complex in Isafahan and British Rail a contract worth £7 million for electrification of the railway between Tehran and Tabriz. GEC was constructing a £30 million power station at Ahwaz, Davy Powergas a £17.5 million fertilizer plant at Shiraz. Marples Ridgeway had a contract worth £125 million to build a highway in Baluchistan.[22]

In addition, as previously mentioned, the British government was very concerned about the reaction of the OPEC countries and the probable refusal of British and foreign banks in the City to comply with any government order to freeze Iranian official assets, so it preferred to stand aside in this matter.

Naturally, similar situations existed in other allied countries. For instance, West Germany, the third largest importer of Iranian goods after Japan and the United States, and the second largest exporter to Iran after the United States, also felt reluctant to be seen to be participating in the American diplomatic initiative. West Germany also had legal difficulties in taking cooperative action with the United States. West German officials explained:

Room for legal and financial manoeuvre is more limited in Europe than in the US. Under German law . . . [the government] would only be able to move against Iranian assets (or take more drastic actions, such as imposing an export embargo) if the security of West Germany or world peace was directly threatened.[23]

Moreover, a trade embargo could have meant much greater hardship for the Germans than for anyone else in the EEC. Nearly half of the EEC's manufactured exports to Iran came from West Germany, with West Germany also depending on Iran for 12 per cent of its oil imports.[24] The industry which would suffer most was steel. In addition to Krupp, Salzgitter, another of the largest steel concerns in West Germany, which was selling one-third of its structural steel to Iran, would be hard hit. Salzgitter's annual sales to Iran amounted to about $50 million, Krupp's to $110 million in 1979.[25]

Italy also had its interests in Iran. The state-owned construction company Società Italiana per Condutte d'Acqua had a contract with Iran for expansion of the port at Bandar Abbas. Another state-owned company, Italimpianti, was to build a steel plant. The total value of these contracts was around $1,000 million.[26]

France had already been hit since the Iranian revolution. At the beginning of 1979, Iran was France's second largest customer for capital goods, next to the USSR, with contracts worth $7,000 million, but 70 per cent of these had been suspended since the revolution. Hardest hit was the nuclear power station group Framatome, whose contract for the construction of up to fifteen nuclear power stations (costing $2,000 million each) had been cancelled. In addition, there was about $2,000 million worth of as yet uncancelled projects (mainly construction, civil engineering, dams and railway projects) also at risk.[27]

Furthermore, although all the EEC countries, except Ireland, had drastically reduced their oil imports from Iran, they still depended on Iran to a considerable extent, far more than the United States. The Netherlands was still buying 6 per cent of its oil from Iran (55 per cent in 1978), Belgium 10 per cent (29 per cent in 1978), France 4 per cent (10 per cent in 1978), Italy 1 per cent (15 per cent in 1978).[28]

For all these reasons, the EEC countries were extremely reluctant to join in US-led trade and financial sanctions against Iran. However, the US Administration was under very great political pressure from the Senate Foreign Relations Committee. Senator Jacob Jacovits had condemned the allies for not doing enough to support the United States during the crisis.[29] The pressure was likely to take more substantial form, as, on 13 December, legislation was introduced into the House of Representatives that would empower the President to raise traffic tariffs on imports of goods from countries seen as not assisting US efforts to free the host-ages in Tehran.

One may assume that Vance's visit to the NATO Council meeting at the end of his tour of Europe to seek support for, and cooperation in, the US economic and financial measures against Iran reminded the allies that there were good reasons to hold that NATO, though primarily directed against the Soviet threat in Europe, also had a global aspect, and that the allies should uphold the honour and credibility of their bloc leader at any time and anywhere. No doubt the United States also argued that its efforts to defend Western Europe from the Soviet threat deserved the allies' support and cooperation when its own honour and credibility were threatened. This pressure will have been most effective in the case of West Germany, given the country's considerable strategic dependence upon the United States and its proximity to the Eastern bloc.

In these extremely delicate circumstances, the outcome of the talks between Vance and the allied leaders was, in essence, diplomatic support for and polite refusal to be involved in the economic sanctions against Iran, though there were differences of degree among the allies. In the case of Britain, Lord Carrington, at the end of the meeting, referred to 'the British Government's wholehearted support of the efforts of the US government to secure the release of the hostages without precondition'.[30] Vance also then said that he was 'very appreciative of the spirit of help-fulness and co-operation'.[31] However, neither side mentioned substantial coercive measures, such as freezing Iranian assets. No pressure seemed to be exerted by America upon Britain. One may assume there were two reasons for this, one that trade with Iran had already shrunk, running at about 25 per cent of the previous year's level, owing to a complex series of factors involving the cancellation of contracts and the general stand-still in the Iranian economy;[32] the other that Britain had not shipped either arms or spare parts to Iran in the preceding six weeks 'because no orders were in the pipeline and not because of any gesture in support of US policies.'[33]

In addition, as one observer pointed out, the British Embassy in Tehran was playing a useful role by keeping an eye on the American hostages on an unofficial basis, and, therefore, in view of this fact, 'it would be difficult for Mr Vance to apply any great degree of pressure on Britain'.[34]

West Germany made a slight further commitment in addition to ex-pressing solidarity with the American position. West Germany made it clear that it would not 'supply military equipment or grant new export credits until the American hostages were released'.[35] These were the only practical expressions of solidarity by the European allies. Nevertheless, the fact was that no German company had applied for official export insurance cover since November 1979, probably because of the high commercial risk in trade with Iran.[36]

The French response after the NATO Council meeting was less co-operative than that of the British. The French government indicated that 'France was reluctant to participate in any action by the Western Powers against Iran',[37] and said nothing about trade with Iran.

The other important US ally was Japan. Since Japan had been the largest importer of Iranian goods and the third largest exporter of goods to Iran, it appeared unlikely that economic sanctions would be successful without its active cooperation. The United States made similar requests to Japan. The first informal meeting between the two took place in Paris on 10 December, between Vance and Japan's Foreign Minister, Saburo Okita, who was in Paris to attend an International Energy Agency meeting. Then, from 16 to 18 December, the US Deputy Secretary of the Treasury, Robert Carswell, made an official visit to Japan to seek cooperation in economic and financial sanctions.

However, in addition to damaging her diplomatic relations with Iran, Japan stood to suffer tremendous economic losses were she to join in economic sanctions. Japan was in a very delicate position, being dependent on imports for almost all her oil supplies, 10 per cent of which normally came from Iran. The position was, indeed, so delicate that, fearing Iran's suspension of oil exports to America's allies, some Japanese oil companies felt it necessary for Japan's economic security to secure Iranian oil on the spot market, regardless of its high price. In addition, more than twenty Japanese companies, among them Mitsui Trading, Chiyoda Chemical Engineering and Construction and Toshiba Electric, were involved in a contract for the construction of the Bandar Khomeini petrochemical complex, worth nearly $3,500 million. Consequently, just like US allies in Western Europe, Japan hesitated to play a significant role in the US-led sanctions.

However, US calls for Japanese support became even more insistent than in the case of the European allies. After the meeting with Japanese Foreign Minister Okita in Paris on 12 December, Vance bluntly accused Japan of undermining US efforts to exert economic pressure on Iran.[38] Referring to the Japanese oil companies' move to secure Iranian oil on the European spot market, Robert Byrd, the Democratic Leader in the Senate, said on 11 December that Japan's aiding Iran in this way was 'disgraceful, an outrage', while his powerful colleague Senator Russell

Long, Chairman of the Finance Committee, hinted at retaliation against Japan, if she did not cooperate with the United States.[39]

The importance of the United States as Japan's major trading partner and as an ally, through the mutual security treaty, prompted Japan in the end to placate the United States by sending a special envoy of the Prime Minister to Washington. Also, after meeting Carswell, Japan's Finance Minister, Noboru Takeshita, expressed, on 18 December, Japan's support for US efforts to press Iran for the release of the US hostages in Tehran, and said that Japan would act with the United States, whenever possible.[40] Prime Minister Ohira also announced on the same day that the government had already decided to instruct oil companies to limit their imports of Iranian crude oil to the levels obtaining before 4 November 1979.[41]

In addition, in order to frustrate any attempt to single out Japan for criticism, Japan made it clear that she would keep step with the European allies in her financial and economic relations with Iran. With respect to the US request to halt financial relations with Iran, Foreign Minister Okita told Carswell that Japan still depended largely on Iranian oil and needed to maintain financial relations with Iran to settle payments for Iranian oil. In another case, where there was US pressure to declare Iran in default, Japan declined to comply, as Iran had been steadily repaying its Japanese loans. Masahiko Seki, President of the Federation of Bankers Association of Japan, regarded the proposal as 'incomprehensible and devoid of common sense'.[42]

To these points should be added the fact that such strong US pressure gave rise to suspicion in Japan that the real intentions of the United States in so insistently requesting cooperation from Japan could be connected with a United States desire not to 'lose' in the 'US–Japan economic rivalry'. Nobuhiko Ushiba, a former trade negotiator and Ambassador to the United States, warned, on 18 December, that 'dissatisfaction with Japan would easily rise again because of the heavy Japanese trade surplus with the United States'.[43]

Finally, attention should be paid to the US approach to neutral Switzerland. In the area of international monetary transactions, the importance of Switzerland is such that Switzerland could clearly not be ignored. The US government, in fact, sent two special envoys to Switzerland: Richard Cooper, Under Secretary of State for Economic Affairs, and Anthony Solomon, Under Secretary responsible for international monetary affairs. On 7 December they flew to Switzerland to explain the importance of freezing Iranian assets in the branches and subsidiaries of US banks in Switzerland, and to seek cooperation from the Swiss government. However, the Swiss government took a dim view of the asset-freezing, 'which is seen as encroaching on its sovereign rights and threatening international monetary stability'.[44] Influenced, no doubt, by the size of deposits by Iran's past and present regimes, Switzerland rejected the idea of such reprisals for the hostage-taking.[45]

Activities similar to those undertaken by the US Administration to mobilize the active participation, or at least the non-participatory co-operation, of as many allies and other countries as possible have been seen in other cases of economic sanctions (see in Part One, Chapter 5). The United States faced enormous difficulty in gaining such cooperation, and, to overcome her allies' reluctance, employed more persuasive measures to get them to participate.

THE US APPROACH TO THE UNITED NATIONS

As seen in the previous section, the United States was not able to obtain full support, even from its allies. One would expect that it would encounter even greater difficulty in rallying support in the United Nations. Before looking at America's request to the United Nations for collective economic sanctions, let us consider two roles which it will have hoped the United Nations would play: first that of giving US policy added legitimacy internationally by a unanimous (or almost unanimous) call for the freeing of the diplomatic hostages and through a favourable judgement in the International Court of Justice; secondly, that of increasing the effectiveness of economic sanctions by means of collective economic sanctions which would make it very much more difficult for Iran to find alternative foreign sources of supply.

Using the United Nations to give added legitimacy to US actions

As far as the first role is concerned, the United States initially brought the case to the UN Security Council at a very early stage in the crisis. On 9 November 1979, the US government addressed a letter to the President of the Security Council, requesting urgent consideration of what might be done to secure the release of the hostages and to restore the sanctity of diplomatic premises and establishments. In response to this request, the Security Council met in closed session on the same day, and the President of the Council, supported by all the Council members, issued a statement declaring that normal international behaviour provided for the inviolability of diplomats, and calling on the Iranian government in the strongest terms to release the American hostages without delay.[46] Also, the President of the General Assembly announced that he was sending a personal message to Ayatollah Khomeini appealing for the release of the hostages.

On 25 November 1979, the Secretary-General of the United Nations addressed a letter to the President of the Security Council requesting an urgent meeting of the Council in an effort to seek a peaceful solution to the problem. In response to this request, the Security Council met twice, on 27 November and 4 December (no representative of Iran was present on either occasion), and at the end of the latter meeting the Council voted 15–0 in favour of a resolution (Resolution 457 (1979)) calling on Iran to release the hostages immediately, also calling on both countries to take steps to resolve the problem peacefully and requesting the Secretary-General to lend his good offices for the immediate implementation of the resolution.

The United States then brought the case to the International Court of Justice (ICJ) at The Hague. On 29 November 1979, the US government requested the Court to consider Iran's multiple violation of the following articles of international agreements, and, pending a final decision, to issue an interim injunction calling on the Iranian government to release the hostages and to restore the Embassy premises to the control of the US government. These articles were:

(a) Articles 22, 24, 25, 27, 29, 31, 37 and 47 of the Vienna Convention of Diplomatic Relations;
(b) Articles 28, 31, 33, 34, 36 and 40 of the Vienna Convention of Consular Relations;
(c) Articles 4 and 7 of the Convention on the Prevention and Punishment of Crimes against Internationally Protected Persons including Diplomatic Agents;
(d) Articles II(4), XIII, XVIII and XIX of the Treaty of Amity, Economic Relations and Consular Rights between the United States and Iran; and
(e) Articles 2(3), 2(4) and 33 of the Charter of the United Nations.[47]

On 30 November 1979, the President of the ICJ sent telegrams to both the United States and Iran, informing them that the matter was now before the Court. But no representative of the Iranian government was present at the public hearing held on 10 December 1979. Instead, on the previous day, the Court received a letter from the Iranian Minister for Foreign Affairs, Sadeq Ghotbazadeh, denying the jurisdiction of the Court over this case, saying that the problem only represented:

A marginal and secondary aspect of an overall problem, one such that it cannot be studied separately, and which involves *inter alia*, more than 25 years of continual interference by the United States in the internal affairs of Iran . . . The problem . . . is thus not one of the interpretation and the application of the treaties . . . Consequently, the Court cannot examine the American Application divorced from its proper context [which] includes . . . all the crimes perpetrated in Iran by the American Government, in particular the coup d'état of 1953 stirred up . . . by the CIA, the overthrow of the lawful national governments of Dr Mossadegh [Mossadeq], the restoration of the Shah . . . under the control of American interests, and all the social, economic, cultural and political consequences of the direct intervention . . . by the United States.[48]

Despite this Iranian claim, the ICJ unanimously accepted its jurisdiction over the matter, and issued an order on 15 December calling for provisional measures requiring the Iranian government to surrender the Embassy to the US authorities immediately, to release the hostages held in Iran, and to afford all diplomatic and consular personnel of the United States full protection, privileges and immunities. In this judgement, the Court also emphasized the importance of the institution of diplomacy and consular relations, stating:

The institution of diplomacy with its privileges and immunities, has withstood the test of centuries and proved to be an instrument essential for effective co-operation in the international community, and for enabling States, irrespective of their differing constitutional and social systems, to achieve mutual understanding and to resolve their differences by peaceful means; . . . the unimpeded conduct of consular relations . . . is no less important . . . in promoting the development of friendly relations among nations . . .[49]

In consequence, the United States succeeded in attaining its goal of aligning itself on the side of justice in the ICJ.

Attempts to increase the efficacy of economic sanctions

Now that the first stage in the sanctions policy within a UN framework had been attained, the United States moved into a more problematic area: it sought to obtain a Security Council decision to impose collective economic sanctions against Iran, and thereby to increase the effectiveness of sanctions.

Notwithstanding the ICJ's provisional judgement on 15 December 1979 requiring the Iranian government to surrender the US Embassy to the US authorities immediately and to release the hostages held in Iran, there seemed to be no progress in Iran. This, however, helped to justify the US government's bringing the matter before the Security Council. Article 94, paragraph 2, of the UN Charter states:

> If any party to a case fails to perform the obligations incumbent upon it under a judgement rendered by the Court, the other party may have recourse to the Security Council, which may, if it deems necessary, make recommendations or decide upon measures to be taken to give effect to the judgement.

On 21 December President Carter called on the United Nations to impose economic sanctions against Iran, accusing Iran of 'arrogant defiance' of the world community.

On the basis of the two precedents for collective economic sanctions by the Security Council – one in the case of Rhodesia in 1966 and 1968, the other *vis-à-vis* South Africa in 1977 – a sanctions decision or resolution requires the approval of nine out of fifteen members and the acquiescence of the Five Permanent Members. Thus, Donald McHenry, the US representative at the United Nations, began consultations with the fourteen other members to line up support for economic sanctions against Iran. The two main difficulties were persuading the Soviet Union not to use its veto, and rallying the support of at least nine members of the Security Council.

America's efforts to induce the Soviet Union to cooperate were initiated by the Secretary of State, Cyrus Vance, who met the Soviet Ambassador in Washington, Anatoly Dobrynin, before setting out on his tour of the EEC capitals. Vance asked the Ambassador not to use the veto on collective economic sanctions in the United Nations. Senator Frank Church, Chairman of the Senate Foreign Relations Committee, publicly warned the Soviet Union that 'the backlash against a Russian veto, or even against a Russian abstention on the sanction issue . . . will almost certainly derail ratification of SALT-II.'[50] The Soviet position remained uncertain until the end of December, but it was very likely that the Soviet Union would use its veto. On 14 December the Soviet Ambassador to the United Nations, Olyeg Troyanovsky, had said that he opposed sanctions because they would not only not help the hostages but might be harmful. And it was generally predicted that, although the Soviet Union had spoken of the violation of international law in holding embassy staff, it had criticized American moves against Iran in an effort to avoid being linked to the United States in Iranian eyes.

There was also difficulty in gathering at least nine affirmative votes for collective economic sanctions. In addition to the five permanent members, the Security Council has ten non-permanent members, at that time Bangladesh, Jamaica, Norway, Portugal, Zambia, Bolivia, Czechoslovakia, Gabon, Kuwait and Nigeria, the President in December 1979 being China. Third World members of the United Nations had actually been warning the United States not to ask the Security Council to impose collective economic sanctions against Iran.[51] Kuwait in particular expressed its opposition to them. On 26 December 1979, Kuwait's Deputy Minister and Foreign Minister, Sheikh Sabah, said that, while the taking of diplomatic hostages was in contravention of international law, 'we reject the punishment of Iran through an economic blockade, especially when it is a neighbour and its people are Muslims'.[52] Therefore, the only votes the United States could count on were those of Britain, France, Norway, Portugal, Bolivia and its own.

In an attempt to obtain support from more countries, McHenry consulted Security Council members to see whether it would be possible to identify a list of items which a majority might be willing to ban. Taking into consideration Western dependence upon Iranian oil, a boycott of Iranian oil imports was excluded. With respect to a food embargo, one argument maintained that such a ban was both immoral and ineffective because it would almost always hurt the wrong people, specifically the poorest and the least powerful. Cuba (not a member of the Council), for instance, expressed its opposition to a food embargo against Iran on 26 December. New Zealand (also not a Council member), though one of America's allies, also opposed using a food embargo to punish Iran. The New Zealand Prime Minister, Robert Muldoon, said on 22 December that 'the Government would not be attracted to any proposal which might prejudice a £45 million deal to export lamb to Iran.'[53] Pharmaceuticals were also dropped from the list of embargoed materials on humanitarian grounds.

Despite all its efforts, the United States failed to find the necessary nine affirmative votes, because 'Third World members expressed general reluctance at sanctions without a "last gasp" to persuade the Iranians that the world was opposed to taking diplomatic hostages.'[54] So the United States had to agree to a proposal to postpone a decision on sanctions for about a fortnight and to send the Secretary-General to Iran again to seek the release of the hostages. One may assume that the United States placed its hopes on the opportunity afforded by the forthcoming replacement of five of the non-permanent members, though the new members did not seem likely to improve the situation. (Of the ten non-permanent members, Bolivia, Czechoslovakia, Gabon, Kuwait and Nigeria were to be replaced by East Germany, Niger, the Philippines, Tunisia and Mexico on 1 January 1980.)

On 31 December 1979, the Security Council passed a resolution (Resolution 461) by eleven votes to none, with four abstentions, deploring the detention of the hostages, calling for their immediate release and requesting the Secretary-General to lend his good offices for a solution.

In accordance with this resolution, Kurt Waldheim flew to Tehran on 1 January 1980 to meet Iranian officials. On 3 January, he also met some of the leading members of the Revolutionary Council, but was unable to see Ayatollah Khomeini. After returning to New York, he told the Security Council on 7 January that 'at present' Iran was 'not prepared to respond to the call from the United Nations for the release of the hostages.'

Since there was no sign of any effort being made by the Iranian government, on 10 January the United States presented to the Security Council a draft resolution for the imposition of collective economic sanctions against Iran. The draft resolution stated that all member states of the United Nations should:

(a) prevent the sale or supply to Iran of all commodities or products 'except food, medicine and supplies strictly intended for medical purposes';
(b) prevent the shipment to Iran of any item covered by (a), or its carriage across their territory;
(c) prohibit the supply of any new credit or loans to Iran and 'not make available any new deposit facilities, or allow substantial increases in existing non-dollar deposits';
(d) 'reduce to a minimum the personnel of Iranian diplomatic missions accredited to them'; and
(e) prevent their nationals from engaging in any activity which would benefit Iran.[55]

With reference to the financial sanction (c), the groundwork for such steps was laid in December 1979, when US Treasury Department officials visited Europe and Japan. But negotiations on concrete measures continued between the United States on the one hand, and the EEC, Switzerland and Japan on the other, and just before 10 January 1980 they reached agreement in principle regarding the measures. Actually, the three measures had been proposed by West Germany on 4 January 1980.

On 13 January 1980, the draft resolution was put to the vote, but was not adopted because of a Soviet veto. The result of the vote was ten countries for the resolution and two against (the Soviet Union and East Germany) with two abstentions (Mexico and Bangladesh). So in the end the United States failed to achieve its second objective: using the United Nations to increase the effectiveness of sanctions.

Appeals to an international political organization had been made for the same purposes, i.e. legitimation and increased efficacy, in other cases of economic sanctions, most notably those of the League sanctions against Italy and the United Nations sanctions against Rhodesia (dealt with in Part One). The US attempt to appeal to the United Nations fell foul of the veto.

US UNILATERAL SANCTIONS

The process of US unilateral sanctions

After America's failure in the Security Council, the Iranian government issued a statement on 14 January calling on other countries 'not to get involved in the United States' political games', and making it clear that 'the sole condition [for the release of the hostages] was the extradition of the deposed Shah . . . and his property'.[56] On 16 January, Oil Minister Moinfar threatened to stop oil supplies to countries that imposed sanctions against Iran.

On 21 January 1980, President Carter announced that 'Sanctions will be pursued by ourselves.' But on 28 January the United States delayed imposition of the planned economic sanctions. One of the main reasons was undoubtedly the landslide victory of Bani-Sadr in the presidential election held on 25 January. He obtained 75.7 per cent of the vote. Bani-Sadr, who was Western-educated, had said during the campaign that 'the question of the American hostages was secondary and should be settled quickly'.[57] Moreover, the evening before the election, Bani-Sadr said, 'If in Iran we have two governments, for example, one the students . . . and the second one the Revolutionary Council, this condition is not acceptable.'[58] Therefore, as expressed on 28 January in a statement by a State Department spokesman, Hodding Carter III, the United States hoped that Iran would end the crisis, though it was 'unable to predict what effect the election results will have on the release of the hostages.'[59]

Another important reason for the postponement of sanctions was presumably that the United States wanted to protect the territorial integrity of Iran against the threat from the Soviet Union (the American response with regard to Afghanistan having a similar basis). Because of the Soviet threat to the Middle East, President Carter wanted 'the matter of the hostages out of the way' and to 'help the Iranian Government . . . in a struggle for survival against the real threat.'[60] This overriding American concern could hardly have been stated more clearly than in the 'Carter Doctrine', proclaimed on 24 January: 'An attempt by any outside force to gain control of the Persian Gulf region will be regarded as an assault on the vital interests of the United States. It will be repelled by use of any means necessary, including military force.'[61] Also, Hodder Carter III said, 'We firmly believe that a democratically stable and economically progressing Iran is the best defense against Soviet expansion.'[62]

The fact that during his campaign Bani-Sadr had emphasized Iran's need for economic and political independence may also have helped to induce the United States to delay imposing sanctions. In addition, in mid-January Ayatollah Khomeini was taken to hospital for treatment for a heart condition. No doubt the United States was hoping for a political change should he die.

American unilateral economic sanctions

Reconciliation was attempted by the Secretary-General, who announced on 25 January that both the USA and Iran had agreed to set up a Commission of Inquiry into the Shah's alleged 'crimes'. By mid-February, both countries had officially announced moves towards a reconciliation, including the establishment of the Commission. This was established in Geneva on 20 February, and included representatives from France, Algeria, Venezuela, Syria and Sri Lanka. On 24 February they arrived in Tehran to begin the inquiry.

The establishment of the Commission as an intermediary would seem to have been a deft diplomatic means of seeking a way out of the political impasse by enabling both the United States and Iran to save face. But from the outset there was major disagreement between the two countries (a) as to whether the Commission's brief should include evidence of American espionage activities under the Shah's regime, and (b) as to when and how the hostages should be released.

Concerning the first matter, on 20 February Tehran radio broadcast a message from Ayatollah Khomeini to the effect that the Commission had been established to investigate not only the Shah's crimes but also America's intervention in Iranian internal affairs through the Shah. President Carter on 19 February, however, had already expressed disagreement with this interpretation, stating that the United States would never apologize to Iran for its previous activities in that country.

Regarding the second matter, the US Administration had demanded the hostages' immediate release in exchange for America's agreeing to consent to the setting up of the Commission of Inquiry, whereas President Bani-Sadr said on 21 February that the Commission had no direct connection with the release of the hostages, and Ayatollah Khomeini also stated in his message that the fate of the hostages would be up to the representatives of the people, who would meet in an Islamic Consultative Assembly.

Notwithstanding these differences of interpretation, the members of the Commission continued with their task, meeting Iranian Foreign Minister Ghotbazadeh several times and taking statements from people who had allegedly suffered torture under the Shah's regime. On 28 February, the Algerian co-chairman of the Commission, Mohammed Bedjaoui, said in a speech that the Commission would tell the world of the unimaginable degree to which, evidence showed, human rights had been violated under the Shah. Circumstances became more favourable for the early release of the hostages. On 6 March, the militant students agreed to turn the hostages over to the Revolutionary Council, announcing that their task was completed. The Commission also tried to see the hostages and to ascertain how they had been treated.

But the situation reversed itself on 8 March, when a member of Ayatollah Khomeini's entourage announced that the transfer of the hostages from the students to the Revolutionary Council had not been approved by Khomeini himself, who had been in hospital until 2 March; the students then refused to relinquish the hostages. As the Commission's request to see the hostages was also refused by the students, the Commission members left Tehran on 11 March.

Thereafter, the situation went from bad to worse. Ayatollah Khomeini had demanded the extradition of the deposed Shah and the return of his wealth as one of the major conditions for the release of the hostages. President Sadat invited the Shah to Egypt, and on 24 March he arrived in Cairo from the United States. This again stirred up anti-American feeling in Iran.

Ayatollah Beheshti, leader of the Islamic Republic Party and the most powerful figure in the Revolutionary Council, said on 26 March that those hostages who were spies should be put on trial, if the Shah and his wealth were not repatriated. On the previous day Ghotbazadeh had said that the Shah's arrival in Egypt would make it extremely difficult to free the hostages. Moreover, it had become clear that Bani-Sadr's power-base was narrow. On 31 March, the day after his meeting with the students, Bani-Sadr announced that the Revolutionary Council would take the hostages under its care and custody, if the United States issued an official statement saying it would refrain from making any provocative moves towards Iran before the new parliament could be convened to deal with the hostage problem. Regarding this as a positive step, the US Administration considered it inadvisable to impose additional sanctions on Iran, and on 2nd April a White House spokesman said that the United States would 'continue to be restrained in [its] words and actions' as long as progress was being made. In the Revolutionary Council meeting on 3 April antagonism between Bani-Sadr and Beheshti surfaced, and it was announced that the Council was not satisfied with the US Statement. On 5 April, the Islamic Republic Party issued a statement that the release of the hostages and the extradition of the Shah were closely connected, and that the hostages should be kept by the students. Since this utterly contradicted Bani-Sadr's policy, the final decision was made by Ayatollah Khomeini, who on 7 April ruled that the hostages would remain in the custody of the students until a new parliament decided their fate.

Considering that the appeasement policy had proved ineffective and insufficient, President Carter decided on a series of sanctions against Iran on 7 April:

(a) severing diplomatic relations with Iran (requiring all Iranian diplomats to leave the United States);
(b) a ban on virtually all exports from the USA to Iran;
(c) a threat to make frozen Iranian assets available to all claimants, including hostages' families, by making a formal inventory of the assets; and
(d) invalidating all visas issued to Iranians for future entry to the United States.

At the same time, Secretary of State Vance called on the ambassadors of nearly twenty-five friendly countries, including the EEC countries, Japan, Austria, Norway, Sweden, Canada, Australia and New Zealand, to match at least some of Carter's measures. On 8 April, the President's plea for support was delivered by the US ambassadors to each of the friendly nations' governments, in a note referring to 'various options for further action by other countries'.[63] In advance of this, American diplomats asked the EEC countries and Japan to collaborate by recalling their ambassadors from

Tehran or lowering their level of diplomatic contact. With a view to ensuring the cooperation of his reluctant allies, President Carter put political pressure on them by announcing on 17 April that whether or not the United States took military action against Iran largely depended upon how far his allies joined in imposing non-military sanctions. In the same announcement he ordered additional punitive steps, which were:

(a) a ban on all imports from Iran;
(b) prohibiting financial transfers by persons subject to US jurisdiction to any person or entity in Iran; and
(c) prohibiting any American citizens (other than members of the press) from visiting Iran.

In Iran, however, this move by the United States was welcomed by Ayatollah Khomeini as a clear victory for Iran. Oil Minister Moinfar threatened to cut supplies of oil to any country which joined in the US-led economic sanctions. On 12 April, Foreign Minister Ghotbazadeh summoned the ambassadors of Spain, Portugal, Sweden, Greece, Finland, Austria and Switzerland and 'asked these countries not to follow the political policy of the United States'.[64] Most of the methods enumerated in Part One, Chapter 3, were employed by the United States.

COOPERATIVE SANCTIONS BY US ALLIES

General reaction to America's demand

In response to urgent requests from the United States for sanctions against Iran similar to those imposed by the United States, the leaders of several countries, including West Germany, Britain, Japan, Canada and Australia, made sympathetic statements about the United States' situation, but most were more or less unenthusiastic and cautious about the imposition of further sanctions. The British Prime Minister, Mrs Thatcher, stressed on the one hand the need for strong backing for President Carter, saying that Americans 'understandably expect solidarity from their allies, and we, for our part, have been giving and will continue to give them our utmost support',[65] but on the other carefully refrained from mentioning any further measures. Italian Premier Francesco Cossiga declared his government's full solidarity with the United States, but did not say what measures Italy was prepared to take. The Japanese Foreign Minister, Dr Saburo Okita, said on 11 April 1980 that Japan:

. . . finds it inexcusable that Iran is still holding the United States Embassy personnel hostage in outright violation of international law. . . . For Japan, oil is a vital issue but, if there are issues which are of greater importance, then we naturally have to think of taking some sort of measures to respond to those lofty causes.[66]

But he also told the Diet Foreign Affairs Committee that 'it will be difficult for Japan at this stage to impose sanctions against Iran'.[67]

One of the main reasons for the allies' unenthusiastic response to the US request was, naturally, as has previously been discussed, that many of them still carried on significant trade and financial dealings with Iran and imported a considerable amount of their oil from that country. British bankers strongly opposed, and might have been able to stop in the courts – or even in Parliament – any action that, by antagonizing a major client, Iran, could damage confidence in London as one of the chief banking centres. The oil-importing position of the main EEC countries and Japan, based on 1979 data, was as follows (figures in parentheses show imports from Iran as a percentage of total imports of crude oil (b/d = barrels a day):

Japan	600,000 b/d	(13.0)
West Germany	228,000 b/d	(12.6)
France	124,000 b/d	(5.4)
Britain	94,000 b/d	(7.1)
The Netherlands	90,000 b/d	(8.2)
Belgium-Luxembourg	52,000 b/d	(7.9)
Italy	48,000 b/d	(2.1)

Oil supplies from Iran had drastically decreased since the Shah's overthrow, but the allies' imports of Iranian oil were still relatively high. The atmosphere of crisis which had brought about the second major increase in the price of oil in the 1970s gave a heightened sense of dependence – indeed, vulnerability.

Another reason for the allies' reluctance was that, as it was put by EEC officials, 'It is unlikely that such action would impress a government driven more by ideological than economic considerations.'[68] Yet another important reason might have been the consideration that a clash between Iran and America's allies would weaken those political forces in Iran which were trying to give the country a democratic constitution and keep it in the non-aligned camp. The Italian Defence Minister, for example, made statements to this effect.[69]

To these factors should be added doubts regarding Carter's tough stand. *Le Monde* suggested in an article of 10 April that America's strong position 'owed as much to [Carter's] calculations about how to get re-elected as to concern for the hostages'.[70] It was probably suspected that it was impatience related to US domestic political considerations that had prompted Carter's criticism of his allies' reluctance. French Foreign Ministry officials 'professed surprise at what they considered to be the US President's unfair criticism'.[71]

However, whatever the differences in their Middle East interests and whatever the resentment felt by the allies at what they saw as high-handed action taken by the United States without prior consultation with them, and notwithstanding any misgivings they felt about US strategy in the Middle East, the allies in fact made great efforts to seek possible co-operative economic sanctions against Iran.

One important reason for their doing so was that, if President Carter had decided to impose a naval blockade on Iran, the allies' oil supplies would have been hit much harder, and the possibility of military conflict in the Middle East would have been increased. It was felt certain that, if President Carter, pressured by the deeply felt certain resentment of the American electorate, were to resort to military action in the Gulf, most Moslem states would align themselves with Iran against the West. Such anti-Western feeling in the region would only reinforce the repudiation of Western-oriented development in the Middle East, and inflict tremendous damage, political and economic, upon America's allies. As a result, they would not only suffer huge economic losses by the loosening of their long-standing economic ties with this region, but Gulf rulers would find it increasingly in their interest to reach an accommodation with the Soviet Union.[72] Therefore, the allies felt it imperative to accommodate the United States in some way or other.

Another reason for their willingness to consider sanctions was probably that, in view of the Soviet intervention in Afghanistan, the allies could not deny the need to reaffirm the solidarity of the free world bloc. Then, too, the possibility of other Middle Eastern oil-producing states' joining forces with Iran and cutting off oil supplies to America's allies would have been felt to have become quite remote, owing to the confrontation between Iran and Iraq.

Moreover, again considering the Soviet incursion into Afghanistan, America's allies, particularly the Europeans, were greatly concerned about the disruption of *détente*. *Détente* had flourished throughout the 1970s, and trade relations between East and West had become closer. These close economic ties had in turn further promoted *détente*. A contraction of trade relations as a result of retaliatory steps by both East and West could threaten an end to *détente*. America's allies probably preferred sanctions against Iran to sanctions against the Soviet Union. Very naturally, 'West German sources have said that officials in Bonn are more sympathetic to economic sanctions against Iran because of the hostages, than to sanctions against the Soviet Union in response to Soviet intervention in, and invasion of, Afghanistan.'[73]

Steps taken by the EEC countries

Deliberations among the EEC countries began on 9 April 1980 in Lisbon, where the EC foreign ministers were gathered for a regular scheduled meeting of the 21-nation Council of Europe to discuss relations between East and West. On the following day the EEC ministers agreed to postpone a decision on whether to back the US economic and diplomatic sanctions against Iran. But they decided that they would instruct their ambassadors in Tehran, in consultation with the Japanese Ambassador, to make another appeal to President Bani-Sadr for the release of the hostages, and that they should decide on their next move after learning of Iran's response to that appeal. On 22 April, the ambassadors of the EEC countries and Japan saw Bani-Sadr, but 'got nowhere',[74] after which they were temporarily recalled for consultation with their respective governments.

At first, joint EEC action was impeded by differences both in the national interests of the nine members and in their interpretation of the international political situation. As previously mentioned, West Germany in particular, being the most exposed to the threat from the Eastern bloc, was readier to prove its loyalty to the leader of the Western world through sanctions against Iran, 'without believing that they will work',[75] than to do so through sanctions against the Soviet Union, 'which will have a chance of making their point'.[76] Therefore, West Germany took the lead in the EEC in working out sanctions formulas.

The United States being her traditional ally, Britain had to, and did actually, express support, but declined to take any action on economic and diplomatic sanctions until the EEC countries collectively had decided what to do. Prime Minister Thatcher said in a television interview on 14 April, 'We have to do two things: do everything possible to secure the release of the American hostages and to show our support for our American allies.'[77]

Moreover, Britain, an oil-producing country, insisted that sanctions would be utterly ineffective without an embargo on oil imports from Iran. One could assume that Britain wanted to protect her political and economic interests by (a) displaying her support for the bloc leader,

(b) trying to evade American criticism of her by participating in collective EEC measures, and (c) attempting within the EEC to make the sanctions formula as little damaging to her own economic interests as possible.

The French government carefully avoided any official statement on the subject.[78] But *The Times* wrote, 'It is pointed out in informed circles [in Paris] that France has repeatedly expressed her solidarity with the United States over the matter of the hostages.'[79] Nevertheless, it was observed that France, partly because of her traditional attitude of 'self-inflicted semi-isolation', would oppose sanctions that could affect her exports.[80]

Despite such conflicting interests, the EEC foreign ministers finally agreed on 22 April, in Luxembourg, 'to seek immediate legislation . . . necessary in their parliaments to impose sanctions against Iran in accordance with the Security Council resolution . . . which was vetoed',[81] and decided that 'these legislative processes should be completed by 17 May', and that 'in the absence of decisive progress on the release of the hostages, they will then proceed immediately to the common implementation of sanctions.'[82] Pending the implementation of such measures, the foreign ministers decided to take the following steps immediately:

(a) to reduce staff at the embassies of the EEC countries in Tehran;
(b) to reduce the number of Iranian diplomats accredited to the EEC countries;
(c) to reintroduce a visa system for Iranian nationals travelling to the EEC; and
(d) to withhold permission for the sale or export of arms or defence-related equipment to Iran.

Moreover, in this text the EEC foreign ministers 'expressed solidarity with the Government and people of the United States', and condemned Iran, stating that the situation was 'intolerable from a humanitarian and legal point of view'.[83] However, they decided against an embargo on Iranian oil imports. The measures adopted were largely cosmetic. For example, arms sales of any size from the EEC to Iran had already ceased.

In accordance with this agreement, each EEC government began examining the intended legislation. West Germany, for instance, decided to issue three decrees, taking advantage of a clause in the 1961 law governing foreign economic relations, without enacting or amending laws, which would have required approval by the Bundestag. Under paragraph 7 of this law, the government was empowered to subject all exports to compulsory licensing arrangements. Under paragraph 23, the government could introduce similar requirements in the areas of finance and banking. Although the export control measure was to be imposed on 17 May if no significant progress had been made by then, on 23 April Chancellor Schmidt called on German concerns not to sign any new commercial contracts with Iran, taking into account the possibility of the retrospective imposition of sanctions decided on by the EEC in the meeting on 17 May.

The Dutch government had prepared itself well in advance. A law governing economic sanctions, passed by Parliament on 13 February, entered into force on 21 April, when it received the royal assent. This law enable the government to restrict 'the movement of goods, services and capital, shipping, air transport, road traffic, posts and telecommunications'. The substantive details of the measure were to be contained in executive orders issued under the law in the light of the decision due to be made on 17 May. The Netherlands Credit Insurance Company (NCM), a privately owned firm which works closely with the government, had ceased to insure trade with Iran in January 1979. Therefore, retrospective sanctions would not cause any undue dislocation in the Dutch economy.

In Britain, the Iran (Temporary Powers) Bill was passed by Parliament, the Act entering into force on 17 May. This Act empowered the government to make necessary provisions by Order in Council in relation to contracts 'Applying either to those for services or those for the sale, supply or transport of goods',[84] provided that the Order in Council should apply neither to any contract 'made before the date on which the Order is made',[85] nor to any contract 'with a bank or other financial institution for the provision of banking or other financial services'.[86] With regard to retro-active legislation, powers already existed under the 1939 Import, Export and Custom Powers (Defence) Act, though the Act does not deal with service contracts and transport. The substance of sanctions would be spelled out in Orders in Council issued in accordance with the decision due to be made at the EEC meeting in Naples. The fact that service contracts and transport were not covered by the two Acts clearly suggests that the British government had no intention of applying sanctions in these areas, whatever agreement was reached at Naples.

In France it was understood that it would take a very long time to enact or amend a *loi*, since it would have to be debated and approved by the National Assembly. So the French government prepared for sanctions by means of a *décret*. Although the *décret* involved a few technical problems with regard to retroactive application, there was no other solution.

Since there was actually no 'decisive progress' by mid-May, the EEC countries proceeded at the special meeting of their foreign ministers at Naples on 17 and 18 May 1980 to determine what form their sanctions should take. It was decided at Naples to prohibit EEC nationals from supplying Iran with goods (except food or medicines) or services (except those relating to food or medicines, or financial and banking services) based upon any contract concluded after 4 November 1979, and to commence such sanctions on 22 May. Despite the declaration made at Luxembourg on the imposition of economic sanctions as provided in the draft UN resolution of January 1980, the sanctions agreed upon at Naples were considerably watered down.

First, the EEC collective sanctions failed to include import embargoes, such as an embargo on oil imports. Second, the EEC ministers did not agree to freeze Iranian assets, or to prohibit financial and banking services. Third, they failed to prohibit the supply of goods and services based on contracts made before 4 November 1979. Although this helped those countries likely to face legal and material problems in cancelling existing contracts, it undoubtedly impaired the meaningfulness of the sanctions. For hardly any contracts had been signed since 4 November 1979 on account of the extreme economic instability in Iran.

Fourth, Britain in the end failed to comply with the EEC agreement and set far slacker sanctions which did not affect any existing contract, including contracts made after 4 November 1979. On 19 May 1980, a 'Statement on Iran' was read by Lord Carrington in the House of Lords and by the Lord Privy Seal in the House of Commons. It stated:

> On the question of existing contracts, it was agreed that contracts for the export of goods to Iran entered into after 4th November, 1979, would be affected by the sanctions . . . However, service contracts will not be affected, except for new service contracts in support of industrial projects which will be banned as from the date of entry into force of the appropriate Order in Council. We shall be coordinating closely with our Community partners to achieve parallel effects on these questions.[87]

Indeed, while the Iran (Temporary Powers) Bill was being debated, the Labour party had insisted that the sanctions should not be extended to any existing contract. Following this, the government had replied that their views would be taken into account. Existing contracts were expressly excluded from the Bill. But on 19 May the government again referred to the possibility of retroactive legislation by invoking the Import, Export and Customs (Defence) Act 1939, under which export of goods under contracts made after 4 November could be prohibited.

MPs, both Conservative and Labour, reacted hostilely to the 19 May statements. David Winnick (Labour) said:

The Government is cheating over the date when sanctions are going to be applied. Those who will suffer and feel most strongly are the people whose jobs could be at risk in this country. It would have been better on the merits of the situation for the foreign ministers to have recognized that sanctions are a farcical gesture which will not help to secure the release of a single hostage.[88]

Sir Nicolas Bonsor (Conservative) said: 'I was not aware that the retrospective element of legislation, now going to be invoked against Iran, is going to do enormous damage to British industry.'[89] The Thatcher government then withdrew the prepared draft of the Order in Council which provided for retroactive legislation.

Strong criticism was naturally levelled by most EEC countries at Britain's failure to live up to the Community agreement. In France, for instance, it was observed that 'British solidarity with the US was less evident when it came to proving it in practice', and 'It was ironic that the UK should be the odd man out when it had been preaching a firm joint Western position on other issues.'[90] The West German Minister of the Economy, Count Otto Lambsdorff, said pointedly that 'The British decision was one of a long line of strong British words and weak actions.'[91] Even within Britain *The Times* referred to the tearing-up of a Community decision without even putting it to the vote in Parliament as 'undignified and lamentable'.[92] It also said, 'The Government should have defended itself and the decision taken, since it was a decision reached . . . by nine governments in close and elaborate consultation, with the British Government insisting particularly that the nine must act together',[93] for 'the number of contracts involved is small and the importance of the sanctions is admitted to be largely symbolic in any case.'[94]

Although Britain failed to comply with the EEC agreement, the position of the EEC countries was not affected by Britain's desertion.

The substance of the sanctions clearly suggests that the European ministers sought to devise ways not so much of putting pressure upon Iran as of demonstrating to the Americans that Europe was a reliable ally and to the Iranians that the leading European countries unanimously and on the grounds of illegality disapproved of the taking hostage of the American Embassy staff. On 19 May Lord Carrington said in the House of Lords:

The nine representatives at Naples all intended to carry out the policies decided. Only time will tell if they are successful. We are part of an alliance and when a friend is in trouble we do not disregard our friends.

The fact that the nine leading European countries have decided to take this action will be noted in Iran as evidence of the Nine's disapproval of Iran's action.[95]

Certainly, as previously mentioned, America's allies had been generally reluctant to join in the US-led economic sanctions, and it was especially so with the EEC countries, which had considerable and long-standing interests in Iran. In 1978, the EEC as a whole was Iran's largest trading partner, exporting to her twice as much as the United States and three times as much as Japan. Indeed, Iran was the EEC's fifth largest export market.[96] It is, therefore, understandable that the EEC leaders wanted to restore close economic relations such as had existed before the revolution, rather than seek to punish her by means of doubtful effectiveness, especially while she was in the grip of religious zeal.

Important at this stage was the failure of a US rescue operation attempted on 24 and 25 April. The resulting fiasco led to the student captors announcing that they had decided to keep the hostages in different cities throughout the country to discourage any repetition of the US attempt to use force to rescue them. This reduced the need for cooperative sanctions by America's allies because one of their principal motives for co-operation had been to dissuade the United States from resorting to military measures which would endanger peace in the Middle East. The need to avoid this had now definitely diminished.

Another point which should be borne in mind is that the second round of elections for the Majlis (Parliament) took place on 9 May (the first had been held on 14 March), the result being that out of 270 seats the Islamic Republic Party gained 112, Bani-Sadr's group 54, and independents 80. The release of the hostages was seen as a decision that would be made by the Majlis. In such circumstances, the EEC countries probably considered that a hard line would generate further antagonism in the Iranian Parliament, harming the chances of the hostages' release.

Measures taken by Japan

Japan applied broader economic sanctions against Iran than those adopted by the nine European states. It was generally believed that the impact of Japanese sanctions should be considerable, given that in the pre-revolutionary period, for instance in 1978, Japan was Iran's largest export market, and her third largest supplier of machinery, cars, steel, clothing and synthetic textiles (after the United States and West Germany).

On 24 April, the Japanese government announced the same sanctions as the EEC countries had decided on at Luxembourg, except for the withholding of permission for the sale or export of arms or defence-related equipment to Iran (such Japanese sales being non-existent). Moreover, like the West German government, the Japanese government advised all major trading companies and large steel, automobile, synthetic textile, electronic, electrical appliance and chemical companies not to sign any new export contracts with Iran.

On 23 May, Japan decided to impose export embargoes on goods and services (except for food and medicines) under any contract entered into after 4 November 1979, to the same degree as the EEC countries (except Britain) had done. To give those sanctions legal effect, Japan issued two Cabinet Ordinances on 26 May – a Trade Control and a Foreign Exchange Control Ordinance. Contracts for a $3,300 million Japanese-Iranian petrochemical complex in Bandar Khomeini had, in fact, been concluded well before 4 November and were, therefore, unaffected by the embargo.

In addition to the measures taken by the Europeans, Japan also imposed financial sanctions. On 22 April the government announced that it would not provide Iran with any new credit.[97] Moreover, supporting America's sanctions, not only against Iran but also those regarding Afghanistan, Japan decided to give aid to the neighbouring states of those countries, such as Pakistan, Oman and Turkey. In close consultation with the United States, Japan had, for instance, decided early in 1980 to extend economic assistance totalling $160 million to Pakistan, and on 15 April she pledged $100 million in emergency assistance to Turkey.[98]

Furthermore, twelve Japanese oil-importing companies suspended purchases of Iranian crude oil. Early in April 1980, the National Iranian Oil Company (NIOC), notified those companies, as well as British Petroleum and Royal Dutch Shell, of increases in the prices of Iranian crude oil (from $32.5 to $35 per barrel for Iranian light; from $31.77 to $34 per barrel for Iranian heavy), making it the most expensive oil sold under contract in the world. The NIOC insisted that shipments to companies not accepting the increased prices would be halted.

Japanese oil companies refused to accept Iran's demands. '[A]cting on the basis of strongly worded "guidance" originating from Prime Minister Masayoshi Ohira',[99] the twelve Japanese oil companies decided to reject the Iranian offer, and on 21 April the supply of crude oil to Japan, amounting to about 520,000 barrels per day (11 per cent of Japan's crude oil imports) was halted.

Japan sought to compensate for these losses in several ways. Under the International Energy Agency (IEA) Scheme, any member is entitled to seek help from others when its supplies fall 7 per cent short of the norm. It was acknowledged that it was indeed possible to compensate Japan for the loss of Iranian crude oil by means of the IEA 'trigger mechanism', should Iran cut off supplies. Moreover, the United States had already given the Japanese government assurances that she would help Japan with her oil needs in the event of the stoppage of oil exports from Iran to Japan. In the meeting between Prime Minister Ohira and President Carter in Washington on 2 May, Carter said, 'If Japan's co-operation in not buying oil at higher prices created special problems for Japan, the United States was prepared to be helpful.'[100] The United States did not, however, make any effort to make available to Japan Alaskan north sea oil, on which the US government still maintains a closed-door policy prohibiting exports. In the end, Japan had to ensure that it would be able to increase its oil imports from other sources, principally from Mexico, in return for loans to finance Mexican projects.

Japan's willingness to accept the loss of Iranian oil might almost have had the Americans jumping for joy. The State Department's spokesman, Hodding Carter III, said that 'Japan's refusal to pay the higher prices could be "the single most significant step taken" toward a peaceful solution to the Iranian hostages crisis.'[101] The US Ambassador in Japan went even further, saying that 'the most important bilateral relationship we have in the world is with Japan.'[102]

The Japanese decision was later followed by those of two European oil companies, British Petroleum and Royal Dutch Shell, which together risked a loss of about 270,000 barrels a day.

Backing from other nations

Other states backing the US-led economic sanctions were Portugal, Norway, Spain, Australia, Canada and the Philippines. On 16 April, the Portuguese government announced that it would sever economic ties with Iran until the American hostages were released. It declared the prohibition of all exports and imports, including oil imports, together with all financial transactions with Iran. It also forbade the use of Portuguese ships to transport, and of Portuguese ports to handle, goods embargoed by other countries. On 24 April, Norway decided to join in the EEC 17 May sanctions, if progress towards the release of the hostages were not made. Greece, which was soon to become the tenth member of the EEC, announced that it would adopt the EEC's position. Spain, which hoped to join the Common Market, also promised to back the sanctions.

Just after US Secretary of State Vance visited the Canadian Prime Minister, Pierre Trudeau, on 23 April, the Canadian government announced a series of economic and diplomatic sanctions against Iran, similar to those imposed by the Europeans and the Japanese. Also, the government told oil companies that 'It would be inappropriate for them to purchase Iranian oil in the current circumstances.'[103] Australia, which was selling Iran about $150 million worth a year of meat, wheat and other food stuffs, had been unenthusiastic about cooperative sanctions. Under strong pressure from the United States, however, the Australian government decided on 21 April that it would impose trade restrictions, falling short of trade embargoes. Under the restrictions, companies trading with Iran in non-food products were denied export subsidies and tax concessions.[104] The Philippines took measures of the same level as the Portuguese, except in respect of oil imports.

SUMMARY

In this chapter various attempts by the imposer – the United States – to ensure the effectiveness of economic sanctions have been seen. One notable feature of this case is that after its diplomats were seized, the US government very swiftly employed three sanction measures: (a) a halt of the shipment of military equipment; (b) a ban on imports of Iranian oil; (c) freezing of Iranian assets. The US decision on such selective sanctions indicates that in its overall strategy in dealing with this crisis the United States must have considered reduction of Iran's purchasing power and restricting its military capability to be of the very greatest importance for effective sanctions and that, therefore, those sanctions had to be imposed at once.

Another key feature of this case is that, as in some cases studied in Part One, the Carter Administration did its utmost to obtain collective economic sanctions by the United Nations. To this end, it worked diligently to establish the righteousness of the imposer's cause in order to justify its call for sanctions against the rule-breaker, Iran. This goal was attained in the United Nations Security Council and also in the International Court of Justice. However, a UN call for collective economic sanctions was in the end blocked by the Soviet veto.

A third key feature of this case is that, as was also seen in Part One, the imposer strove, following the failure in the UN collective sanctions, to ensure not merely verbal or moral support from its allies but their actual participation in the sanctions against Iran. The advocate of sanctions did not merely request or call for their cooperation, but employed pressure, even threats. For example, President Carter hinted at the possibility of military action against Iran unless the allies failed to join in the sanctions.

Fourthly, also noteworthy are the facts that the imposer took urgently necessary measures at an early stage and kept emphasizing its intention of going on to full-scale economic sanctions if the target failed to yield, and then, towards the end of January 1980, delayed resorting to all-out sanctions, despite the failure to attain UN collective sanctions, doing so partly because it saw the possibility of positive developments, perhaps as a result of Bani-Sadr's victory in the presidential election in late January. Nevertheless, one could argue that it was felt that gradually intensifying sanctions might help the sanctions to work more effectively than imposing them all at once.

What is certain is that in this case almost all the means of economic sanctions found to be used in the earlier cases studied in Part One have been seen to be employed.

9 Effect of the Economic Sanctions Against Iran

THE GENERAL STATE OF IRAN'S ECONOMY AND TRADE

Long before the Islamic Revolution the Shah embarked on economic modernization plans backed by oil production amounting to 6 million barrels a day (b/d). Between 1968 and 1973, the years of the fourth five-year plan, economic growth was in excess of 10 per cent per year. By the years of the fifth five-year plan (1973–1978), the Iranian economy had changed in character, from a traditional economy based on such products as foodstuffs and textiles, to one based on heavy industry, mainly in such fields as oil refining, petrochemicals and steel-making. This industrial reform inevitably made Iran highly dependent on the Western industrial countries, principally the United States, the EEC and Japan. Table 9.1 shows that the total volume of imports grew by nearly 20 per cent each year from 1976 to 1978, with imports from the major industrial states growing at about the same rate. In 1978, imports from the USA, the EEC countries and Japan accounted for 78.5 per cent of total imports, with those from the Soviet bloc accounting for no more than 5.5 per cent.

Table 9.1   Sources of Iranian imports, 1976–8 ($ million)

Source	1976	1977	1978	%(1978)
USA	2,133	3,004	4,053	21.6
West Germany	2,304	3,014	3,719	19.6
Japan	2,098	2,136	2,991	16.0
UK	992	1,256	1,585	8.5
Italy	686	996	1,173	6.7
France	630	751	970	5.2
Switzerland	434	400	423	2.3
Belgium	421	266	358	1.9
Holland	394	349	346	1.8
Spain	125	119	285	1.5
Total	12,894	14,070	18,733	100.0 (85% up to Spain)

Source: *Direction of Trade Statistics (IMF)*, 1979.

Iran's main imports were metal products (including iron and steel), machinery, chemical products and food (this last principally from the United States). According to a May 1980 statement by the Bank Markazi (the Iranian central bank), Iran's manufacturing industries largely depended upon imported semi-finished goods, chiefly from the West. The rate of dependence upon semi-finished products was about 80 per cent for metal goods and machinery, 75 per cent for pharmaceuticals, 71 per cent for textile goods, 59 per cent for building materials, with a similar pattern in other areas. Iran produced cars, but most of the parts, from engines to tyres, were imported. This fact, characteristic of the Iranian economy, suggests the key role joint-ventures with Western capital played. Moreover, Iran was buying over a quarter of its grain from abroad – half of its wheat and three-quarters of its rice from the United States, and much of the rest from countries such as Australia that were allies of America. Also, vital supplies of dairy products came from Western Europe, particularly from Britain.

Considerable dependence upon the Western countries was also conspicuous in Iran's exports, as shown by Table 9.2.

Oil and oil products accounted for a very large percentage of these exports. According to the annual report issued by the Iranian Central Bank, the national revenue in fiscal years 1978–9, 1979–80 and 1980–1

Table 9.2   Iranian export markets, 1976–8 ($ million)

Market	1976	1977	1978	%(1978)
Japan	4,049	3,881	3,869	17.2
USA	1,483	2,756	2,876	12.8
West Germany	1,807	1,696	1,910	8.5
Italy	1,155	1,356	1,421	6.3
Holland	1,565	1,454	1,362	6.1
France	1,309	998	1,093	4.9
UK	1,709	1,254	928	4.1
Spain	842	1,078	829	3.7
Belgium	432	680	707	3.1
Canada	677	506	523	2.3
Total	23,500	24,250	22,449	100.0 (69% up to Canada)

Source: *Direction of Trade Statistics (IMF)*, 1979.

was 1,598.9, 1,699.6 and 1,325.9 billion rials respectively, of which income from oil sales accounted for 1,013.3 (63.3 per cent), 1,219.7 (71.7 per cent) and 888.8 (67.0 per cent) billion rials. Table 9.3, showing contract crude oil exports at 1 May 1980, clearly illustrates how substantial a part of the Iranian national reserves had come from the advanced industrial countries.

Table 9.3   Iranian contracted crude oil exports at 1 May 1980

	Amount of contract (ten thousand b/d)	%
Contracts with developed countries:	94.6	72.2
Japan	52.6	40.1
BP (UK)	15	11.4
The Royal Dutch Shell (UK and Holland)	12	9.2
Belgium	5	3.8
Spain	3	2.3
West Germany	2	1.5
Sweden	2	1.5
Finland	2	1.5
Portugal	1	0.7
Contracts with developing countries:	23.5	17.9
India	12.5	9.5
Brazil	6.0	4.6
Turkey	4.0	3.1
Bangladesh	1.0	0.7
Contracts with Communist countries:	11	8.4
Romania	3.6	2.7
Yugoslavia	1.9	1.4
Poland	1.4	1.1
Czechoslovakia	1.1	0.8
Bulgaria	1.1	0.8
Hungary	1	0.7
East Germany	0.9	0.6
Others	2	1.5
Total	131.1	100

IRAN'S VULNERABILITY TO ECONOMIC SANCTIONS

Even the most cursory glance at the general characteristics of Iran's trade pattern reveals several points clearly indicating that the economic sanctions imposed by the United States and its allies must eventually have had a considerable effect.

First, the fact that Iran had depended largely upon the Western economies, almost all of which participated in the US-led sanctions against her, must eventually have reduced her to an extremely vulnerable position, the nations in question having accounted for over 80 per cent of Iran's total exports. Second, Iran's importing a huge volume of semi-finished articles meant that an almost immediate result of the sanctions would be the collapse of Iranian industry. There would also be acute shortages of plant and parts for new factories. The oil industry would be particularly hard hit by the cut-off of plant and spare parts. Third, the fact that since November 1979 US ports had stopped loading grain for shipment to Iran might cause one to expect food shortages, since, as already mentioned, Iran had bought half its wheat and three-quarters of its rice from the United States. Even though America's allies did not, for humanitarian reasons, include food in their embargoes, the effect of that halting of shipments ought not to be underestimated.

Fourth, freezing Iranian assets must have made it extremely difficult for Iran to finance essential foreign trade. Of $15,000 million in foreign currency reserves, some $9,000 million was said to be frozen. (The correct figure for assets frozen was later found to have been over $12,000 million.)

Fifth, the substantial oil-import boycott by the twelve Japanese oil companies, BP and Royal Dutch Shell no doubt led to a sharp reduction in oil revenues and, thus, to serious external payment problems. Undoubtedly, this must have further exacerbated the difficulty of financing foreign trade, and made it hard for Iran to obtain both the necessities of life and materials for industry. When Japan decided on the oil-import boycott, industrial analysts in Tokyo said that the Iranians 'could not afford to lose their revenues from Japan'.[1] Both American and British oil officials and diplomats also stressed that 'Iran was more dependent than ever on revenues from oil exports, which have dropped to 1.5 million barrels daily from 5.5 million in 1978 and 3.2 million a year ago [i.e. in 1979].'[2]

Then, too, even before the unrest of late 1978 and early 1979, the Iranian economy had been entangled in many difficulties, caused primarily by an over-ambitious five-year plan from 1973 to 1978. This plan to turn Iran into a leading industrial nation in the 1980s failed, bringing the annual rate of inflation to nearly 30 per cent. The industrial and civil unrest of late 1978 and early 1979 seriously disrupted the country's economy, particularly the oilfields and refineries, the banks, the national airline and the railways, which suffered long periods of inactivity. In these circumstances, the Bakhtiar government in some cases cancelled and in others revised the main military and nuclear contracts, and also development projects. Following the assumption of power by Ayatollah Khomeini and his followers, the Barzargan government made it clear that it would continue the policy already initiated by the Bakhtiar Cabinet of reviewing all foreign contracts with a view to cancelling or reducing most of the large-scale projects undertaken by the Shah.

Given these blows to the Iranian economy, foreign suppliers would naturally have been reluctant to fulfil even existing contracts. As a result, the number of joint ventures, on which the Iranian economy depended, would have been expected to drop considerably.

ACTUAL EFFECT OF THE ECONOMIC SANCTIONS

Though the conventional wisdom of recent years has it that economic sanctions are mere ritual without real effect, the sanctions against Iran did, in fact, have very considerable effect, but they were certainly not effective enough to force Iran to give in quickly. Early in 1980, before the EEC countries joined in the sanctions, the Bank Markazi issued a report stating that financial problems, a lack of skilled manpower and shortages of raw materials were seriously affecting many areas of industry. The report covered output of cars, tractors, tyres, electrical appliances and non-electrical household goods. Shortages of raw materials were the corollary to difficulties in buying from abroad and exchange and customs delays. Some 80 per cent of the managers surveyed were facing financial difficulties, while 56 per cent had difficulty in finding jobs. One could argue that, as this report was released before the Iranian presidential election, it is possible that by emphasizing economic hardships the Bank Markazi was seeking to help Bani-Sadr, who seemed likely to pursue more rational economic policies. But ensuing developments tended to confirm this report.

The Iranian government has published no official facts and figures indicating the effect of the US-led sanctions. Nor has any participating country released sufficient data to show how well sanctions worked. However, there is quite a considerable body of reliable data evidencing the large drop in trade between Iran and the Western allies.

America's exports to Iran in the first four months of 1980 fell to $8.7 million, compared with $349 million for the same period of the preceding year.[3] Japan's exports to Iran dropped by half after she joined in the sanctions. According to the figures issued by the Japanese Ministry of Finance, exports to Iran totalled $304 million in May 1980, dropping to $135 million in June and to $74.4 million in July. It was pointed out that the sanctions would cause a drop of roughly $2,700 million in Japan's exports of industrial plant in 1980, from the 1979 figure of $11,700 million.[4]

Speaking for the EEC countries, a Dutch official calculated that EEC sanctions had been so diluted that the effect would just 'lower the Nine's exports to Iran by only 8% below their previous likely levels'.[5]

Nevertheless, as Table 9.4 shows, EEC–Iran trade had already fallen in 1979 after the Shah's departure. Until 1979 Iran had been the EEC's fifth largest export market, but in that year it slid to twenty-second place, accounting for less than 1 per cent of total exports.[6]

Iran's economic difficulties gradually increased as a direct effect of the sanctions. According to the Bank Markazi, between 21 May and 21 June 1980 wholesale prices of industrial raw materials increased by 33 per cent, those of chemical products and petrochemicals by 30 per cent, those of paper and paper products by 36 per cent, and those of steel products by 29 per cent.[7] This situation, which cannot have failed to cause great difficulty and hardship, existed all over the country. The consumer price index in January 1980 was 12.1 per cent higher than in January 1979, 18.1 per cent, if housing is excluded.[8]

Table 9.4   EEC Exports to Iran in 1979

	Index *(1978 = 100)*
EEC total	38
West Germany	35
Britain	32
France	44
Italy	36
Belgium-Luxembourg	45
Denmark	90
Ireland	48

Source: *The Economist*, 24 May 1980, p. 67.

According to the Bank Markazi, in the first quarter of the Iranian year (starting on 21 March 1980), 'prices for food and clothing were up by 48 per cent, while agricultural goods and livestock showed a 56.5 per cent increase' compared with the corresponding period of 1979.[9]

That the rate of inflation was so high was partly owing to shortages of imported goods, and partly because middlemen in the Gulf, who sheltered Iran from the full impact of the sanctions by re-exporting embargoed goods to the Gulf ports going up by 30 per cent. Moreover, the bazaar merchants, who had traditionally controlled Iran's retail outlets, began hoarding. This accelerated, first, further shortages of goods and then inflation.

Along with soaring inflation, the falling output of Iran's factories inflicted severe damage on the Iranian economy. According to the Bank Markazi, factories were operating at only 30–40 per cent of capacity in June 1980. One reason for this was that the supply of semi-finished goods, on which Iran had depended, was drying up – partly on account of the export embargo by the United States and her allies, partly because exporters were unwilling to send goods to a country in such confusion, and partly also because of price increases. Naturally, this reduced both the production and supply of goods, making inflation even worse.

At the same time, shrinking industrial operations resulted in massive unemployment. The Iranian government took the earliest opportunity to ensure that workers who had been laid off were paid with bank advances. However, protracted under-utilization of industrial capacity eventually made it impossible to continue this assistance. Moreover, since the victory of the revolution at the beginning of 1979, most Iranian managers closely connected with the Shah's regime (accounting for a significant percentage of the country's managerial expertise) had been expelled from Iran and their companies nationalized by the new government. Following nationalization, many employees had been dismissed for ideological reasons or because of cancellation or reduction of projects.

Furthermore, work on existing joint projects was not pushed ahead positively, or, worse, projects (sometimes actually joint-ventures already operating commercially) were even suspended or abandoned. General Motors, for instance, closed a car plant producing 11,600 cars a year. IBM continued to run a service facility for its computers, but as the supply of spare parts from abroad had been halted by the sanctions, its future was precarious. Ford Aerospace and Communication had pulled out of a one-third completed, but uninsured, $300 million telephone cable contract.[10] Krupp postponed its decision whether to be involved in the

Sar Chesmeh copper project. The $3,000 million petrochemical complex at Bandar Khomeini, 50 per cent owned by a Japanese consortium led by Mitsui, was also suspended, though already 85 per cent complete.[11] Obviously, the suspension or abandonment of these projects exacerbated unemployment. Although almost no report has been found indicating the numbers unemployed, the Iranian Ministry of Labour disclosed in autumn 1979 that it was about 1–1.5 million. In June 1980 it was revealed in Tehran that it was more than 3.5 million. People gathered in front of the Ministry of Labour demanding jobs, and street stalls run by un-employed people were seen everywhere in Tehran.

The shortages of goods from outside and the temporary shutdown or permanent closure of factories were accelerated by the expectation that Iran would become insolvent on account of the freezing by the United States of perhaps $11,000 million of Iran's total foreign currency hold-ings of about $15,000 million. Misgivings were increased by the virtual boycott of Iranian oil applied by Japanese and European oil companies. This boycott meant that Iran lost sales of about 900,000 b/d of crude oil, which meant a loss to the national revenue of $11,500 million in a full year. This could not fail to create tremendous difficulties, not only with external payments but also for the government's own budget.

In fact, Oil Minister Moinfar said on 28 April that oil exports had dropped from 1.7 million b/d to 1.35 million b/d, following a halt in supplies to Japan and Western Europe. On 13 May, he added that oil exports, which had dropped by nearly fifty per cent since April, were then averaging about 1 million b/d. According to Moinfar, oil produc-tion itself would be reduced to 2 million b/d, almost one-third below the government target and two-thirds lower than the pre-revolution figure.[12] The *Petroleum Intelligence Weekly* of New York predicted that April and May exports might be even lower, as Iran faced difficulty in finding new markets for 850,000 b/d previously supplied to the Japanese oil companies, British Petroleum and Royal Dutch Shell.[13]

The financial difficulty was first officially acknowledged in the an-nouncement on 27 May of an emergency budget to replace the ordinary one approved earlier that month. This emergency budget incorporated drastic cuts in public spending intended to permit exclusive reliance on domestic revenues. After the announcement, the Plan and Budget Organ-ization Chief, Ezzatollah Sahabi, said that, if the emergency budget were adopted, some major development projects would have to be dropped. Such a cutback, or even the prospect of it, must have created yet more unemployment and increased shortages of goods, thus driving inflation yet higher.

Iran now appeared to be caught in an economic vicious circle and to be on the verge of economic collapse.

SUMMARY

Judging from all the evidence, all the conditions conducive to the effectiveness of economic sanctions in Chapter 4 in Part One except (f) – ease of monitoring sanctions – were satisfied. The sanctions' impact upon the Iranian economy was considerable. Shortages of imported commodities caused inflation and reduced industrial activity, leading to vast unemployment. Falling production, the freezing of assets and the disastrous drop in oil export revenue brought about serious budgetary deficits compelling the Iranian government to cancel some major development projects. This seemed likely to make the future for Iran's economy even darker. So, clearly, the economic sanctions against Iran achieved considerable effectiveness.

10 Limitations of the Economic Sanctions Against Iran

IRAN'S EFFORTS TO AVOID THE IMPACT OF SANCTIONS

Reporting to President Carter on 6 January 1980, the UN Secretary General, Kurt Waldheim, said that economic sanctions were unlikely to secure the release of the hostages, and that Iran would not be intimidated by economic embargoes; any such action would merely serve to harden attitudes to the United States.[1] Despite the successes recounted in the previous chapter, the evidence available is not sufficient to prove that the sanctions were effective enough to force the release of the hostages. There are, indeed, several indications to the contrary.

In July, shops in Tehran were still full of Western goods.[2] In August, the shortages of eggs, detergents, vegetable oil and milk ended; there was no shortage of meat; the bare essentials of life, such as wheat, were not difficult to obtain. The unemployment problem was indeed acute, but some urban workers who had lost their jobs went back to the countryside, which partly alleviated the situation.

One could argue that in countries, such as the Iran of 1980, where a modern economic system does not yet fully exist and the minimum standard of living has been low, it will be some time before people really come to feel threatened by economic collapse. It is, therefore, not really surprising that the sanctions failed to secure the quick release of the hostages.

Moreover, one should note that, as has been seen in almost every case of sanctions, there were loopholes which reduced the efficacy of the sanctions. Iran's domestic efforts to mitigate the impact of the sanctions will now be considered.

Increasing economic independence

If the target is, or becomes, economically independent of the nations imposing sanctions, this will, naturally, save it from being vulnerable to external economic pressure. This premise was to underpin President Bani-Sadr's approach to his own country's economic policy. First, with

162

regard to the encouragement of domestic production in general, Bani-Sadr said in February 1980 just after he had been elected that one of the priorities of his administration would be the revitalization of the economy by increasing domestic production, while at the same time reducing imports.[3] Beginning in early 1980, the Iranian government organized a number of exhibitions and seminars to encourage local production of as much as possible of the machinery that had previously been imported. The government claimed that these events had attained their purpose, and that Iranian industrialists would soon be able to supply the bulk of the equipment and spare parts needed,[4] though there have been no official reports as to how far they succeeded in doing this.

Second, in the area of financial policy, President Bani-Sadr insisted that international loans would no longer be sought, as such financial arrangements would create further dependence.[5] As a gesture of political independence, it was decided in May 1980 to disengage the Iranian rial from the US dollar and establish a link between the rial and the Special Drawing Rights (SDR).[6]

Third, the Iranian government attempted to reduce the number of joint venture projects. Late in February 1980, the Islamic Revolutionary Council approved the cancellation of joint venture projects for oil exploration and production, for example, the Iran Pan-American Oil Company and the Société Irano-Italienne de Pétroles.[7]

Fourth, long-term energy policy was re-assessed. The nuclear power programme initiated by the Shah was cancelled, and Iran decided to sell its 10 per cent stake in the Eurodif uranium enrichment consortium. Eliminating such means of generating electricity entailing considerable dependence upon advanced technology and financial assistance, Iran sought to ensure an adequate supply of electricity with its own resources and technology. Accordingly, Iran formulated a plan intended to give, within four years, oil-fuelled generating stations with a total capacity of 5,000 megawatts, as compared with the 3,621 megawatts of February 1980.[8]

Fifth, to reduce Iran's heavy dependence on other countries for its supplies of food, the government increased subsidies to farmers by up to 50 per cent – which did, in fact, help to increase food supplies. In addition, the government promoted food production by making land available for cultivation through official confiscation and redistribution and by permitting company takeovers where they would increase the food supply. In April it was said that 'Iran's agriculture is having an extraordinary boom which should make the country self-sufficient in food in a year and help plans to revamp the economy.'[9]

Sixth, more skilled workers were definitely needed if Iran was to attain industrial self-sufficiency. President Bani-Sadr announced that Iran should adopt the policy of inviting back as many skilled Iranians as possible.[10] It should be noted that the Iranian government was reluctant to turn to the Soviet Union because of the fear of exchanging dependence on one power bloc for dependence on the other. In April, however, Iran signed a protocol on economic and technical cooperation with the Soviet Union (understood to cover spare parts, raw materials and land supply routes), but she refused a Soviet offer to sell Iran weapons to counterbalance Soviet supplies to neighbouring Iraq.[11] Iran needed the Soviet Union to eliminate the economic threat posed by Western sanctions, not for arms.

Iran's attempts to protect and recover her assets in the EEC and Japan

The Iranian government's second measure to counter the sanctions was to try to transfer $4,000 million in bank deposits from the EEC countries and Japan to pre-empt any Western efforts to freeze them. In January 1980 Iranian funds in Europe and Japan were about to be switched to Libyan and Algerian banks, and it was believed that at least $300 million in yen and dollars were involved in instructions to the branches of Japanese banks in London.[12] There were other efforts to transfer funds from British banks. In April, an estimated $1,500 million held in British banks, mostly with the Midland and National Westminster Banks, was transferred to Switzerland.[13]

Iran also repatriated some of its gold deposited abroad. In the first half of 1980, withdrawals from Britain amounted to about 30 tons, valued at more than $500 million.[14] If the EEC countries and Japan had gone along with the United States by freezing the Iranian assets under their jurisdiction, Iran would have been confronted with much more serious gold and foreign currency shortages.

Guaranteeing transport routes

Even after economic sanctions had been imposed, goods were still flowing into Iran through, for example, middlemen in the Gulf. The Bahrain weekly *Gulf Mirror* reported in February 1980 that supplies of food, clothing and electrical goods were increasingly being obtained from Dubai in the United Arab Emirates, and that traders were working night and day to meet Iran's 'insatiable demand'.[15] Dubai was regarded as the leading Gulf centre for re-exports to Iran, a thorn in the side of the US-led embargo. Dubai's ruler, Shaikh Rashid, took a free trade, *laissez-faire* attitude, and did not join in the boycott of Iranian trade. Moreover, the Dubai merchants, who often had close family and religious ties with Iran, were unlikely to obey any boycott call from outside. In addition, most of Dubai's trade with Iran was carried on by dhow and would, in any case, have been very difficult to police, even if the Dubai government had wished to do so.

The other possible entrepôt was Kuwait, which had criticized the United States for trying to punish Iran over the hostage issue and said that it would not comply with any request from the United States for restrictions.[16] Many prominent Kuwaiti businessmen were of Iranian origin and supported Iran, increasing their stocks of and providing almost any goods Iran might need in the event of expanded Western economic sanctions. The Iranian Ambassador in Kuwait said on 26 April, 'huge offers have been made by Kuwaitis'.[17]

There was, of course, the possibility that the United States might undertake a naval blockade of the Gulf or of Iranian ports and oil terminals, especially if its allies proved unwilling to cooperate fully in imposing sanctions. However, the chances of such a measure being adopted were probably remote. Iran could retaliate by shelling any ship in the Gulf or at its mouth with its coastal artillery. An American task force in that region could have done little to prevent this, and a blockade would also have further endangered the hostages' lives.

Nevertheless, the possibility of a naval blockade made it necessary to secure other trade routes, mainly by land through Turkey to Eastern and Western Europe, through Pakistan to India, and via the Soviet Union to Europe and even to China and North Korea.

Turkey was taking Iran's side. In February, Turkey's Defence Minister, Ahmet Ihsan Birincioglu, said Turkey had turned down an American overture concerning the possible use of a Turkish airbase in Washington's contingency plans regarding Iran. According to an interview with the Ankara daily *Milliyet* in January 1980, President Bani-Sadr said, 'Turkey and Iran can create a common front against the superpowers.'[18] On 29 April, Turkey's Foreign Minister, Hayrettin Erkmen, said, 'It is impossible for Muslim Turkey to join US-requested sanctions against neighbouring Iran.'[19] He added that 'Turkey is prepared, if asked, to mediate between Iran and the US.'[20]

Turkey was indeed the most attractive route for Iran, not only because it saved Iran from overdependence upon the Soviet Union, but also because the Pakistani route did not lead directly to European countries. In February, a road transport agreement with Turkey was initialled which provided for waiving of transit duties on goods transported between the two countries or passing through either of them to or from a third country.[21] In accordance with this agreement, border trade was discussed on 13 April: flour, fruit, soap, meat, etc., were to be supplied in exchange for oil products.

The second possible route was through the USSR. Early in 1980, when it appeared that the United States might impose a naval blockade, the Soviet Union indicated that Iran could count on massive transshipments of goods from both Eastern and Western Europe through Russian territory. The Soviet press referred to the land and rail route from Europe to Jolfa, and to the attractions of a 'reliable and beneficial' trans-Siberian container service linking the Far East and Iran.[22] On 21 April Iranian Finance and Economy Minister Reza Salami announced that Iran and the Soviet Union had concluded an agreement for the transit of goods through the Soviet Union in the case of a US blockade of the Gulf.[23] In May, Iran and the USSR also agreed to expand Iranian Caspian Sea port facilities to accommodate the growing number of Soviet ships carrying goods to and from Iran.[24]

The clear Soviet willingness to help Iran came despite, or because of, the friction between the two countries over Soviet intervention in Afghanistan and Iran's consequent halting of natural gas supplies to the Soviet Union. Iran's view of the Soviet Union was, as previously mentioned, that the Soviets were not happy about the Iranian revolution, which provided an example of a Moslem people freeing itself from domination, and that, in the light of the Soviet intervention in Afghanistan, their ultimate aim would be to try to destabilize Iran.

Moreover, there were two factors which clearly made Iran suspicious of Russian intentions. One was Soviet supplies of arms to Iraq, when that country and Iran were at war. The other was the Soviet Union's intervention in Iran by sending arms to Arabic-speaking dissidents in the southern part of the country, and the upgrading of the Soviet Consulate in Resht, following the closure of the consulate in Isfahan. In Isfahan there were 2,000 Soviet citizens, as against only 200 in Resht; the latter was, however, a centre of leftist activity.

The reason why Iran, nothwithstanding all the above factors, reached agreement with the Soviet Union for the transit of goods was partly that Iran thought she would certainly need the Soviet Union in the case of a US naval blockade, partly that a good relationship with the Soviet Union might prevent the USA from resorting to further 'aggression', partly that the agreement might promote good economic relations with the East European countries, and partly that Iranian moves towards dependence upon the Soviet Union would frighten the West, show it that sanctions could not be effective but would indeed be counterproductive, and make the West reluctant to start or continue sanctions.

The last route was through Pakistan, an Islamic country. Its head of state, General Zia-ul-Haq, said in April 1980 that relations with Iran were quite good, and promised Iran all possible assistance.[25] Pakistani ports could be used by Iran to circumvent a naval blockade of the Gulf. But, as road links were poor and a railway link on the Iranian side was not yet complete, Iran could not rely solely upon the Pakistan route.

Pakistan made two great efforts to improve communications. First, discussions were begun in April with a view to setting up a joint cargo company plying European and Gulf routes, using several of the nine Boeing 747s and thirteen Boeing 707s belonging to the Iranian Air Force and two 747s belonging to Pakistan International Airlines (PIA). Also, Pakistani railway specialists worked on a feasibility study with French railway consultants with a view to giving good rail communication between Quetta in Pakistan and the Iranian border town of Zehidan. Since India was both favourably disposed towards Iran and a large trading partner of hers, the route through Pakistan must have had great attractions.

COUNTRIES HELPING IRAN

In addition to Iran's own efforts to reduce the impact of sanctions (discussed in the previous section), there were countries that helped her to bypass them. These countries can be most conveniently dealt with in four categories: Eastern bloc states, Middle Eastern states (including India and Pakistan), neutral states, and Western bloc states.

Eastern bloc states

Although Iran's political relations with the Soviet Union had deteriorated following the Soviet invasion of Afghanistan, economic ties improved. As we have seen, Iran looked very cautiously at Soviet economic offers and was rather reluctant to accept them, as she desired to attain economic self-sufficiency and maintain political independence. But trade with the Soviet Union significantly increased at the beginning of 1980.[26]

There were numerous Soviet offers. In February 1980 contracts for the supply of timber products, including logs, boards and railway sleepers, were signed. In March, Soviet technicians arrived at Isfahan to help to build an 800-megawatt gas-fuelled power station. The plant, designed by the Moscow branch of the Soviet Thermoelectric Design Institute, was to use natural gas and heavy petroleum distillates from a nearby oil refinery.[27] However, negotiations for a financial and commercial traffic agreement – the expression of greater overall economic cooperation between the Soviet Union and Iran – were not concluded until September 1980, when it was felt a war between Iran and Iraq was about to begin.[28] Iran's reluctance to enter into closer economic relations reveals her fear of being involved with another superpower.

Notwithstanding this hesitation, Iran was not backward in accepting offers of help from other Eastern bloc countries. Trade links with those states had already improved since February 1979, when the Islamic revolution occurred.[29] In January 1980 Czechoslovakia signed an agreement with the Agronomic Company of Iran for the construction of a sugar refinery at Karun and the supply of equipment to process 2,000 tons of sugar cane a day. The Polish national vehicle export enterprise Pol-Mot decided in February 1980 to conclude an agreement for Polish vans and buses to be assembled in Iran.[30] Production at Iran's vehicle plants had dropped significantly since the revolution because of shortages of skilled manpower, spare parts and raw materials. Japanese firms' refusal to meet Iran's request for 30,000 small trucks had also reduced the availability of commercial vehicles. Poland also decided to buy significant amounts of Iranian oil under a ten-year contract. This agreement also covered investment in Iranian mining, agriculture and industry.[31]

Late in January 1980, Bulgarian and Iranian officials agreed to increase trade, particularly imports of Bulgarian meat and other foodstuffs. Bulgaria also announced that she would help Iran to produce cigarettes to replace the popular US-made Winston brand.[32] Rumania agreed to deliver some 100,000 tons of wheat to Iran by the end of March 1980.[33]

There was already considerable cooperation between Iran and Yugoslavia in a wide range of areas – agriculture, infrastructure and power engineering, as well as trade in oil. A $29 million contract under which the Yugoslavs were to construct a network of high-tension electric cables was signed in March 1980. Yugoslavia also took over projects abandoned by Western companies, such as the Sar Cheshmeh copper complex near Kerman. According to an ADU (the East German news agency) release of 23 April, East Germany was to help Iran in the areas of energy, industry, foreign trade, agriculture, food and transport.[34] Hungary's Transelectro signed a $5.5 million contract to supply of transformers.[35] Iran also agreed to supply North Korea with 500,000 tons of crude oil in 1980.[36]

The Eastern bloc states were also major participants in an international trade fair held in Tehran from 19 September 1980, the first such fair since the Islamic revolution. The Soviet Union was the principal foreign participant. Other socialist states attending the fair were Hungary, Poland, Bulgaria, Yugoslavia, Czechoslovakia, East Germany and Cuba.

Nevertheless, the Eastern bloc's ability to pay for Iranian oil at world market prices appeared to be limited, and so Iran could not dispose of all the oil it would normally have sold to Japan, the USA and Western Europe. Also, Iranian leaders would still have been anxious lest an increase in deals with Eastern Europe should lead to overdependence on the Eastern bloc. One may assume that there was an element of bluff, with Iranian officials attempting to alarm the West about the consequences of its actions.

Middle Eastern states (including India and Pakistan)

As has already been seen, some Moslem states, such as Kuwait, the United Arab Emirates, Turkey and Pakistan, helped Iran by providing entrepôt or transportation links with the outside world. Although the conservative and pro-Western Gulf States were considered not to be friendly to Iran's revolutionary regime, it was highly unlikely that they would side with the United States. Anti-Western feeling had been growing throughout the Islamic world, with the revolution in Iran serving, as it were, as a catalyst, bringing anti-Western Islamic feeling and resentment nearer the surface. So even Saudi Arabia, which was possibly, after Iraq, the country second most hostile to Iran in the area, could not help the West against fellow Moslems. On the contrary, it seemed probable, though in the event it did not happen, that to prevent popular protest at home the Saudi government would consider retaliatory measures against the West in the form of reducing oil exports. Such moves might have materialized, if the United States had undertaken full-scale, or even only larger-scale, military action against Iran (as the West European countries and Japan in fact feared).

Moreover, according to an announcement by Iranian Plan and Budget Organization Chief Ezzatollah Sahabi there were also plans to combat sanctions by importing through other friendly countries, such as Libya, Algeria and India.[37] India's help was particularly noteworthy. In April, Iran sent India a list of goods which she wanted to buy as part of her plan to move away from her traditional Western sources of supply. The list ranged from eggs, meat, edible oils, rice and soap to machinery, chemicals, diesel engines and spare parts.[38] India also agreed to export motorcycles, bicycles, car parts, agricultural equipment, refrigerator components, steel pipes, etc. India also decided to import 5 million tons of crude oil and 300,000 tons of furnace oil from Iran in 1980.[39] In addition, Indian doctors and technicians were invited to replace Western staff in Iranian hospitals, etc.

Neutral states

International law provides for the rights and duties of states neutral in a war. Corresponding rights and duties have, however, not yet been established for economic warfare, specifically economic sanctions. The Constitution of Switzerland does, however, forbid it from associating itself with collective sanctions against a single country. Early in May, the Swiss government announced that it would 'not join the economic and trade boycott of Iran but the Government [had] decided that the country would not profit from the action by expanding its commercial relations with the Iranians.'[40]

The Austrian Chancellor, Bruno Kreisky, criticized the American sanctions in mid-April 1980, calling them 'unreasonable despite Iran's breach of international law in taking the hostages'.[41] The Head of the Foreign Trade Department of the Trade Ministry, Josef Meisl, said that Austria, being a neutral country, would not join any embargo, and would not stop the Iranian Embassy in Vienna from buying embargoed goods in Austria, or financing their purchases through Austrian banks (a special bureau attached to the Iranian Embassy in Vienna bought West European goods).[42]

Western bloc states

As we have seen, Western bloc countries had decided to cooperate with the Americans. Still, a great many loopholes became apparent.

First of all, the United States refrained, in view of humanitarian considerations, from asking the other Western bloc countries to impose a food embargo, and was not, therefore, in a position to criticize them for exporting food to Iran. However, it is even possible that supplies of food from those countries saved Iran from having to yield. America's wheat exports, 1.1 million tons a year, stopped in November 1979 because of a ban by American longshoremen. But Australia and Argentina leaped to fill the gap. Australia undertook to export 500,000 tons of wheat, 500,000 tons of maize and 200,000 tons of barley by the end of the Iranian year ending 20 March 1981.[43] Iran also ordered 900,000 tons of wheat from Argentina for the year ending June 1981. Both countries seemed eager to take over America's share of the Iranian market.

Iran's meat imports came principally from Australia and New Zealand. According to figures released by the Australian Meat and Livestock Corporation, Australian exports to Iran in the year ending June 1980 totalled 31,980 tons, compared with 4,678 tons in the year ended June 1979. This represented more than a quarter of all Australian meat sales to the

Middle East.[44] The Meat Producers' Board of New Zealand said on 11 January 1980 that New Zealand's meat sales to Iran between December 1979 and July 1980 would increased by 10 per cent, to 49,500 tons, and that a further increase was being sought[45] (figures are available showing the target was attained). Both Australia and New Zealand, which had meat contracts with Iran totalling over $100 million, were thought to be under pressure from the United States to restrict trade, but they announced that most of their exports to Iran were of food, to which the US-led collective sanctions did not apply.

The largest EEC supplier of food was France, followed by the Netherlands and Denmark. France exported agricultural goods valued at $119 million, principally sugar, followed by cheese, butter and vegetable oil. Some 36,900 tons of white sugar were sent to Iran, which became France's second largest customer for sugar.[46] Eggs were also exported from the EEC: the Netherlands supplied 2,200 tons, West Germany 2,000 tons, Britain 250 tons.

Moreover, European and Japanese companies also exploited loopholes, using non-EEC and non-American subsidiaries, for deals with Iran to 'revamp existing contracts [by] shipping through middlemen in a third country'.[47]

SUMMARY

A number of the circumstances which limit the effectiveness of economic sanctions seen in Chapter 5 in Part One existed in the case of the US against Iran. As the present chapter has revealed, Iran managed to find alternative trade partners willing to help it for commercial or political reasons – Eastern bloc countries, Arab nations, neutral states (such as Switzerland and Austria), and even a few Western bloc countries. For humanitarian reasons, the EC countries and Japan hesitated to halt exports of food and pharmaceuticals to Iran. As to legal limitations, the United States' allies opposed the extraterritorial application of US laws ordering the freezing of Iranian assets deposited in US-affiliated banks outside United States jurisdiction.

The imposer did not, in fact, greatly fear that the target might be embraced by the other bloc, but did fear that the dismemberment of Iran would invite Soviet intervention, not just political but also military, first in Iran and then in the Persian Gulf. So, in the midst of the Iran–Iraq war, which no doubt increased the effectiveness of sanctions, the United States softened its stance towards Iran, in mid-October of 1980 declaring itself to be neutral with respect to the war and even indicating readiness to accept Khomeini's conditions as a basis for a settlement.

Various efforts were also made by the Iranian government to protect its economic interests, by, for instance, increasing economic independence in a variety of fields, such as agriculture, electric power generation and banking. The Iranian government very quickly sought to repatriate money and gold deposited in Europe and Japan. It also endeavoured to secure transport routes for trading, through Turkey, Pakistan, Kuwait, and the Soviet Union.

11 Factors Contributing to the Solution

GENERAL

The various limitations of the economic sanctions notwithstanding, the hostage crisis was brought to a happy conclusion, the hostages being finally released on 20 January 1981, not by force but through negotiations between Iran and the United States, with Algeria as mediator. The major concern of this chapter is to establish whether or not it was the economic sanctions which led to a settlement, or, more precisely, to what extent the economic sanctions contributed to the eventual peaceful settlement.

The death of the Shah

One might suppose that the death of the Shah on 27 July 1980 was one important contributory cause, given the fact that it was his admission to the United States for medical treatment that had occasioned the seizure of the hostages and that their release was stated to be dependent on his extradition. However, the fortune which Iranian public opinion was convinced the Shah had stolen from the Iranian people was still mainly in the United States. According to the Iranian central bank, the Bank Markazi, the Shah's assets totalled over $32,000 million, of which roughly $20,000 million was outside Iran.[1] Hassan Ayat, a member of the Islamic Republic Party, for example, demanded that these assets be returned to Iran.

Also, the Shah's death could not cancel out the alleged US crimes of espionage. Former Foreign Minister Yazdi said that the hostages should be tried and American interference in Iran exposed. President Bani-Sadr stated that an American apology for past misdeeds was an indispensable prerequisite for the hostages' release. An article in *The Economist* said:

> Many Iranians generally believe that the Americans murdered the Shah to rid themselves of an embarrassment and to try to secure the release of the American hostages in Iran. Iranian government officials were quick to say that his death would make no difference, even though his extradition was the main condition originally posed for the release of the captive diplomats.[2]

173

In fact, the reaction in Iran to the news of his death appears to have been one of indifference, and his death cannot be considered a major factor leading to the final settlement.

Condemnation by world public opinion

One might also think that pressure exerted upon Iran by what is termed international public opinion contributed to a large extent to the release of the hostages. As has already been seen, the UN Security Council passed a resolution on 31 December 1979 deploring the detention of the hostages and calling for their prompt release (although the draft resolution proposing economic sanctions was vetoed by the Soviet Union on 13 January 1980). It had the backing of all the Third World members except Bangladesh and Kuwait, the ambivalence of whose feelings towards Moslem Iran led them to abstain rather than vote against the motion. The USSR also merely abstained. China voted in favour. But the resolution failed to elicit any response from Iran.

Further international pressure was exerted in the form of the final judgement of the International Court of Justice, arrived at on 24 May 1980, which proclaimed that Iran's violations of her international obligations to the United States 'engage the responsibility of the Islamic Republic of Iran'[3] towards the USA.

This judgement was passed by thirteen votes to two, the Soviet and Syrian judges dissenting. The Court went on to decide that Iran should 'immediately terminate the unlawful detention'[4] of US diplomats, and return the US diplomats, and return the US Embassy and consular premises to the US authorities – this decision being unanimous.

Nevertheless, the general reaction to the judgement in Iran was to stigmatize it as totally invalid, as being a judgement by default (however, Article 53 of the Statutes of the ICJ permits the Court to decide a case even when 'one of the parties does not appear before the Court, or fails to defend the case'). Foreign Minister Ghotbazadeh announced on 25 May that the ICJ had no jurisdiction over the dispute. The contribution of the ICJ judgement to the final settlement, therefore, would appear to have been minimal. Moreover, the fact that even after the judgement many states continued to help Iran to resist economic sanctions indicates that such pressure had little practical effect.

The economic sanctions

As we have already seen, the economic sanctions adopted by America and her allies would appear not to have been directly instrumental in bringing about a settlement, owing to a number of defects. Although it is true that economic sanctions work slowly and gradually, one would hesitate to argue that economic sanctions alone brought about the release of the hostages.

Despite the limited effectiveness of all three factors (the death of the Shah, international condemnation and economic sanctions), there was what appeared to be a turning point early in September 1980, as Warren Christopher, US Deputy Secretary of State in the Carter Administration revealed in January 1981, after the release of the hostages. On 1 September, the Foreign Affairs Commission of the Majlis made the first authoritative proposal for the resolution of the hostage crisis, following a long silence since Ayatollah Khomeini had instructed the Commission in February 1980 to set terms for the release of the hostages. The proposal called for the United States to acknowledge responsibility for its past role in Iran and return the wealth of the late Shah and his relatives, together with the frozen Iranian assets.[5]

A few days later, a message from Sadegh Tabatabai (head of the Prime Minister's Office and a relative of Ayatollah Khomeini) offering to hold talks with an American official was conveyed through the West German government. This choice of route was presumably connected with the fact that Tabatabai had formally been a press attaché in Bonn under the Shah, and that the West German Ambassador to Iran, Gerhard Ritzel, had had talks with the US Secretary of State, Edmund Muskie, in Vienna in mid-May 1980.

Following this, on 12 September Ayatollah Khomeini issued a public statement through the state radio, setting out four conditions for the release of the hostages. This was understood to imply his desire to see the issue settled. The conditions were that the US government should:

(a) return all property belonging to the former Shah and his relatives;
(b) unblock all Iranian assets;
(c) cancel all claims against Iran; and
(d) undertake not to interfere politically or militarily in Iran's affairs.

There was no mention of his previous demand, which the USA was highly unlikely to accept, that America should apologize for her involvement in Iran's affairs under the Shah.[6] Moreover, Ayatollah Khomeini said that he had entrusted the duty of deciding the fate of the hostages to the Majlis, and did not refer to the threat to put the hostages on trial.

By mid-September, Ghotbazadeh, too, had changed his mind. In a letter to Parliament on 15 September he said that Iran should seek a way to release the hostages, since evidence of the American diplomats' espionage activities was insufficient and because Iran's treatment of them gravely damaged her international standing and lost her much sympathy. On 16 September the Majlis voted to form a special commission to consider the matter of the hostages, and on the 30th decided to set up a seven-member commission which would study (but not make a final decision on) the question. Nevertheless, a great majority of Majlis members voted against the holding of talks with the United States, whether direct or indirect (i.e. through a third party).[7] In particular, the spokesman of the militant students, Hojatoleslam Moussavi Khamen'ei, said in the debate, 'We are fighting America . . . how can we have talks with our enemies?'[8]

Despite such strong anti-American feeling in the Majlis, further progress was seen in mid-October. On 16 October, the US Deputy Secretary of State, Warren Christopher, offered to hold talks with Prime Minister Radjai during his visit to New York to present Iran's case in the UN Security Council debate on the war with Iraq. Christopher's message was conveyed to Radjai through the UN Secretary-General, Kurt Waldheim, and also through the Algerian permanent representative to the United Nations. Although Radjai refused to talk to any American official, on his way back he stopped briefly in Algeria, where the Algerian government was understood to have urged him to seek an early solution to the issue. Before Ayatollah Khomeini made his four-point statement on conditions, Radjai had stressed the need for the United States to 'repent' her past role in Iran, saying 'If we were sure you had repented, we would talk.'[9] But after his return from New York via Algeria, he said merely that, now that the United States was ready to meet the four conditions, 'The hostages are not really a problem for us; we are in the process of resolving it.'[10] 'The nature of the hostage-taking was important for us. We got the results long ago.'[11]

On 2 November (just two days before the US presidential election) the seven-member Majlis commission finally announced Iran's official conditions for the release of the hostages, which were essentially based upon those laid down by Ayatollah Khomeini. On the following day the conditions proposed were conveyed to the United States through the Algerian Ambassador in Washington. On the same day, the militant students stated that they had transferred control of the 52 hostages to the Iranian government, as they had been instructed by the Majlis to do so. This time Ayatollah Khomeini approved the transfer.

Such conciliatory moves were presumed to be attributable principally to the anticipation and, since September 1980, the materialization of full-scale fighting with Iraq. We shall now consider how the war between Iran and Iraq influenced Iran's attitude and contributed to the release of the hostages.

THE IRAN–IRAQ WAR

Origins of the war

The dispute between Iran and Iraq had a long history and deep roots. The dispute had two aspects, one legal and technical concerning the delimitation of the border, particularly along the Shatt-al-Arab river, the other relating to inflitration and other activity of a subversive character by both sides, mainly in Kurdistan, the Kurdish areas of the two countries.

The Shatt-al-Arab dispute stems from the Treaty of Erzerum of 1847, under which the whole of the river was allotted to the Ottoman Empire, of which Iraq was then part. Following the discovery of oil at Masjid Sulaiman in 1908 and the expansion of the port of Khurramshahr, a new boundary treaty which left the port under Persian jurisdiction was concluded in 1913 and reconfirmed in 1937. However, in 1969, after the Iraqis had substantially raised river tolls, the Iranian government abrogated the treaty and the border was subsequently in dispute.

The subversive activities in Kurdistan are connected with the long-standing sectarian and cultural tensions between the two countries. Iranians consider Iraq an integral part of the Iranian cultural sphere. Shia Moslems constitute roughly 65 per cent of the Iraqi population.[12] The principal shrines and pilgrimage centres of Shia Islam are all in Iraq. However, ever since the modern state of Iraq was created by Britain in 1921, the rulers of Iraq have been Sunni Moslems, a minority in the country, and, therefore, 'no 20th century Iranian ruler has ever considered the Iraqi leadership legitimate.'[13] On the other hand, the Iraqi leadership has always endeavoured to emphasize Iraq's Arab identity and enhance its Arab credentials, by, for instance, calling for the 'liberation' of Khuzestan (called by the Iraqis Arabistan), and by calling the Persian Gulf the 'Arabian Gulf'. It was against this background that the Shah sought military superiority to Iraq and supported Iraqi Kurds in their struggle for autonomy. In the Kurdish provinces of Iraq, therefore, there had been sporadic revolts (the two most serious occurring in 1961 and 1974).

At an OPEC meeting in Algiers, an agreement between the Shah of Iran and President Hussein (then Vice-President of the Iraqi Revolutionary Command Council) settled both disputes. This agreement adopted the so-called Thalweg Line, i.e. the middle of the deepest navigable channel, as the demarcation line in the Shatt-al-Arab, and provided that the Shah and President Hussein would undertake to exercise a strict and effective control to stop 'all infiltration of a subversive character from either side'.[14] The outcome, then, was that Hussein made concessions on the frontier issue in return for an end to the Shah's intervention in the Kurdish provinces of Iraq.

Armed clashes occurred intermittently along the border from May 1980, with casualties on both sides. Seeing the fall of the Shah and the probable disarray of Iran's military forces and threatened by Ayatollah Khomeini's policy of spreading his Islamic revolution, and perhaps also prompted by the ambition to gain regional leadership, Saddam Hussein's Iraq abrogated the 1975 agreement on 31 October 1979 and demanded autonomy for the Arabs in Iran. The Iranian government rejected these demands on 1 November 1979, and the old dispute not only revived but gradually intensified. In April 1980, each side expelled the other's diplomatic representatives, and this was followed by skirmishes, albeit fitful, along the border between the two countries.

Course of the war

On 2 September 1980, clashes between Iranian and Iraqi forces occurred along the border near Qasr-i-Shirin, Nasrabad and Karantari. By early September, full-scale fighting was imminent, breaking out on 21 September with a major Iraqi offensive. Much of the Iranian territory adjacent to the border was soon occupied by Iraqi troops. The key Iranian oil-producing province of Khuzestan was the centre of the conflict. The province and its cities, particularly Abadan and the oil port of Khurramshahr, came under heavy attack by Iraqi forces.

Attacked by Iraqi infantry supported by heavy artillery barrages, both Abadan and Khurramshahr were in flames by 3 October. But, owing to 'tenacious resistance'[15] by the Iranian forces in those cities – Revolutionary Guards, some regular troops, naval cadets, militia and volunteers[16] – as well as the difficult terrain (mountains in the central sector and swamps in the south), the initial Iraqi *Blitzkrieg* had slowed to a war of attrition within six weeks. Having failed to take either city, the Iraqi High Command appeared to change its plan of campaign. It now avoided frontal attacks, and concentrated on damaging Iran's oil production by attacking refineries and pipelines – a strategy of siege and attrition.[17] By mid-October, pipelines from Abadan to Ahwaz, Dizful and Tehran were burning in several places. The towers and pipes of the Abadan refinery were also in flames.[18] The Iraqi offensive was extended to Ahwaz, the provincial capital of Khuzestan, a communications and oil installation centre. The Iraqi forces also hammered Dizful with heavy artillery and mortars. Dizful was the junction of most of the major pipelines running north from Khuzestan, and, moreover, the

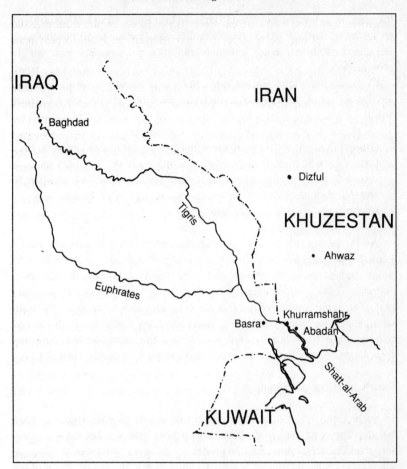

Map 11.1   Iran–Iraq war zone

site of a huge oil-pumping station. Above all, it had one of the largest
airbases in the Middle East.[19]

As the war progressed, ground skirmishes escalated into air attacks on
population centres and economic targets. On 3 October, the petrochemical
complex at Bandar Khomeini (almost completed under a Japanese and
Iranian contract) was heavily shelled and strafed by Iraqi artillery and
aircraft, nearly 700 Japanese engineers being evacuated. Moreover, in mid-
October Iraqi warplanes bombed Tehran, setting fire to oil storage tanks
there, also striking at two major Iranian army camps near Khurramshahr.
On 24 October, the oil installations at Masjid Sulaiman were attacked. On

the same day, Iranian jets raided Baghdad and Basra (Iraq having large oil refineries at Basra).[20] Also on 24 October, the first air-to-air combat took place in the southern sector, and thereafter air activity became increasingly pronounced.[21]

Commenting on the damage suffered by both sides in these air raids and air battles, the American magazine *Aviation Week* reported on 7 October 1980:

> Citing Pentagon and congressional analysts . . . , Iran was known to have lost at least 50 aircraft and perhaps as many as 100. The bulk of these were F4 and F5 fighter bombers. By contrast, Iraq had lost between 30 and 50 aircraft, with the losses spread among MIG 21 and MIG 23 fighters, and Tupolev Tu 22 bombers.[22]

As far as the tide of the war was concerned, military analysts in the United States and Western Europe were beginning, early in November, to doubt Iran's ability to prevent the occupation of Khuzestan, the main source of Iran's oil. The analysts, allowing for Iraqi exaggeration, said that 'The reports emphasized that the Iranian attempts to break the Iraqi stranglehold on Khuzestan's chief cities had been ineffective.'[23] It seemed that there was 'little that the Iranians, faced with superior artillery and tank forces, can do to counterattack.'[24] Thus the outlook appeared bleak for Iran.

Iran's wartime predicament

In such a war of attrition the full consequences of economic sanctions became apparent. Before the Shah's overthrow, the Iranian forces, 'being larger and better equipped, could probably have got the measure of Iraq's in a few days'.[25] By the time full-scale fighting began, the armed forces of the two countries were about numerically equal in terms of men and equipment, and, by and large, in terms of the quality of their equipment.[26] However, because of the US-led sanctions, the supply of spare parts and maintenance support for almost all Iranian equipment had been suspended, with the result that the effectiveness of the Iranian forces was greatly reduced.

On 27 September *The Economist* reported:

> [Iran] has plainly managed to keep some of its Phantom and F-5E fighter-bombers flying (although all its advanced F-14 Tomcat interceptors are grounded). However, as combat losses build up and irreplaceable parts wear out, the numbers of flyable aircraft could drop rapidly.[27]

According to *The Times* of 24 September 1980:

> The main problem confronting the Iranian armed forces is a shortage of spare parts, particularly for 77 F14 fighter jets delivered to the late Shah by the United States. It is believed [in Washington] that most if not all of these jets are grounded because of a lack of maintenance and the loss of the sophisticated equipment needed to make them combat-worthy.[28]

According to NATO sources, the other Iranian deficiency seemed to be trained pilots and navigators. With regard to ground forces, it was reported that:

> [The Iranian] army's main striking force is a fleet of British Chieftain tanks, backed up by some older American M-60s and M-48s. The Chieftain is as good as any that Iraq possesses, but has an engine that can be kept going only with meticulous maintenance. Now that the spare parts have stopped coming it is unlikely that Iran's tank force could last for more than a few days of hard fighting.[29]

According to NATO sources, early in November 1980, the Iraqi forces were confident that 'although Iran apparently possesses large stocks of ammunition and arms it will not be able to use them'.[30] The sources added that 'there has not yet been any deployment of tanks in a strength that would affect the engagement'.[31] *The Times* reported on 23 October that 'military observers have been surprised by the small part so far played in the fighting, . . . and by the little use of . . . its air force for tactical ground attack missions'.[32] This clearly indicates the existence of shortages of military equipment on the Iranian side.

By contrast, the Iraqi forces had no such problems with arms supplies and maintenance. This was largely because Iraqi armament came mostly from the Soviet Union, the East European countries and France.[33] Although Iran had urged the Soviet Union to halt shipments to Iraq, some arms were apparently still being sent.[34] Iraq had a treaty of friendship with the Soviet Union and most of the Iraqi arsenal was Soviet-supplied. Early in October two Soviet freighters carrying heavy military equipment were sighted in the Red Sea. Passing Aden, they headed for the Jordanian port of Aqaba.[35] In view of the fact that Jordan's King Hussein whole-heartedly supported Iraq (welcoming the opportunity to demonstrate his Arab solidarity), the supposition was that the ultimate destination of the equipment was Iraq. *The Times* of 23 October cited 'unconfirmed reports' suggesting that 'the

Soviet Union has already been making routine stocks available to Iraq through the Jordanian port of Aqaba'.[36]

Taking into account the fact that, since the US sanctions, the Soviet Union had approached Iran and offered not only economic but also military aid to help Iran out of the difficulties caused by the sanctions, Moscow may well also have sent arms to Iran. On 15 October 1980, the CBS television network quoted 'a high State Department official' saying, 'Moscow is not sending more military supplies to Iran and had also given permission to . . . Libya to fly transport planes through Soviet airspace with equipment destined for Tehran.'[37]

Even if Iran accepted the Soviet offer, it is still doubtful whether the supplies from the Soviet Union did much to improve matters. One report said:

> The Iranian military, except for some British tanks and a few hovercraft, is armed almost exclusively with American equipment. In peacetime, the hardware might well have sufficed for many years, or at least until replacement by Soviet or French equipment. Given the attrition of a war using sophisticated weaponry, within a matter of weeks the Iranian army and air force will be in dire need of replacement aircraft and weapons.[38]

For instance, the Iranian Phantom jets fired Sparrow and Sidewinder air-to-air missiles and could be fitted with Maverick air-to-surface missiles, but they were not compatible with Soviet Aphid or Atoll missiles, or with equipment the Iranians might have wished to purchase from Western Europe. Nor were their J-79 engines obtainable anywhere but America.[39]

Furthermore, Iraq also hoped for military aid from France. There were reports that Iraq was to 'receive from France the first of the 60 Mirage F-1 fighters it has ordered', and that 'Iraqi pilots are known to be undergoing training on the F-1s in France.'[40] In *Strategic Survey 1980–1981* it was reported that '100 or more Soviet T-54 or T-55 tanks from Eastern Europe were shipped to Iraq via Saudi Arabia during the course of the war.'[41]

The Iran-Iraq war naturally added to Iran's economic difficulties. In fact, the war significantly weakened the Iranian economy, which had been making a gradual recovery from the effects of the sanctions. As we have already seen, Iraqi bombing damaged Iran's oil installations and oil-refining facilities and severed pipelines. In wartime, when oil is desperately needed, such damage inevitably causes potentially fatal shortages.

The government imposed petrol rationing on 15 October, but the fighting caused a 70 per cent drop in the output of refined petroleum products.[42] The price of petrol for private vehicles was raised by 300 per cent, and the use of private cars between sunrise and 2 p.m. was prohibited. Despite such measures, the shortages persisted.

The shortage of refined oil was aggravated by the lack of spare parts to repair refinery facilities destroyed by the Iraqi bombing and artillery bombardment. According to Reuter reports, Tehran experienced long queues at almost every petrol station, and domestic heating fuel was to be rationed in the coming winter to half the estimated normal needs.[43] Iran's shortage of refined oil was so critical that even Japanese refineries had been approached concerning the availability of kerosene and other oil products.[44]

The shortage of oil led to difficulties in electric power generation. The government announced plans to cut electricity use by imposing a surcharge on consumption above certain levels. Tehran suffered two or three power cuts a day, 'apparently because of a shortage of oil at the city's power station'.[45] The Energy Minister called on people to save energy and to find ways of reducing electricity consumption. Moreover, the damage to Iran's oil refineries also brought about a shortage of aviation fuel. In October 1980, aviation fuel became a matter of grave and urgent concern, as without continued adequate supplies the Iranian Air Force could not continue fighting.[46]

Another economic difficulty engendered by the war was the rapidly increasing financial deficit. On 9 October, 1980, the Governor of the Bank Markazi, Ali Reza Nobari, said that Iran had $8,000 million in foreign currency reserves, which could last for about six to seven months without any oil sales, and was still selling oil, though less than before the war. However, in reality, the situation turned out to be much more serious than he suggested.

Financial difficulties were caused by both the fall in revenue from oil sales, which dropped because of the damage to the oil installations and pipelines, and the increase in government spending on the war effort. It was reported in mid-November 1980 that Iran had 'been starved of oil revenue since the war brought exports to a halt'.[47] In fact, by early 1981 Iran's oil production had dropped to 600,000 b/d, compared to 1.4 million b/d before the war (in the third quarter of 1980 – less than a quarter of its 1977 peak); crude-oil exports amounted to only a few thousand barrels per day.[48]

In addition to the damage to oil production, four Japanese firms, Mitsui, Marubeni, Mitsubishi and C. Itoh, which had been importing Iranian heavy fuel oil under contracts signed earlier in 1980, decided not to renew contracts which were due to expire at the end of September 1980. These contracts involved the shipping of about 2.8 million tons of fuel oil over nine months.[49] The Minister of State for Executive Affairs, Behzad Nobari, said on 3 April 1981 that 'the war had resulted in a loss of the equivalent of

some $15,000 million in the past six months – five-sixths of this amount
in loss of revenue and the remainder in increased government expenditure.'

It is still not possible to assess Iran's war expenditure with accuracy. One
can, however, arrive at a rough estimate from the budgetary figures for
the following fiscal year, which began on 21 March 1981. On 26 April
1981, Nobari said nearly $7,300 million, 16.6 per cent of Iran's budget
of $44,000 million, would be allocated to the war effort.

The financial situation deteriorated further because of massive withdrawals of savings from the banks after the outbreak of war. On 20 September, the Governor of the Bank Markazi, Nobari, urged Iranians not to
withdraw money from their banks except in an emergency. He went on
to point out that restrictions on domestic flights and on the sale and transfer
of oil had delayed the circulation of money in the country, so that some
branches were short of cash.[50] The government also ordered all foreign
exchange offices to close. This step was taken to restrict the amount
of currency leaving Iran and to channel more foreign currency into the
official banking system.

Such financial shortages, exacerbated by the war, hit very hard at the
Iranian economy, which had already been put under severe strain by economic sanctions. On 29 March 1981, President Bani-Sadr described the
plight of the Iranian economy during the war, saying:

> Inflation was running at an annual rate of 27 per cent, with the poor
> certainly suffering from a much higher rate of price increase on essen-
> tials . . . rationing introduced at the start of war had made matters worse
> by creating a black market and fuelling a smuggling boom. High govern-
> ment spending, increasing unemployment, political instability and lack
> of law and order . . . could lead to wide-spread social and political
> tension . . .[51]

Here, the effect of the financial deficit upon purchases of military equipment should be considered. As has already been pointed out, Iran must
have been faced with serious shortages of military *matériel*. However,
Iran's Chargé d'Affaires in Belgium, Mohammed Hassan Mohazed, said
on 9 October that 'Iran was still receiving spare parts for much of its
Western-built military equipment . . . on the free market', and added that
there was 'no spare parts problem for the moment or in the long-term,
except for some air force equipment'.[52] The *Financial Times* of 1 October
1980 reported that Iran was 'scouring the . . . arms market for aircraft
spare parts and anti-aircraft ammunition'.[53] Nevertheless according to a
statement of 23 September 1980, issued by a State Department spokesman,

Jack Cannon, the Iranian authorities had already admitted that military spare parts from third parties were 'obtained only at a considerable premium'.[54] Therefore, bearing in mind Iran's financial difficulties, the Iranian diplomat's statement appears exaggerated.

Another factor which should be mentioned here with regard to the economic effect of the war is the fact that the physical dangers of the war, together with the possibility of Iran's insolvency, would certainly have discouraged foreign traders from dealing with Iran. In September 1980, for instance, underwriters at more than 100 London insurance companies and at Lloyd's of London increased cargo insurance premiums on vessels sailing to Iran by 300 per cent. The customary methods of minimizing commercial risks in wartime further worsened the situation.

Another problem faced by Iran after the outbreak of the war was her considerable international isolation – not only from the United States and its allies, which had already been imposing sanctions upon Iran (though they did not support Iraq either), but also even from neighbouring countries, most of which had supported Iran with regard to the US-led sanctions. In the early stages of the war, many Arab states expressed support for Iraq, though the support varied in warmth, depending on their differing political circumstances, internal and external.

The conservative Arab states in the Gulf certainly had no liking for the idea of living under Iraqi hegemony. They feared that 'a dominant Iraq would also pose a direct threat to their existence. Iraq had not abandoned her Ba'athist ideological orientation and would, if victorious, emerge as the main regional power.'[55] But for the Camp David Agreement, they would have been more 'attuned to the moderate politics of Egypt than to the militant radicalism of Iraq'.[56] But, of the two duelling powers in the Middle East, Iran represented the graver threat to the other states.

The principal reason was that, since the outset of the Islamic revolution, Ayatollah Khomeini had insisted that a new standard for Islamic piety and behaviour, one in accordance with strict Shia doctrine, should be spread through all the Moslem countries. The Arab states of the Gulf and the Arabian Peninsula, with considerable Shia populations, had been annoyed by Iran's incitement of their Shia communities. In Bahrain, for instance, Shia Moslems (constituting a majority of the island's population) were courted by Khomeini's Iran in daily propaganda broadcasts. The Khomeini regime also sought constantly to stir up the significant Shia minorities in the United Arab Emirates and Kuwait and on the east coast of Saudi Arabia (where the country's oil fields are concentrated).

Moreover, many of the rulers of the Arab states of the Peninsula were modernizing (their Moslem critics would say 'westernizing') monarchs who felt that their status had been threatened by the fall of one of the area's apparently most firmly established monarchies, that fall suggesting that neither modernizing and westernizing policies nor powerful military forces could protect a throne.

Consequently, many Arab states in the Peninsula expressed support for Iraq in the early stages of the war. These countries included Saudi Arabia, Kuwait, Qatar, the United Arab Emirates and North Yemen. Of the other Arab states, King Hussein of Jordan was the most whole-hearted supporter of Iraq, even permitting the stationing of Iraqi fighter-bombers at Jordanian airbases to safeguard them from Iranian strikes, and transporting *matériel* to Iraq. Jordan's attitude to some extent reflected its traditional posture of 'Arab solidarity', but one cannot ignore the fact that its neighbour, Syria, ruled by a branch of the Ba'ath Party (which combines socialism and Arab nationalism) which was deeply hostile to the Ba'ath Party ruling Iraq, was at odds with Jordan. Morocco and Mauritania also supported Iraq.

By contrast, only Syria and Libya backed Iran. Syria was a strong supporter of Khomeini's Islamic regime; its relations with Iraq had long been at a low ebb because of the rivalry between the Syrian and Iraqi wings of the Ba'ath Party. Their relations worsened when Syria alleged that 'Iraq had been supporting the outlawed Moslem Brotherhood'.[57] However, feeling threatened by the fact that the Soviet Union did not back Syria against Jordan, despite the Soviet-Syrian Treaty of Friendship and Co-operation, and mollified by funds from Saudi Arabia, Syria later pulled back its forces and 'even allowed the renewal of the flow of Iraqi oil through the pipeline over her territory'.[58] Though an Arab country, Colonel Qadhafi's Libya supported Iran, sharing the Ayatollah Khomeini's ideal of an 'Islamic renaissance'.

Algeria, Egypt, Turkey, Pakistan and the PLO declared their neutrality. The United States and her allies (except France) also remained neutral. However, the Iranian government believed that the United States had 'encouraged the Iraqis indirectly through surrogate countries which also have an interest in the fall of the Khomeini regime'.[59] Pakistani President Zia-ul-Haq, who attempted to act as an intermediary in his capacity as Chairman of the Islamic Conference, was described in Tehran as 'a US puppet' and 'a butcher of Muslims'.[60] The Soviet bloc called for a peaceful settlement, but it seemed more or less one-sidedly to favour Iraq. Naturally, since Iran had virtually no foreign support, the Soviet Union would lose nothing by this gesture.

The psychological pressure of isolation manifested itself when Prime Minister Radjai went before the Security Council to present Iran's case on the Iran–Iraq war. It was the first time an Iranian official representative had attended a meeting of the Council since Iran had boycotted it because of its condemnation of the seizure of the American hostages. Prime Minister Radjai wanted the Council to condemn Iraq for invading Iran, but many delegates warned that 'Iran [could] expect little sympathy from the Council as long as it [continued] to defy the Council's repeated calls for the hostages' release.'[61]

It is extremely difficult to assess the effect of isolation upon Iran, or, more precisely, upon Iran's leaders. Nevertheless, there is some evidence of an Iranian feeling of 'claustrophobia'. Despite his long-standing desire and efforts to solve the hostage issue by means of negotiated agreement and despite his popularity among the Iranian people, the voice of President Bani-Sadr had not been heeded, and his desire thwarted by clerical factions in the Iranian power structure. However, after having tirelessly conducted the war, flying to the battle front and mapping strategy with his command-ers, he raised his voice in mid-October, and blamed Iran's isolation in the conflict with Iraq 'on the fact that [Iran], largely as a result of the hostages issue, is regarded as being beyond the pale in international terms.'[62] He laboured to convince his countrymen that they could not 'go it alone', claiming that Iran 'was the first country to wage war with no outside help'.[63] His adviser on foreign affairs, Mansour Farhang, went further, saying, 'It is the affair of the hostages which has largely contributed to our isolation. We must be realists and draw the conclusions of the objective conditions in which we find ourselves.'[64]

The semi-official daily newspaper *Etallaat*, in its issue of 15 October 1980, gave vent to Iran's frustration and chagrin: 'Now we know that all those professions of Arab fraternity were filthy lies. Now we know that our sincere support for the Arab cause is rewarded by treachery and naked aggression.'[65]

AMERICA'S ACCEPTANCE OF KHOMEINI'S CONDITIONS

While Iran was struggling to surmount this predicament – shortages of military equipment, economic difficulties (particularly financial problems) and international isolation – the United States in mid-October informed the Iranian government, through the Swiss Embassy in Tehran, that it was ready to accept Khomeini's four conditions as a suitable basis for negotiat-ing the release of the hostages. At the same time, President Carter and the Secretary of State, Edmund Muskie, publicly confirmed that, if the hostages were released, the United States would be willing to lift the trade embargo, allow the shipment of military spare parts already paid for by Iran, permit the unfreezing of Iranian assets, and assure Iran that the USA would not interfere in Iran's internal affairs.

As far as the return of the Shah and his relatives' assets was concerned, however, the Administration said that it was considering 'ways of aiding the Iranians . . . to locate holdings and to seek through the courts to retrieve them if they can prove that they rightfully belong to the Iranian Government', because 'the United States did not know where the Shah's assets were kept and had no legal way of giving them to Iran'.[66]

On 20 October, Muskie further stated that the 'integrity of Iran' had been threatened by what he referred to as the 'Iraqi invasion', and warned that America was opposed to the 'dismemberment of Iran'.[67] Although he insisted that the United States would be strictly neutral with regard to the war, he suggested that the Administration held Iraq responsible for the outbreak of the hostilities. This statement, made by the Secretary of State in a speech to the Chicago Council of Foreign Relations, was the most strongly worded and most favourable to the Iranians the Administration had made since the outbreak of the Gulf War. His words were later reinforced by President Carter during the campaign in Ohio. He said the United States wanted 'a strong, peaceful and united Iran'.[68]

Naturally, Iraq accused the United States of planning 'to buy the hostages by offering arms to Iran' – particularly in *Al Thawa*, the organ of the ruling Ba'ath Socialist Party.[69] On the other hand, it appeared that the general climate in Iran improved as a result of the conciliatory and pro-Iranian remarks by American leaders. Their publication coincided with Radjai's attendance at the UN Security Council meeting. As we have already seen, after returning to Tehran, and perhaps also because he was given the cold shoulder at the meeting, he changed his tone to a considerable degree about the conditions for solving the hostage issue. Bearing in mind that Radjai was an Islamic fundamentalist, a senior member of the Islamic Republic Party (IRP) and said to be very close to Ayatollah Khomeini, one may assume that his readiness to solve the hostage issue exerted considerable influence upon discussion in the Majlis, where the IRP and clerics constituted the majority.

According to Reuters, Hojatoleslam Moussavi Khamen'ei, one of the seven members of the special commission, spiritual leader in Tehran and a close confidant of the young militants, said on 22 October that the terms for the release of the hostages would be announced on 26 October, and that the hostages could be 'released as early as [27 October]' if the Americans 'accept the conditions and put them into action'.[70] On the same day, the young Moslem militants who had taken the hostages stated their position –

namely that they would accept the conditions announced by the Majlis 'even if these conditions are against our views'.[71]

Some fundamentalists were still sceptical about the change in America's attitude. In particular, Ayatollah Mohammed Beheshti, the influential leader of the IRP, said on 22 October that the Commission's terms might differ in detail from those of Ayatollah Khomeini.[72] *The Sunday Times* of 26 October referred to the fact that 'Official propaganda, however, is cautious not to create undue expectations. The US is still referred to as "the enemy".'[73]

Nevertheless, a majority of the Iranian leaders began to realize that the hostage crisis was no longer yielding dividends and that it was time to be rid of this time-consuming problem and to get on with more pressing matters, i.e. reducing the shortages, which caused considerable hardship, improving Iran's ability to repulse the Iraqis, and preserving the gains of the Islamic revolution. Therefore, although some division continued within the Iranian leadership on the question of the release of the hostages and the benefits that might accrue from freeing them, on 2 November 1980, after repeated adjournments, the Commission announced Iran's official conditions for the release of the hostages, based upon those laid down by Ayatollah Khomeini on 12 September 1980. As previously stated, the United States was immediately notified of these proposed conditions by the Algerian Ambassador in Washington, while in Iran the militant students, instructed by the Majlis and having received Khomeini's approval, transferred control of the hostages to the Iranian government.

What now needs to be examined is why the United States also adopted a conciliatory approach. One probable reason is that, as the superiority of the Iraqi forces gradually manifested itself, fears grew that the war might spread eastward as the Iranians retreated, and that, in desperation, Iran would be tempted to close the Persian Gulf to shipping. Arab states in the Gulf, including Saudi Arabia, whose oil fields are mostly in the Eastern Province, exported virtually all their oil through the Gulf, which accounted for 60 per cent of the world's oil trade.[74] As most of the oil was bound for Western Europe, Japan and the United States, such desperate action by Iran would have resulted in a severe oil shortage that would have undermined Western economic strength and political cohesion.

In this light, President Carter had declared on 24 September that, 'while the West could cope with an interruption of Iranian and Iraqi supplies . . . it is imperative that there be no infringement of the ability of other suppliers to ship oil out of the Persian Gulf.' He added that America's neutrality in the war did not rule out all direct military action against Iran, should Iran attempt a blockade of the Strait of Hormuz.

President Bani-Sadr, however, said in an interview with *Newsweek* towards the end of September that if Iran was attacked 'from all sides' – implying the possibility of other Arab states supporting Iraq – it would block shipping in the Strait. In fact, several tankers were reported to have been intercepted by the Iranian Navy and interrogated about their destination (though none was forced to stop).[75]

In such circumstances, the US government on 26 September proposed the convening of a meeting of six nations – the United States, Italy, Britain, Japan, France and West Germany – to review how to 'minimize the economic effects of the conflict on international shipping and the world petroleum market'.[76] Prudent silence was maintained by these states in order not to give rise to rumours that they were planning direct military intervention, which would damage their political relations with the Third World, particularly the Arab states in the Gulf. However, according to the *International Herald Tribune*, the USA, France and Britain were determined, if necessary, to take military steps to protect the Strait: for instance, by escorting tankers, driving off Iranian naval vessels, sweeping mines or ensuring the silence of Iranian guns and missile batteries able to attack vessels in the Strait.[77]

Moreover, in view of the need to protect other sources of oil, especially those of Saudi Arabia, the United States on 30 September sent four AWACS early-warning planes to that country to coordinate air defence of its oil fields. Saudi Arabia, the world's largest producer of oil, was then producing 9.5 million b/d, or one-third of OPEC's total production. However, her armed forces were relatively small – 44,500 regulars and 26,500 paramilitary troops, including the National Guard charged with protecting the royal family – owing to the royal family's fear that large military forces would encourage coups. Therefore, though well equipped, the Saudi forces were no match for Iraq, or even for the combined forces of the two Yemens.[78]

The Iranian government later undertook not to block the Strait, but, in fact, the possibility of a blockade eventually appeared less remote principally because it became increasingly clear how great a threat the Iraqi forces posed to Iran. Probably because of this last development, the Americans, indeed, appear to have come to feel it necessary to reduce the very great strain under which Iran was labouring.

A second reason for America's conciliatory attitude was that the US government considered that an Iraqi victory in the war would endanger the lives of the 52 Americans held hostage. For Iranians had been told that the Iraqi invasion had been ordered by President Carter. Ayatollah Khomeini had said on the first day of the fighting with Iraq, 'We are at war with America, . . . and today the American hand is showing through the sleeve of Iraq.'[79] On 23 September, Tehran Radio alleged that 'the current Iraqi attack was part of a US plan to free the captives', and went on:

Three days ago President Carter announced that the US was considering a plan to break the hostages deadlock. Its plan is now being implemented by the Baghdad Government. . . . Brave Iraqi soldiers, do not turn yourselves into tools for Carter's fiendish plans. Do not kill yourselves for the sake of Carter and Saddam's overlords, who are . . . sending Muslims to fight fellow Muslims. . . Direct your guns at the enemies of your people – Carter and his agents.[80]

The Iranian government then issued a statement that the Majlis on 23 September had 'decided to freeze the issue of the hostages'.[81] Moreover, a broadcast announcement by the militant students on the same day said that, in order to 'foil any plot', they had 'transferred the spy hostages from Qum, Esfahan, Mashhad, Tabriz, Kerman, Yazd and Jahrom to other sites'.[82]

Iran's suspicion of America's intentions was increased by the fact that, despite the lack of full diplomatic relations between the USA and Iraq since the 1967 Arab–Israeli War, the Carter Administration had decided in early 1980 to approve the sale of $11.2 million worth of military equipment to Iraq, for the Iraqi Navy. The equipment comprised eight turbine engines for Iraq's Italian-made frigates, though the sale had not yet been finalized.[83]

So President Carter announced US neutrality on 23 September and endeavoured to convince Iran of the genuineness of United States neutrality by attempting to obtain a Senate amendment denying Iraq the turbine engines and rejecting an Iraqi request for five Boeing jetliners worth $23 million.[84] US officials were still worried about the disruptive effect of the Iran-Iraq war on the efforts to free the captive diplomats.

A third concern of the US government was the strategic implications of Iraq's slow but steady advance into Iran. It recognized that the military and political disintegration of Iran could lead to the growth of Soviet influence in the region.

The Soviet Union's strategic interest in areas adjacent to her southern borders and in access to the Indian Ocean necessarily implies a strategic interest in Iran, and has a long history going back long before the Russian Revolution. The Persian Gulf, which Iran dominates, will continue to be a geo-political cornerstone, and not merely because it is the major source of petroleum. Iran's anti status quo stance and the West's economic and political sanctions against her were a 'fortuitous bonus' for the Soviet Union. Iran's foreign policy at times proclaimed fraternity with the Arab states, but at other times called for expansion of Islamic revolution, which isolated her politically in the Gulf region. The more isolated Iran became, the more dependent, at least, potentially, she became on the USSR.

Post-revolution Iran had never tilted towards the East, though she had on occasions accorded the Soviet Union special treatment. As Chubin points out:

> The first ambassador received by Khomeini was Vladimir M. Vinogradov of the USSR. When foreign banks were nationalized, the Russo-Iran bank, the only bank exclusively foreign-owned, was exempted. When all secular political parties were banned, the Tudeh's activities were still permitted until January–February 1983. Iran has often shown uncharacteristic patience and restraint regarding Soviet activities in Afghanistan.[85]

In the military area, Iran's conflict with Iraq had exposed her northern border and so laid her dangerously open to Soviet military intervention. The Soviet Union had consistently maintained that the 1921 Soviet-Iranian Treaty gave it the right to intervene in Iran, an interpretation successive Iranian governments had rejected. In such circumstances, a further weakening of the Iranian military machine in the war with Iraq could encourage minority groups in Iran, such as the Kurds, to break away from central control, and such fragmentation could facilitate Russian intervention. Chubin notes:

> Soviet military maneuvers could tie down Iranian forces on the northern frontiers, or make the prosecution of the war with Iraq, or assistance to the Afghan resistance, more difficult and onerous. Overflights and incursions slice away at the sovereignty of the government which, once lost, may be difficult to reclaim.[86]

In late 1980 the possibility of actual Soviet military intervention was in fact rather remote, particularly as the US Navy had already dispatched an aircraft carrier, the USS *Kittyhawk*, and its battle group to join the carrier USS *Midway* and its battle group already in the area. This was the largest naval force assembled in the Indian Ocean since World War II. Avoidance of direct military confrontation with the United States had always been Soviet strategic policy, but, had the Soviet Union been tempted to move into Iran, the Carter Administration would have been under such strong domestic pressure to meet the threat directly that it would hardly have been able to avoid a military response. In a 6 October 1980 television interview in Milwaukee, President Carter remarked that, 'the biggest threat to American security would arise if the Soviets should be tempted to move into Iran or to move into an area where they can control the Persian Gulf itself or access to it.'[87]

Moscow had greater latitude in the Iran-Iraq War than the United States. As in the war between India and Pakistan in 1971, the Soviet Union could offer her services as a mediator in peace talks between Iran and Iraq, thereby seeking to acquire increased political influence in the Middle East. By contrast, the United States could scarcely be a mediator. For she had had no diplomatic relations with Iraq since Iraq had severed them after the 1967 Arab–Israeli War. As has already been seen, diplomatic relations with Iran were severed in April 1980.

With all these considerations in mind, it was obviously vital for American strategic interests in the Middle East *vis-à-vis* the Soviet Union that settlement of the hostage problem be expedited.

A fourth factor that should be taken into account is that the US presidential election scheduled for 4 November 1980 gave President Carter and his Administration a powerful incentive to conclude the hostage crisis by that time. He might well have thought that, if the hostages were to return before polling day, it would give his campaign an enormous boost. Such a tactic, known in American politics as 'the October surprise', was, of course, what Ronald Reagan, the Republican candidate, and his advisers had long feared most.

A convention had grown up in US presidential elections of there being one or more subjects that were too sensitive to be debated during the election campaign, as, for instance, when in the election of 1944 both Roosevelt and Dewey avoided any repetition of the arguments about what had been wrong with the Versailles Treaty at the end of World War I. In the 1980 presidential election, however, such restraint appeared to slide away early in September 1980, as far as the hostage issue was concerned.

On 9 September, Reagan harshly criticized the Carter Administration, saying that 'the Administration was "responsible" for the situation that led to the taking of the hostages because it had not strengthened the Marine guard at the United States Embassy, or moved personnel from the Embassy following an earlier seizure by Iranian militants.'[88] On the following day, he also said that 'The way to deal with the hostage situation was to give the Iranian Government an ultimatum', and added that 'the United States should have stood by the Shah before he was forced from power.'[89]

Moreover, as soon as Ayatollah Khomeini announced the four conditions on 12 September, Reagan stated that the United States 'can and should' agree to three of them and that whether to return the Shah's property or not was for American courts to determine. He went on, 'Having agreed to these points, we must above all insist that the hostages be released immediately upon conclusion of an agreement, that there be no delays, introduction of additional demands or waiting for fulfilment of an agreement.'[90] In this way, Reagan probably attempted to 'offset the Carter campaign's characterisation of him as a dangerous, warmongering hothead', and 'to demonstrate . . ., in defiance of innuendoes from the Carter camp, that he is capable of presidential decisiveness.'[91] Meanwhile, the reaction of the Carter Administration to Khomeini's offer was one of extreme caution, perhaps too cautious to appeal to the US electorate. A *New York Times*-CBS national opinion poll taken towards the end of September gave Reagan a five-point lead. Thus, President Carter was under strong political pressure, and probably felt a need to settle the hostage issue before election day.

However, another *New York Times*-CBS national opinion poll, in late October, found Carter edging ahead of Reagan in the race for the presidency for the first time. This time, there was a nine-point lead in Carter's favour. Most of the other opinion polls confirmed his recovery of popularity. It should be remembered that the change occurred after the Carter Administration's overtures to the Iranian government – if the hostages were released, the United States would lift the sanctions – had produced a conciliatory response from Iran.

With regard to this change, the *Financial Times* wrote on 24 October that the result of the polls 'shows that Mr Carter has succeeded to a degree in painting Mr Reagan as the candidate more likely to lead the country into war.'[92] It went on:

> This is certainly what the Ronald Reagan camp fears, and it explains why the Republican candidate has sought to launch a pre-emptive strike by charging this week that the crisis was a national humiliation and disgrace, brought on by Mr Carter's ineffective foreign policies.[93]

Moreover, former Republican president Gerald Ford spoke critically of any Carter 'October surprise', saying that 'such a move purely for short-term political advantage could prove to be a disaster for the United States in the long term.'[94]

Given these facts, the importance of the hostage issue in the presidential campaign is evident, also the strength of the political pressure that might have made the Carter Administration desperate to find a solution. One can also infer the importance of the hostage issue in the election campaign from, for instance, the *National Journal* of 7 November 1980, which carried a survey of what Americans thought might have been the most decisive factor in Reagan's victory. According to the survey, the Iranian hostage crisis ranked first and the loss of prestige by the United States fourth.[95] The combination of these two should clearly be seen as significant.

It should also be added that there were those in Iran which called for an early end to the hostage crisis, preferably before the American presidential election, or at least before Carter left office. Sadeq Ghotbazadeh, for instance, had, on 16 September (well before the result of the election was known), underscored the importance of settling the problem before 4 November, the reason being that 'obviously Mr Reagan, supported by Kissinger and others, had no intention of resolving the problem. They will do everything in their power to block it.'[96] On 24 October, in an American television programme, he warned American voters that they would do better to elect Carter, whom the Iranian leaders appear to have thought, as the *New York Times* put it, 'a weak and manageable US President'.[97]

12 The Settlement of the Crisis

THE PATH TO A SOLUTION

Things finally began to move towards a settlement on 2 November, when, as we have seen, the Majlis approved a report by the Special Commission endorsing the four conditions for the release of the hostages laid down by Ayatollah Khomeini. On the same day, President Carter announced that these conditions appeared to offer a positive basis for a solution. On the following day, Prime Minister Radjai and US Deputy Secretary of State Christopher met Algeria's ambassadors in Tehran and Washington respectively and agreed to Algerian mediation.

Following this, several official letters were exchanged for clarification through the Algerian authorities. In these negotiations, Algeria played an essential role as mediator, one involving not only its ambassadors in Tehran and Washington but also Algeria's President Chadli and Foreign Minister Yahia. For weeks Algerian diplomats shuttled between Tehran, Algiers and Washington, trying to 'straddle the wide gulf of mistrust that separated the two sides'.[1] Algeria was well placed to act as negotiator and had exceptional qualifications for serving as a bridge between a revolutionary Third World country and the United States. To this was added the extraordinary skill and patience of the Algerian diplomats, without which the negotiations might not have succeeded. Algeria was understood to be eager to gain a leading position among the Third World nations, particularly among the non-aligned countries. At the same time, its relations with the United States had improved considerably (for example, the USA had been its largest trading partner for the previous two years). It was against such a background that the Algerian government endeavoured to play a decisive role in settling the hostage dispute, partly in an attempt to wipe out its old image as 'an unwavering supporter of revolutionary movements, and . . . a haven for hijackers and odd-ball revolutionaries'.[2]

Behind the scenes of such official negotiations, bankers were 'at the centre of the bargaining from the beginning', because they realized that 'the frozen assets could be the crucial bargaining counter in trying to achieve the release'.[3] Since May 1980, discussions had been carried on between a Citibank lawyer, John Hoffman, and Iran's lawyers in Frankfurt,

Paris, New York, London and Bermuda. Hoffman took on this role at the request of Citibank, but at the same time kept in close touch with the Administration, discussing various ideas with the Administration, especially with Deputy Secretary of the Treasury Robert Carswell. The discussions were based on Hoffman's proposal, which was that the frozen assets should be used to pay off Iran's debts to the US banks. But progress was very slow, until a basis for diplomatic negotiations was created after the Iran–Iraq War had put a serious strain upon Iran's resources.

Despite some progress after September, the discussions ground to a halt in mid-November, when Iran's lawyers told Citibank that Iran had decided not to pay any of its debts to the banks. When delivering to Algerian officials in Algiers a memorandum of reply to Iran clarifying the US position, Deputy Secretary of State Warren Christopher warned that the negotiations could be held up considerably, if the matter was not resolved by 20 January, since the new administration was likely to appoint a new negotiating team. Towards the end of December, Reagan displayed his hardline attitude, referring to the hostages' Iranian captors as 'nothing better than criminals and kidnappers who have violated international law totally in taking these innocent people and holding them this long', and that he did not think 'ransom' should be paid for people who had been 'kidnapped by barbarians'.[4]

Whatever Reagan's intentions were in making these statements – whether he intended to concentrate the government's efforts to reach a solution or was attempting to avoid any commitment on the hostage issue in order not to be bound by a solution concluded under the Carter Administration – he clearly appeared to be seeking to put pressure on Iran. Sampson notes, 'by early January the Iranians showed signs of wanting to settle before Reagan took office'.[5] On 15 January, the news came from the Algerian government that Iran had accepted Hoffman's proposal. This broke the impasse. In the end, an agreement resolving the issue was signed on 19 January, and on the following day the 52 hostages left Tehran at approximately 8.55 p.m. (25 minutes past noon of the same day in Washington), about half an hour after the transfer of power in the United States.

OUTLINE OF THE AGREEMENT

The Agreement comprised two declarations of intent. The first, the Declaration of the Government of Algeria, provided for commitments with regard to future political relations between the two countries, the release of US nationals in Iran and the end of US sanctions against Iran.[6] The second, the Algerian Declaration Concerning the Settlement of Claims, set forth procedures for the settlement of claims between the two parties, including the establishment of an international tribunal and its terms of reference.[7]

The first declaration stipulated the following undertakings by the United States in exchange for the release of the hostages:

(a) a pledge not to intervene, directly or indirectly, politically or militarily, in Iran's internal affairs;

(b) to end all trade sanctions;

(c) to release all Iranian assets frozen by the Administration;

(d) to freeze the property of the late Shah and his close relatives pending resolution of the Iranian government's lawsuit to obtain it;

(e) to prohibit all future lawsuits against Iran in the United States arising from the seizure of the hostages or from the Islamic revolution; and

(f) to withdraw US claims against Iran before the International Court of Justice.

The total amount of frozen Iranian assets released was $7,977 million. Of this, Iranian deposits in foreign branches of American banks accounted for $5,500 million[8] (chiefly the Bank of America (about $2,000 million), Manufacturers Hanover Trust ($416 million), Bankers Trust (about $330 million), the Chase Manhattan Bank ($320 million), Morgan Guaranty Trust ($200–300 million), and Citibank ($225 million)), Iranian deposits with the Federal Reserve (US Treasury Securities and bills) for $1,400 million, $940 million represented the equivalent of 1.6 million ounces of Iranian gold held with the Federal Reserve, the remaining $137 million consisting of other Iranian assets not the subject of lawsuits, such as the Iranian military trust fund.

This amount was first transferred to an escrow account at the Bank of England. However, a total of $3,700 million was returned to the United States to pay off syndicated loans involving American, European and Japanese banks. One example was the 1977 $500 million loan, syndicated among eleven American and West European banks by the Chase Manhattan's Bahamas affiliate for the purpose of helping the Shah to balance the budget. These syndicated loans included loans to Iranian banks, many of which had been privately owned before the revolution.[9]

Moreover, $1,400 million was kept in the escrow account to cover non-syndicated American loans made to the Iranian government, quasi-governmental entities or Iranian banks that had been nationalized. For

instance, William Bikoff and George Eisenpresser, two American finan-
ciers, were seeking $450 million in compensation for nationalization of a
32 per cent stake (16 per cent each) in the Zarshouran copper mine. Sedco
was seeking compensation of $175 million for sixteen drilling rigs and
assorted construction equipment which had been nationalized. General
Telephone and Electronics was also seeking $100 million for breach of
a contract worth $500 million. Further claims had been presented by Xerox,
General Motors and others.[10] Disputes over these claims were to go to
the international arbitration commission in The Hague established under the
Algerian Declaration Concerning the Settlement of Claims. As a consequence, the Iranian assets immediately transferred back to Iran totalled
no more than $2,850 million.

As for the estimated $2,200–2,600 million in Iranian deposits with
domestic branches of US banks, these also were to be handed back to
Iran under the Agreement. The Administration requested the banks to
transfer the deposits to the Federal Reserve. The Iranian deposits concerned
were to be sent to the Algerian central bank within six months. $1,000
million of the deposits would be put into a 'security account' for the
settlement of arbitration proceedings; the rest would go straight back to
Iran.

Part Three

Conclusion

13 Conclusion

Any society is held together by rules of behaviour, and will seek to uphold those rules by sanctions when they are flouted by a member. The day when the society that is the international community is able to compel members' compliance with its rules seems still far distant. In the international community today no grouping of nations or international organizations, be it general or regional, can be sure that it will be able to employ sanctions effectively. On the other hand, no country can merely do nothing if it is the target of what it considers an unlawful, rule-breaking act on the part of a state or states. It will try to impose sanctions, and if it cannot muster collective support for such action, may still do so unilaterally. Inevitably, too, states, individually or collectively, have to accept the consequences of imposing sanctions on 'wrong-doers'.

The sanctions available range from verbal appeals to international public opinion or expulsion of the wrong-doer from a regional or general international grouping of states to coercive military action against the offender, with economic sanctions coming somewhere in between. Verbal appeals or ostracism may seem unlikely to inflict enough damage upon the target to have any real effect. On the other hand, military action, which presupposes the destruction of life and property, will in today's world tend to expose the initiator, rather than the wrong-doer, to serious international criticism on humanitarian grounds. The imposer will also fear that military action may invite a quid pro quo escalation, possibly even ending in nuclear warfare. Hence, the importance of ensuring the effectiveness of economic sanctions in the world today.

Among the various cases of economic sanctions, the still recent Iranian case deserves special attention. The outcome was certainly that desired by the imposer, the United States, with the hostages returning home sefely, and that outcome was attained in very difficult circumstances. If, or to the extent that, the outcome is to be attributed to the economic sanctions, the Iranian hostages case is clearly an instance of the successful use of economic sanctions.

The Iranian population was in the grip of emotional and religiously fanatical anti-Americanism and to yield to any foreign pressure could have endangered the Iranian leaders' hold on power, which was then newly established and still uncertain after the revolution. The Iranian case is, indeed, one of the most important of all those deserving close and detailed investigation regarding the role of economic sanctions in settling international disputes in the world today.

Economic sanctions are not new, but they have undoubtedly increased in importance in the twentieth century, for both political and economic reasons. They were an essential part of the concept of collective security as it was embodied in the League of Nations. They appeared to provide a means by which, without recourse to arms, an aggressor could be contained and his aggression reversed by the collective action of the international community. Despite the failure of sanctions in the cases of Manchuria and Ethiopia, the idea was refurbished with the establishment of the United Nations. Very importantly, economic sanctions are attractive when a government, sometimes for domestic political reasons, determines that some action is necessary, but shrinks from the cost and the risks of using military force.

The growing attraction of sanctions as a lever against alleged rule-breakers derives also from the growing economic interdependence of states. If states were self-sufficient, no state could hope to employ economic sanctions against another to any effect. Economic sanctions can, clearly, only be effective where the target is part of a fabric of international economic transactions.

No state can afford to discount entirely the possibility of suspension of economic transactions with other states in an emergency, whether natural or 'man-made'. Consequently, states usually seek to maintain a certain level of domestic production of basic necessities, even where this runs counter to the principle of comparative advantage in international economic theory. At the same time, however, trade has undoubtedly become indispensable for virtually all countries in the world today. There can be few countries which are not, in effect, part of the world trade network and, therefore, few which might see themselves as being totally insulated from pressure in the form of economic sanctions.

Also, since the Industrial Revolution, as a result of the discovery of new sources of energy and technological advances in the transport and communications fields, an increasingly diverse range of materials, products and services has constantly been exchanged in international trade. International capital transactions have also attained vast dimensions.

The cases examined in this study reveal that virtually every kind of international economic transaction, be it the flow of goods, services or money, has actually been suspended, and that a variety of means have been employed, ranging from import and export embargoes to the stoppage of air transportation services to and from the target state, from the suspension of conversion of the target's currency to the freezing of its assets. They also reveal that the more diverse the objects and methods of international economic transactions have become, the greater the range of means available as economic sanctions. It was, for instance, only with the advent of the internal combustion engine, the arrival of plastics and the large-scale use of oil as a source of energy for the generation of electricity and for transportation that the modern industrial economy became so dependent upon oil that oil export or import embargoes could be seen to constitute a major threat. A 'high-tech' embargo could be attractive only after a certain dependence on such technology had developed. The same is true of air transportaion. The recent rapid development in tele-communications and the fact that traders, bankers and other business-men are greatly dependent on international telex and telephone systems for their day-to-day business transactions suggest that the severing of international lines of telecommunication can be another promising form of economic sanctions. The use of this means was, in fact, urged by African States in the case of Rhodesia, but was not adopted because of British and United States opposition. The recent rapid growth in the volume of monetary transactions increases the importance of boycott measures in that area. In the case of Iran, we saw almost all the means available for economic sanctions in today's world deployed.

The present study has identified a number of cases in which economic sanctions inflicted severe damage upon the target's economy. Wide-ranging economic encirclement of Japan by the United States, Britain and others was effective enough to bring Japan's trade almost to a standstill, and seriously aggravated her financial position. British sanctions against Iran in 1951, based on a claim to continuing ownership of Iranian oil, were not effectively challenged. Oil exports from Iran virtually came to a halt. The Iranian economy suffered the shock of suddenly reduced revenue and the budget deficit soared. Britain's import ban on tobacco and other goods from Rhodesia in 1966 reduced Rhodesia's exports by nearly 40 per cent in value terms. Britain's freezing of Rhodesia's assets in London and expulsion of Rhodesia from the sterling area precipitated a crisis in Rhodesia's foreign exchange position. The Arab 'oil weapon' – production cuts plus an embargo on exports to the United States and the Netherlands – caused alarm in the OECD countries. It contributed to the West Euro-pean countries' refusal to provide staging bases for the United States' resupply of Israel and brought a change in Japan's Middle East policy. It prepared the ground for OPEC's imposing of a fourfold increase in the price of oil, which in turn contributed to the inflation and recession of the following years.

The impact of economic coercive measures upon a target country will differ greatly, depending, for example, on the relative importance of foreign economic transactions in its economic activities and the relative importance of its economic transactions with the sanctions-imposing state(s) in its external economy. The cases studied in Chapter 4 in Part One indicate that: (a) the greater the importance of foreign trade for the target's domestic economy, the greater the economic impact; (b) the smaller the target's GNP, the more effective are sanctions likely to be; (c) the more closely interknit the target's trade with specific partners, the more vulnerable it is, should those partners join in the sanctions; (d) the more difficult it is for the target to find alternative foreign sources of supply or alternative markets, or a substitute (domestic or foreign) for goods previously imported, the greater will be the impact; (e) the smaller the target's foreign exchange reserves, the more difficult it will be for it to resist economic sanctions; (f) the easier it is to monitor, or even control, the target's trade with other countries, the more effectively will sanctions work; (g) state-trading countries are less vulnerable than those in which foreign trade is carried on by the private sector. Similarly, where what might, very loosely, be described as the reverse circumstances are in the imposer's favour, the probability of economic sanctions being effective is increased.

All of the above conditions except (f) were satisfied in the case of US-led economic sanctions against Iran in 1980. In fact, their impact upon the Iranian economy was considerable. Shortages of imported goods caused soaring inflation and declining industrial activity created huge unemployment. Falling production levels caused by factories having to operate below capacity, or even close down, together with the freezing of Iranian assets in the USA and the oil import boycott by the USA, the EEC and Japan, resulted in large budgetary deficits, forcing the Iranian government to cancel some major development projects.

Notwithstanding such serious impacts upon the target countries, economic sanctions have only rarely attained the declared goals. In nearly all cases they have been designed to reverse a course of action already undertaken and to persuade the target country to withdraw from a position it has taken, or, at least, to negotiate a compromise. However, the League of Nations' economic sanctions against Italy did not reverse the Italian invasion of Abyssinia, and before oil sanctions could be implemented, Britain and France offered Italy a compromise in the Hoare-Laval plan, which Italy in the end rejected. The Arab oil weapon, which was triggered by the US supply of arms to Israel during the Yom Kippur War, did nothing to stop it, that sanction being discontinued, in part because Saudi Arabia was alarmed at the possible consequences of continuing the boycott, as soon as a disengagement agreement between Israel and Egypt was signed.

A yet more outstanding case was that of the sanctions against Japan, which, rather than dissuading it from doing so, actually prompted that country to expand its campaign in order to secure the oil supplies which the United States, Britain and Holland were trying to cut off. The Soviet Union was unable to change the independent stance of Tito's Yugoslavia. Castro's Cuba was not prevailed upon to change. Even the United Nations' collective economic sanctions against Rhodesia failed to topple the Smith regime.

Even in the few cases where economic sanctions appear to have attained their goals, it is often questionable whether it was the economic sanctions or other measures, or a combination of the economic sanctions and other measures, which brought ultimate success. In the case of the Soviet sanctions against Finland in 1958, the 1956 Soviet intervention in Hungary and the 1958 Berlin crisis may be presumed to have suggested the possibility of a military threat influencing the Finnish government's response. The successful outcome when economic sanctions were initiated by Britain against Iran in 1951 is to be attributed largely to the subsequent coup engineered by British and American intelligence which overthrew the Mossadeq regime. Without the assassination of Trujillo, the OAS's collective sanctions against the Dominican Republic might well not have produced results, or at least not so soon, though it might also be argued that the assassination itself was caused by the economic coercive pressure exerted by the OAS members.

The apparent success of the US-led economic sanctions against Iran would seem to be attributable less to economic sanctions than to the war with Iraq, together with the approaching American presidential election and the expectation that the next President would be much less open to compromise and would take a much tougher line towards Iran than President Carter. Also, Iran's foreign trade had already declined before sanctions were imposed, mainly because of the political instability before and after the Islamic Revolution. EEC–Iran trade, for example, had already dropped considerably more than a year before the actual imposition of sanctions. Financial difficulties, manpower problems (though there was serious and growing unemployment, there was also a shortage of skilled manpower) and shortages of raw materials had already been reported by the Iranian Central Bank.

Moreover, economic sanctions have a number of inherent drawbacks. The target state can employ various countermeasures to circumvent the attempted economic stranglehold. These are not limited to domestic economic adjustments to increase self-sufficiency, or at least reduce dependence upon the imposer. They also include external measures, specifically efforts to find alternative markets and sources of supply. Finding new trading partners is usually fairly easy, since other countries, and possibly even the commercial enterprises of the country imposing sanctions, will be tempted by the profits and other advantages to be gained by helping the target.

Owing to the lack of an established body of international law concerning the rights and duties of countries that are neither imposer nor target, corresponding to that concerning neutral states in the international law of war, there are no legal restrictions on helping the target.

In order to close gaps, therefore, the imposer state attempts to mobilize other countries, particularly friendly nations or allies, to join in the sanctions. It sometimes takes the issue to international organizations, regional or general, seeking to make the sanctions collective. However, even where an international organization has decided to impose mandatory economic sanctions, not all members have acted in accordance with the decision. Difficulties in attempting such mobilization lie in the fact that, because of the interlinked character of international trade, economic sanctions have a double-edged effect: upon the target's economy and upon that of an imposer. If the cost appears unacceptable to a potential participating state or politically unsustainable domestically, any such diplomatic effort, even if accompanied by quite considerable 'arm-twisting', tends to fail. In fact, unequal distribution of the burden can constitute a serious problem, even within the country of the principal imposer. The imposition of economic sanctions obviously tends to affect different groups in a country in different ways. Groups (as it might be, American farmers) which will suffer may be expected to be opposed to sanctions, and will often prevent their governments from resorting to them.

Moreover, polarization, the prime example being East–West confrontation, makes it easier for a target to find new trading partners. It will also tend to deter the imposer from making its economic coercive measures as devastating as they might be. If there is the fear that the target may be drawn into the embrace of the other bloc, losing a political partner or ally may well be less acceptable than having to tolerate its wrong-doing. This study has revealed that where a group of states employs sanctions against a member of that bloc, the other bloc has attempted to seize the opportunity to weaken the first bloc by assisting the target of the sanctions.

Another limit to the efficacy of economic sanctions stems from recent developments in international law, which has been following a course tending to (a) restrict the right of a state to use force (even economic force) against another and (b) ensure the maximum possible freedom for international economic transactions. Such development of the international legal system has limited both the means available for use as economic sanctions and the situations in which the use of sanctions is seen as being permissible. Articles of the GATT make discriminatory export prohibitions or restrictions illegal. Exemption from these rules necessitates the proving of the target's prior illegal act, which is not always easy. In various cases examined in this book states have refrained from extending export embargoes to food and pharmaceuticals on humanitarian grounds, though it is still debatable whether international law in fact forbids such embargoes. On the other hand, traditional international law itself also tends to limit the effectiveness of economic sanctions. Although the increasing economic interdependence of the world's states and the growing diversity of international economic transactions have presented states with attractive new ways of applying economic pressure, some of those methods are said to violate traditional international law, the prime example being extraterritorial application of domestic laws and regulations.

Another inherent limit to the efficacy of economic sanctions is related to the fact that they tend to hit the wrong people within the target state. Because of the difficulty of hitting a specific group of people in the target state, sanctions tend to bring pressure to bear on the whole population of the target state, those most severely hit on occasion being those whom the sanctions are meant to help, as in the case of UN sanctions against Rhodesia. Also, middle-of-the roaders in the target country will tend to support their government. The political leaders of the target state can, therefore, the more easily enhance national unity in the face of outside pressure by, for instance, exciting the patriotic, or nationalistic, feelings of the entire population.

Such limitations of economic sanctions were also seen in the case of the US-led sanctions against Iran. As Chapter 10 in Part Two reveals, Iran made strenuous efforts to mitigate the impact of the sanctions by increasing the country's economic independence, by protecting its assets abroad and by attempting to ensure that there would be routes open for her foreign trade. Iran had no great difficulty finding trade partners willing to increase trade with her. Some of them helped Iran for commercial reasons, others from political motives.

In the midst of the Iran–Iraq war, which undoubtedly increased the effectiveness of the attempted economic stranglehold on Iran, the US Administration softened its stance towards Iran in mid-October of 1980 by declaring its policy of impartiality with regard to the war and sending the message that it was prepared to accept Khomeini's four conditions as a basis for negotiating a settlement. One important reason for this shift was that the dismemberment of Iran would invite Soviet attempts to increase Russian influence, first in that country and then in the Persian Gulf. America's attempt to freeze Iran's assets in Europe by applying US law extraterritorially was opposed by the EEC countries, which claimed that such application was incompatible with current international law. During the course of sanctions against Iran, the United States for the first time called on her allies – the NATO countries and Japan – to participate in cooperative economic punitive measures in connection with an issue not directly related to East–West confrontation – in fact, an issue beyond the scope of the Western Alliance. The United States took it for granted that NATO had a global aspect and that America's efforts to defend Western Europe from the Soviet threat deserved the allies' support and cooperation whenever the bloc leader might need them. However, as was seen in Chapter 8 in Part Two, those allies, particularly certain EEC members, showed considerable reluctance.

Economic sanctions' critics have maintained that, even if economic sanctions are imposed, in the end they either peter out or become an embarrassment, and at best they are a clumsy way of signalling disapproval of the target's action. Such critics assert that the chances of a successful international venture in the area of sanctions are remote. Many would also stress that, regardless of the chances of success or failure, exploiting economic links for political or strategic goals may well hamper the development of a free-trade network linking all blocs and nations, which has been seen as a means not only of increasing economic efficiency but also of enhancing world political stability and peace.

Nevertheless, there have so far been no signs that states are becoming any more reluctant to use economic sanctions, quite the contrary. It would, moreover, appear that, while economic sanctions may only rarely have attained their declared objectives, states have perceived other, hidden, objectives. By applying economic sanctions, the imposer can proclaim what it deems to be the rules of the group to which it belongs (which may be the international community as a whole), and let all other members know that any attempt to violate them will be met resolutely. This purpose can be seen in the cases of US sanctions against Cuba and the Dominican Republic and that of the Soviet sanctions against Yugoslavia. Economic sanctions may also serve to discredit the target and gain the support of world public opinion, the aim being to bring to bear on the target the concerted pressure of international public opinion, even to call on other nations to form a unified front against the target. The Arab oil embargo did, in fact, draw world attention to the Arab cause in the struggle against Israel.

Placating domestic public opinion or international demands can be an objective of economic sanctions. Before a general election, for example, a government may feel compelled to take some form of 'concrete' action against a wrong-doer in order to satisfy public opinion calling for it to be punished. The demands of another country cannot be ignored when, for instance, failure to satisfy them will anger or disappoint the country calling for support, or will cause it to turn to the other bloc for help. The British government in 1935 and the American administration in 1960 were influenced by this factor in imposing economic sanctions against Italy and Cuba respectively. Also, Britain and other industrialized countries were certainly influenced by the need to do something in the face of the African countries' demand that the Smith regime be brought down. Economic sanctions can be a means of releasing the pent-up feelings of anger or frustration of the people of the imposer country and preventing their calling on their government to have recourse to more substantial means, military force. Participation in economic sanctions is useful as a proof of friendship (or loyalty, if the initiator is a bloc leader) when there is a strong demand by the initiator to do so, but it can also be useful as a means of reducing the initiator's sense of isolation and preventing it from becoming enraged or desperate and taking up arms.

In the case of US-led economic sanctions against Iran, however, to punish Iran by damaging its economy would have fallen far short of a solution to the problem for America. So would merely demonstrating the righteousness of the United States case against Iran. The Carter Administration may have felt that even such effects would favourably affect the approaching Presidential election, but it is all too obvious that with 52 US nationals held hostage, sanctions alone, even with the effects mentioned, would by no means have satisfied the American people. The essential objective was the release of the captured Americans.

From that perspective, the economic sanctions can be seen as having been useful in that the lifting of the sanctions could be used as a bargaining counter. This use of economic sanctions can also be seen in the cases of British and French sanctions against Italy in the 1930s and the Western sanctions against Poland in the 1980s. This tactic, first imposing sanctions and then offering to lift them if the target ceases its wrong-doing, can obviate a complete severing of communications or too harsh an emotional confrontation with the target, thereby making the way to a settlement easier.

If the imposer foresees that military action by the target seems imminent, or if the imposer for some other reason perceives the need to weaken the target state's capability in general, be it by reducing the target's economic production, political influence or whatever, economic sanctions are useful in undermining that capability. The sanctions imposed against Italy were directed at reducing its economic potential, which would hamper military build-up. The sanctions against Japan had the same purpose. The main objective of the Western embargo policy regarding high-technology exports to the Warsaw Pact countries was to ensure the latter's continued military inferiority and to prevent them from being tempted to indulge in adventures, whether directed against the West itself or other countries.

The *time-frame* is also important in evaluating success or failure. The Soviet economic sanctions against Yugoslavia indicate that a target state which at first stubbornly resists the imposition of any humiliating measures from outside may in time come to view the situation more 'objectively' and become conciliatory, at least to the point of accepting some of the demands presented by the imposer state. Yugoslavia found it too costly to continue to be so at odds with the Soviet bloc and to increase military spending when she was pursuing industrialization. It was also unacceptable politically, as well as economically, in that accumulating debts to the West, mainly to the United States, might, Yugoslavia's leaders thought, be turned by the lenders into a means of control. Thus, economic sanctions can restrict the policy options of the target in such a way that it cannot elect to pursue the optimal policy.

Yugoslavia's case further suggests that while pursuing a vital national goal, for Yugoslavia industrialization, states may not be able to afford to fight a prolonged battle resisting the imposer of economic sanctions. No doubt, the fighting of a war can be such a vital national goal to which a state must give top priority.

That a belligerent will try to undermine its opponent's economic base with a view to reducing its military strength, or its willingness to continue the war, as in the cases of Napoleon's Continental Blockade and Britain's naval blockade of Germany during World War I, is taken for granted. As action to cut off an enemy's foreign trade weakens its military strength, any actual fighting which coincides with the imposition of economic sanctions will increase their effectiveness. As far as the efficacy of economic sanctions is concerned, the fighting need not necessarily be between the imposing and target states.

In the case of the USA and Iran, a military conflict happened to occur while the economic sanctions were being imposed, not with the imposer but with a third country, Iraq. This fighting, in fact, further aggravated Iran's budgetary deficit and accelerated depletion of her foreign exchange reserves. It may well be that Iraq, which had vehemently attacked Ayatollah Khomeini's policy of spreading his revolution, sought to take advantage of Iran's economic difficulties caused by the US-led economic sanctions. Economic sanctions employed by one country against a wrong-doer may, in fact, trigger a chain reaction, inviting another country to take punitive action against that wrong-doer for completely unrelated reasons.

To these merits of economic sanctions should be added another reason for states' advocacy of them: economic sanctions, even if second best, are the instrument of choice when, for whatever reason, military action seems too costly. Because of the horrifyingly destructive power of nuclear weapons, it seems highly unlikely that a nuclear state will dare to use military action against another nuclear state. Naturally, states militarily weaker than their target states are unable to resort to military action. The surprising fact is, however, that in most of the cases in recent years the economic sanctions were imposed by nations stronger militarily than the target states. The reason for this is that, in addition to any military cost, there is also the political, legal and moral price the imposer of military sanctions has to pay. Owing particularly to the diminished legitimacy of the use of force and the growing importance of international public opinion, the price in these three important areas has increased so greatly that, unless the target has been guilty of an act that is flagrantly illegal or one that constitutes an imminent danger to the national security of the imposer country – for instance, when the target state attacks the imposer's territory or its armed forces – the imposer state tends to avoid military action and demonstrates its determination to punish the wrong-doer by means of economic sanctions.

Finally, as this study has shown, there were several features of the Iranian episode which were distinctive and which illustrate the more general points about sanctions by their exceptional character. These special characteristics did not all operate in the same direction.

Generally speaking, the sanctions had a damaging effect upon the Iranian economy. But their impact upon ordinary Iranians was limited, in part probably because ordinary Iranians, because of religious and re-volutionary fervour and because they were accustomed to a relatively low standard of living, would not soon have their morale destroyed by economic hardship. Of the various means employed, the freezing of its assets was a particularly serious blow to Iran, but Iranian holders of assets abroad, one may reasonably assume, will have been on the whole not ordinary Iranians, but the newly established revolutionary government itself and government-affiliated companies – and, of course, a fairly small number of rich Iranians, probably anyway all too conscious of the dangers of appearing unpatriotic or un-Islamic. Consequently, the sanctions did not hit the 'wrong people' – which in several other sanc-tions cases has been seen to be one of the defects of economic sanctions – and did not give rise to criticism of the government among the Iranian people strong enough to pressure the government to change its stance towards the United States. Rather, the regime very effectively took advantage of the sanctions to advocate the need for national unity in the fight against the United States.

The effect of the sanctions was yet further limited because the efforts of the United States Administration to enlist the support of its allies were met with considerable reluctance. Iran, by contrast, had little difficulty in finding trading partners willing to increase trade with it. A further difficulty for the United States was that the sanctions had a precise objective, i.e. the release of the hostages. Punishing Iran by damaging its economy or merely demonstrating the righteousness of the United States' case against Iran – though in certain other cases of economic sanctions these were the, or at least two of the, declared goals – would by no means have satisfied the American people. Therefore, unless and until the sanctions attained the safe return of the diplomats held hostage, they would not be regarded as a success, at least not in the United States. For the Carter Administration, the need to secure the release of the hostages was the crucial constraint, with nothing short of that being in any way adequate.

In addition, the Administration had to be cautious about the possibility of Soviet intervention in Iran, as is clear from the President's warning regarding doing anything that might lead to the dismemberment of Iran. Iran's previous secular hostility to Russia had not disappeared but was, indeed, enhanced by the Islamic regime's hostility to communism. Iranian anti-American feeling could, however, easily and with impunity be fanned and exploited by the revolutionary regime.

Notwithstanding such various factors unfavourable to the sanctions imposer, the United States, the objective was attained, with all the hostages returning home safely. What contributed most to this outcome was the coinciding of the economic sanctions with the outbreak of the Iran-Iraq War. The freezing of assets, which had not directly hit ordinary Iranians hard, hit the Iranian government severely by causing serious shortages of foreign currency reserves, which became of critical importance after the outbreak of war with Iraq. The oil import boycott by American, Japanese and European buyers, already imposed before the war began, further aggravated the Iranian government's budgetary deficits. The embargo on exports of military equipment to Iran, whose effectiveness seems to have been limited before the war began, suddenly became extremely effective once the war started. The shortages of foreign reserves mentioned above made this embargo even more effective, because they very seriously restricted Iran's imports of arms from other sources.

The fighting also resulted in physical damage to economic facilities. This caused further shortages of goods and services (for example, petrol and electric power), increasing the need for economic transactions with foreign countries. The physical dangers of a war zone, together with the possibility of Iran's insolvency, discouraged foreign traders from dealing with Iran. This narrowed the 'loopholes' in the economic sanctions, and consequently very significantly increased their impact.

The onset of the war with Iraq, thus, made it very much more important for Iran to free itself from the shackles of economic sanctions. Two aspects of the role of the war with Iraq in bringing about a solution to the hostage crisis should be emphasized particularly. First, if Iran had been at war with the imposers of economic sanctions, i.e. the United States and its allies, rather than with Iraq, Iran would not have been creating more opponents by losing the friendship of most of the neighbouring Arab countries, which had hitherto supported Iran, the target of US wrath and sanctions. One concludes that the war between Iran and Iraq, by further isolating Iran, contributed very much more to the effectiveness of the sanctions than would have been the case had the United States itself been at war with Iran. Secondly, if Iran had been at war, not with Iraq, but with the USA and its allies, Iranian anti-American feeling would have become so bitter that Iran might not even have been tempted to seek compromise with the United States. Although it was indeed alleged in Iran that the Iraqi attack was part of a US plan to free the hostages, settlement through negotiation would have been far less likely to occur had there been direct military engagement between Iran and the United States.

Some have argued that the international community should have been far more active in seeking to contain the Iran–Iraq war in those early years, in which case sanctions against Iran or Iraq, or both, might have been proposed. Instead, ironically enough, the war had the important effect of adding to the incentives for Iran to reach a settlement with the United States.

In the end, the hostages were released through negotiation (Algeria acting as an intermediary), with the timing of the US presidential election expediting the negotiations. In those negotiations, the release of the hostages was attained in exchange for the lifting of economic sanctions. The usefulness of economic sanctions as a bargaining counter could hardly be more clearly exemplified.

Notes

CHAPTER 2

1. A general definition of sanctions containing similar elements is given by Hans Kelsen in *Collective Security under International Law* (Washington, DC, 1957), p. 101.
2. A very useful account of positive and negative sanctions in society is to be found in A.R. Radcliff-Brown, 'Sanctions, Social', *Encyclopaedia of the Social Sciences* (New York, 1934), Vol. 13, pp. 531–4.
3. A similar definition is offered by J. Galtung in 'On the Effects of International Economic Sanctions', *World Politics*, Vol. XIX, No. 3 (April 1967), p. 379.
4. Max Beloff, *The Foreign Policy of Soviet Russia 1929–1941* (London, 1949), Vol. 1, p. 35.
5. Rita F. Taubenfield and Howard J. Taubenfield, 'The Economic Weapon: the League of Nations', *American Society of International Law*, 1946, p. 185; Royal Institute of International Affairs, *International Sanctions* (London, 1938), pp. 1–205; other materials (see Chapter 4, notes 13 and 14).
6. William N. Medlicott, *The Economic Blockade*, Vol. 1 (London, 1952), pp. 475–99; Richard Storry, *Japan and the Decline of the West in Asia 1894–1943* (London, 1979); other materials (see Chapter 4, notes 20–2).
7. Donald L. Losman, 'The Effects of Economic Sanctions', *Lloyd's Bank Review*, October 1972.
8. Gunnar Adler-Karlsson, *Western Economic Warfare 1947–1967: A Case Study in Foreign Economic Policy* (Stockholm, 1968) gives a comprehensive account.
9. Robert Owen Freedman, *Economic Warfare in the Communist Bloc: A Study of Soviet Economic Pressure Against Yugoslavia, Albania, and Communist China* (New York, 1970), Chapter 2; Barry Farrell, *Yugoslavia and the Soviet Union 1948–1956* (Hamden, Conn., 1956); other materials (see Chapter 4, note 23).
10. D.J. Harris, *Cases and Materials on International Law*, 2nd edn (London, 1979), p. 775; other materials (see Chapter 4, note 3).
11. Losman, op. cit, p. 30.
12. Paul Y. Hammond, *Cold War and Detente: The American Foreign Policy Process since 1945* (New York, 1975), pp. 101–4.
13. Raimo Väyrynen, 'A Case Study of Sanctions: Finland–the Soviet Union in 1958–59', *Co-operation and Conflict* (Nordic Studies in International Politics, March 1969); other materials (see Chapter 4, note 6).
14. Anna P. Schreiber, 'Economic Coercion as an Instrument of Foreign Policy', *World Politics*, Vol. XXV No. 3 (April 1973), pp. 387–413; other materials (see Chapter 4, note 24).
15. Alexander Eckstein, *Communist China's Economic Growth and Foreign Trade* (New York, 1966), Chapter 5.

16.   Freedman, op. cit., Chapter 3.
17.   The economic sanctions are counted a success by R.St.J. MacDonald in 'The Organization of American States in Action', *University of Toronto Law Journal*, Vol. 15, No. 2 (1964), p. 370; Jerome Slater, *Intervention and Negotiation: The United States and the Dominican Revolution* (New York, 1970).
18.   UN Security Council Resolution 218, 23 November 1965.
19.   Galtung, op. cit., pp. 378–416.
20.   Ibrahim F.I. Shihata, 'Destination Embargo of Arab Oil: Its Legality under International Law', *American Journal of International Law*, Vol. 68, No. 4 (October 1974), pp. 591–629; other materials (see Chapter 4, notes 7–12).
21.   UN Security Council Resolution 418, 4 November 1977.
22.   James Barber and Michael Spicer, 'Sanctions against South Africa – Options for the West', *World Politics*, April 1967, gives the background to the sanctions.
23.   *Strategic Survey 1981–1982* (International Institute of Strategic Studies), pp. 54–61.
24.   *Strategic survey 1982–1983*, pp. 116–21; Report of a Committee of Privy Councillors, *Falkland Islands Review* ('Franks Report') (London, 1983).
25.   Muriel J. Grieve treats this case as a typical example of economic pressure in 'Economic Sanctions Theory and Practice', *International Relations* (David Davies Memorial Institute of International Studies), Vol. III, No. 6 (October 1968), p. 434.

CHAPTER 3

1.   Royal Institute of International Affairs, *International Sanctions* (London, 1938), pp. 79–81.
2.   Margaret P. Doxey, *Economic Sanctions and International Enforcement*, 2nd edn (London, 1980), p. 68.
3.   The Control of Gold, Securities, Payments and Credits (Argentine Republic) Directions 1982, Paragraph 2.
4.   Paul Y. Hammond, *The Cold War Years: American Foreign Policy since 1945* (New York, 1969), p. 89.

CHAPTER 4

1.   Max Beloff, *The Foreign Policy of Soviet Russia 1929–1941* (London, 1949), Vol. 1, p. 35.
2.   Ibid., p. 32
3.   Alan W. Ford, *The Anglo-Iranian Oil Dispute of 1951–1952* (Berkeley, Calif., 1954); R. Bullard, 'Behind the Oil Dispute in Iran', *Foreign Affairs*, April 1953; S.H. Longrigg, *Oil in the Middle East* (London, 1968); N.S. Fatemi, *Oil Diplomacy* (New York, 1954).
4.   Ford, op. cit., p. 250. This shows the corresponding figures for the preceding years: £10.3 million in 1946–7, £12.4 million in 1947–8, £16.2 million in 1948–9 and £18.9 million in 1949–50.

5.   Ibid., p. 157.
6.   Raimo Väyrynen, 'A Case Study of Sanctions: Finland–the Soviet Union in 1958–59', *Co-operation and Conflict* (Nordic Studies in International Politics, March 1969); J.M. MacKintosh, *Strategy and Tactics of Soviet Foreign Policy* (London, 1962).
7.   Ibrahim F.I. Shihata. 'Destination Embargo of Arab Oil: Its Legality under International Law', *American Journal of International Law*, Vol. 68, No. 4 (October 1974); J.E. Akins, 'The Oil Crisis: This Time the Wolf is Here', *Foreign Affairs*, Vol. 51 (1973), pp. 463–80; E.M. Shamsedin, *Arab Oil and the United States: An Admixture of Politics and Economics.* University of South Carolina, (April 1979); Jordan J. Paust and Albert P. Blaustein (eds), *The Arab Oil Weapon* (New York, 1977).
8.   *Middle East Economic Survey*, Vol. XVI, No. 52 (19 October 1973), pp. iii and iv.
9.   *International Energy Statistical Review* (National Foreign Assessment Center), 30 January 1980.
10. 'OECD Oil Statistics 1973', *Quarterly Oil Statistics* (OPEC), pp. 26 and 27.
11. *Middle East Economic Survey*, Vol. XVII, No. 4 (16 November 1973), p. 27.
12. Shihata, op. cit., p. 597.
13. The Royal Institute of International Affairs, *International Sanctions* (London, 1938); A.J. Barker, *The Civilizing Mission: The Italo-Ethiopian War 1935–36* (London, 1968); A.J. Toynbee, *Survey of International Affairs 1935*, Vol. II: *Abyssinia and Italy* (London, 1936); and G.W. Baer, *The Coming of the Italo-Ethiopian War 1935–1936* (Cambridge, Mass., 1967).
14. Margaret P. Doxey, *Economic Sanctions and International Enforcement,* 2nd edn (London, 1980), pp. 47–8.
15. Royal Institute of International Affairs, *op. cit.*, p. 93.
16. Ibid., p. 78.
17. Ibid., p. 79.
18. M.J. Bonn, 'How Sanctions Failed', *Foreign Affairs*, Vol. 15, No. 2 (January 1937), p. 354.
19. According to *Statistical Year Book of the Trade in Arms and Ammunition* (The League of Nations, 1935).
20. William N. Medlicott, *The Economic Blockade*, Vol. 1 (London, 1952), Jun Tsunoda, *Nichi-Bei Kosho* (Tokyo, 1960).
21. Medlicott, op. cit., pp. 122–3.
22. Ibid., p. 478.
23. Robert Owen Freedman, *Economic Warfare in the Communist Bloc: A Study of Soviet Economic Pressure Against Yugoslavia, Albania and Communist China* (New York, 1970); Barry Farrell, *Yugoslavia and the Soviet Union 1948–1956* (New Haven, Conn., 1956); Louis J. Halle, *The Cold War as History* (London, 1967), pp. 227–33.
24. Anna P. Schreiber, 'Economic Coercion as an Instrument of Foreign Policy', *World Politics*, Vol. XXV, No. 3 (April 1973); R.F. Smith, *The United States and Cuba: Business and Diplomacy 1917–60* (New York, 1961); A. Schlesinger, *A Thousand Days* (Boston, 1965); D. Larson (ed.), *The Cuban Crisis of 1962* (Boston, Mass., 1963).
25. Doxey, op. cit.; J. Galtung, 'On the Effects of International Economic Sanctions', *World Politics*, Vol. XIX, No. 3 (April 1967); P. Keatley, *The Politics*

of Partnership: The Federation of Rhodesia and Nyasaland (1963).
26. United Nations Security Council, *Resolution 660 (1990)*, 2 August 1990.
27. United Nations Security Council, *Resolution 661 (1990)*, 6 August 1990, p. 2.
28. Ibid.
29. United Nations Security Council, *Resolution 665 (1990)*, 25 August 1990, p. 1.
30. Väyrynen, op. cit., p. 210.
31. Klaus Knorr, *The Power of Nations* (New York, 1975), pp. 151–2.
32. Roy Parviz Mottahedeh, 'Iran's Foreign Devils', *Foreign Policy*, No. 38 (Spring 1980), p. 24.
33. Adam B. Ulam, *Expansion and Co-existence: The History of Soviet Foreign Policy 1917–67* (New York, 1968), p. 543.

CHAPTER 5

1. Anna P. Schreiber, 'Economic Coercion as an Instrument of Foreign Policy', *World Politics*, Vol. XXV, No. 3 (April 1973), p. 398.
2. *New York Herald Tribune*, 19 November 1961 and 7 February 1962.
3. *New York Times*, 17 September 1963.
4. Schreiber, op. cit., p. 399.
5. See Chapter 4, Table 11.
6. Schreiber, op. cit., p. 407.
7. Schreiber, op. cit., p. 396.
8. Ibid.
9. T.H. Bingham and S.M. Gray, *Report on the Supply of Petroleum . . . to Rhodesia* (Foreign and Commonwealth Office, 1978).
10. Barker, A.J., *The Civilizing Mission: The Italo-Ethiopian War 1935–36* (London, 1968), p. 378.
11. J. Galtung, 'On the Effects of International Economic Sanctions', *World Politics,* Vol. XIX, No. 3 (April 1967), p. 382.
12. Ibid.
13. Muriel J. Grieve, 'Economic Sanctions Theory and Practice', *International Relations* (David Davies Memorial Institute of International Studies), Vol. III, No. 6 (October 1968), p. 440.
14. Margaret Doxey, 'Economic Sanctions: Benefits and Costs, *The World Today*, December 1980.
15. James Barber and Michael Spicer, 'Sanctions against South Africa – Options for the West', *World Politics* (April 1967), pp. 393–4.
16. Ibid., p. 389.
17. Ibrahim F.I. Shihata, 'Destination Embargo of Arab Oil: Its Legality under International Law,' *American Journal of International Law*, Vol. 68, No. 4 (October 1974), p. 593.
18. *Zycie Warszawy*, 3 August 1983.
19. *Rzeczpospolita*, 20 October 1983.
20. Statement by the President on 18 June 1982.
21. John Plender, 'Coming Clean on the Pipeline', *Financial Times*, 23 September 1982.
22. Ray Dafter, 'Yesterday, 32 Kilometres More', *Financial Times*, 5 April 1983.

23. Ibid.
24. David White, 'French May Take Action to Force Work on Pipeline', *Financial Times*, 23 August 1982. $700 million was then equivalent to £402.3 million.
25. Ibid.
26. Edward Townsend, 'British Pipeline Turbines Ready for Shipment', *The Times*, 26 August 1982.
27. David Simpson, 'Pym Stresses Britain Made No Concessions over Pipeline', *The Guardian*, 15 November 1982.
28. Kevin Done, 'Sanctions Cloud Lifted from Kohl Talks', *Financial Times*, 15 November 1982.
29. 'Lessons from the Pipeline Débâcle', *The Guardian*, 15 November 1982.
30. 'Declaration on China', agreed in the Paris Economic Summit Meeting held on 14–16 July 1989.
31. Winston Lord, 'Extend equal trade status for a year – conditionally', *New York Times*, 10 May 1990.
32. Steven E. Plant, 'Economic Warfare: Costs and Benefits?', *Washington Quarterly* (Center for Strategic and International Studies, Georgetown University), Spring 1981, p. 190.
33. *Keesing's Contemporary Archives*, 22 May 1981, p. 30, 883.
34. Harold Jackson, 'Moscow Presses US for Fair Balance on Trade', *The Guardian*, 23 August 1983.
35. *Executives*, 10 May 1990. (Bureau of National Affairs, Inc.).
36. *House of Lords Debates*, Vol. 99, col. 352 (December 1935).
37. Leonard Downie, Jr. 'US Calls on its Allies to Back Moves on Iran', *International Herald Tribune*, 9 April 1980.
38. Otto Wolff von Amerongen, 'Economic Sanctions as a Foreign Policy', *International Security* (Harvard University) Vol. 5 (Fall 1980), pp. 162–5.
39. This article provides for non-military enforcement action by the United Nations to deal with a threat to the peace, breach of the peace or acts of aggression.
40. L.M. Goodrich, E. Hambro and A.P. Simons, *Charter of the United Nations: Commentary and Documents*, 3rd edn (New York, 1969), pp. 312–13.
41. UN General Assembly, GA Res. 2131, 20 UN GAOR Supp. 14, p. 11, UN Doc. A/6014 (1965).
42. GA Res. 2625, 25 UN GAOR, Supp. 28, p. 121, UN Doc. A/8028 (1970).
43. GA Res. 3171, 25 UN GAOR, Supp. 30, UN Doc. A/9030 (1974).
44. GA Res. 3281, 29 UN GAOR, Supp. 31, at 50, 55, UN Doc. A/9631 (1974).
45. UN Doc. A/AC, 125/SR 25, p. 16, para. 39 (1966), quoted by Richard B. Lillich in 'Economic Coercion and the International Legal Order', *International Affairs* (Royal Institute of International Affairs), Vol. 51 (1975).
46. Derek W. Bowett, 'International Law and Economic Coercion', *Virginia Journal of International Law*, Vol. 16, No. 2 (1972), p. 252.
47. Quoted from the Summary of Amendment of the Export Administrative Regulations, issued by the US Department of Commerce on 22 June 1982.
48. Townsend, op. cit.
49. For the legal arguments regarding jurisdiction see F.A. Mann, *Studies in International Law* (Oxford, 1973), pp. 39, 88; L.F. Oppenheim and H. Lauterpacht, *International Law*, Vol. I, 8th edn (London, 1974), pp.

331–3; D.P. O'Connell, *International Law*, Vol. II, 2nd edn (London, 1970), p. 599; M.M. Whiteman, *Digest of International Law*, Vol. 6 (Washington, DC, 1968), pp. 88–91; I. Brownlie, *Principles of International Law*, 3rd edn (Oxford, 1979), p. 302.

50. Paul Webster and Alex Brummer, 'French Break US Pipeline Embargo', *The Guardian*, 24 August 1982.

51. James Barber. 'Economic Sanctions as a Policy Instrument,' *International Affairs*, July 1979, p. 372.

52. Samuel Hoare (Viscount Templeford), *Nine Troubled Years* (London, 1954), p. 152.

53. Winston Churchill, *The Second World War*, Vol. I: *The Gathering Storm* (London, 1948), pp. 131 and 136.

54. Margaret P. Doxey, *Economic Sanctions and International Enforcement*, 2nd edn (London, 1980), p. 50.

55. Schreiber, op. cit., p. 405.

56. Ibid., p. 404.

57. Ibid., p. 404.

58. Ibid., p. 405.

59. Galtung, op. cit., p. 395.

60. Barber and Spicer, op. cit., p. 389.

61. Ibid.

62. Ibid., p. 392.

63. David Baldwin, 'The Power of Positive Sanctions', *World Politics*, Vol. XXIV, No. 1 (October 1971), pp. 19–38.

64. Klaus Knorr, *The Power of Nations* (New York, 1975), p. 154.

65. Galtung, op. cit., pp. 395, 398, 399.

66. 'Soviets Step up US Grain Purchase' *Financial Times*, 26 August 1983.

67. Grieve, op. cit., p. 439.

CHAPTER 6

1. *Declaration on Events in Poland*, approved at a special NATO foreign ministerial meeting on 11 January 1982.

2. Gunnar Adler-Karlsson, *Western Economic Warfare 1947–1967; A Case Study in Foreign Economic Policy* (Stockholm, 1968), p. 210.

3. *Middle East Economic Digest*, 22 March 1974.

4. Official text issued by the American Embassy in London, quoted in 'Reagan: Crime against Humanity Must Never be Forgotten', *The Guardian*, 7 September 1983.

5. Stephen W. Roskill, *Hankey: Man of Secrets* (London, 1974), p. 187.

6. Ronald Hilton, 'Castrophobia in the United States', *The Yearbook of World Affairs 1964* (London, 1964), pp. 56–72.

7. Statement by George Sokolsky, spokesman for National Conservatives, quoted in Anna P. Schreiber, 'Economic Coercion as an Instrument of Foreign Policy', *World Politics*, Vol. XXV, No. 3 (April 1973), p. 391.

8. Tad Szulc and Karl E. Meyer, *The Cuban Invasion: Chronicle of a Disaster* (New York, 1962), p. 62.

9. Ibid., pp. 65–72.

10. Richard Crossman, *The Diaries of a Cabinet Minister,* Vol. I: *Minister of Housing 1964–66* (London, 1975), pp. 397–8.
11. Reginald Dale, 'Reagan's Response Disappoints the Right', *Financial Times*, 7 September 1983.
12. Ibid.
13. Ibid.
14. Julius K. Nyerere, 'Rhodesia in the Context of Southern Africa', *Foreign Affairs*, April 1966, pp. 385–6.
15. UN Doc. S/Res/232.
16. *Hansard*, Vol. 720, No. 3 (11 November 1965).
17. James Barber and Michael Spicer, 'Sanctions against South Africa – Options for the West', *World Politics*, April 1967, p. 397.
18. Ibid., p. 395.
19. Ibid., p. 397.
20. *Keesing's Contemporary Archives,* 30 April 1982, p. 31, 457.
21. Jerome Slater, *The OAS and United States Foreign Policy* (Columbus, Ohio, 1967), pp. 135–74.
22. William N. Medlicott, *The Economic Blockade*, Vol. 1 (London, 1952), p. 110.
23. Ibid.
24. Samuel Hoare (Viscount Templeford), *Nine Troubled Years* (London, 1954), p. 152.
25. Samuel P. Huntington, 'Trade, Technology and Leverage: Economic Diplomacy', *Foreign Policy*, No. 32 (Fall 1978), p. 65.
26. Medlicott, op. cit., p. 478.
27. Ibid., p. 480.
28. US Department of State, *American Foreign Policy: Current Documents 1964* (Washington, DC, 1967), pp. 323–4.
29. Edward Gonzales, 'Castro, the Limits of Charisma', *Problems of Communism,* Vol. XIX (July–August 1970), pp. 13–14.
30. Klaus Knorr, *The Power of Nations* (New York, 1975), p. 112.
31. CD/417 Annex 1, pp. 1–2, Committee of Disarmament.

CHAPTER 7

1. *Keesing's Contemporary Archives*, 21 March 1980, p. 30, 150.
2. R.K. Ramarzani, 'Iran's Revolution: Patterns, Problems and Prospects', *International Affairs*, Summer 1980, p. 445.
3. Alvin Z. Rubinstein, 'The Soviet Union and Iran under Khomeini', *International Affairs*, Autumn 1981, p. 599.
4. Ibid.
5. Ibid., p. 604.
6. Ibid.
7. *Keesing's Contemporary Archives*, 21 March 1980, p. 30, 148.
8. Ibid., p. 30, 149.
9. Ibid., p. 30, 145.
10. Ibid., p. 30, 150.

CHAPTER 8

1. Case Concerning United States Diplomatic and Consular Staff in Tehran, Judgement, *ICJ Reports 1980*, p. 16.
2. Quoted in Steven Rattner, 'The Economic Warfare Was Also Psychological', *New York Times*, 18 November 1979.
3. Calculated on the basis of $23 per barrel.
4. Ian Mather, 'Iran May Face Sanctions Campaign', *Observer Foreign News Service*, No. 39, 222 (13 November 1979), p. 1.
5. *Middle East Economic Digest*, Vol. 25, No. 4 (23 January 1981), p. 9.
6. *New York Times*, 25 November 1979.
7. 'Wider Boycott by Unions Possible', *New York Times*, 26 November 1979.
8. David Buchan and Andrew Whitley, 'Trade Ban Would Cut Food and Fuel Supply', *Financial Times*, 14 November 1979.
9. Rattner, op. cit.
10. Ibid.
11. 'US May Call for Sanctions on Iran', *Financial Times*, 14 December 1979.
12. Richard Burt, 'NATO supports US on Iran Sanctions', *New York Times*, 14 December 1979.
13. 'Little Help from US Friends', *International Herald Tribune*, 13 December 1979.
14. Patrick Keatley, 'Britain Declines to Get Involved in Iran Sanctions', *The Guardian*, 11 December 1979.
15. Paul Lewis, 'US Urges Iran Sanctions, but Whom Will They Hurt?', *New York Times*, 16 December 1979.
16. Richard Evans and Andrew Whitley, 'Support for Iran Trade Sanctions Sought by Vance', *Financial Times*, 11 December 1979.
17. Peter Norman, 'Mr Vance Seeks Allies in Bonn and London Over Iran Money War', *The Times*, 8 December 1979.
18. Anthony Sampson, *The Money Lenders: Bankers in a Dangerous World* (London, 1981), pp. 247–8.
19. Ibid., p. 248.
20. Patrick Keatley, 'Vance's Freeze Strategy Shunned!', *The Guardian*, 8 December 1979.
21. Ibid.
22. 'Iran Boycott: Britain May Set the Pace', *The Sunday Times*, 23 December 1979.
23. Roger Boyes, 'Bonn Halts Iran Trade Credits', *Financial Times*, 10 December 1979.
24. 'How to be a Good Ally without Putting Oneself Out', *The Economist*, 19 April 1980, p. 48.
25. 'How Much Will Sanctions Cost Us?', *The Economist*, 26 April 1980, p. 54.
26. Ibid.
27. Ibid.
28. *The Economist*, 19 April 1980, p. 48.
29. Boyes, op. cit.
30. Patrick Keatley, *The Guardian*, 11 December 1979.
31. Ibid.

32. John Miller, 'Britain Keeps out of Row', *Daily Telegraph*, 11 December 1979.
33. Ibid.
34. Ibid.
35. Lewis, op. cit.
36. Boyes, op. cit.
37. Evans and Whitley, op. cit.
38. Jurek Martin, 'Carter May Take Tougher Action', *Financial Times*, 12 December 1979.
39. Ibid.
40. 'Japan Asked to Aid Iran Asset Freeze', *Japan Times*, 18 December 1979.
41. Ibid.
42. 'Japan to Co-operate in US Iran Sanctions', *Japan Times*, 19 December 1979.
43. Robert Rumball, 'Japanese Assure US of Support in Moves to Put Pressure on Iran', *New York Times*, 19 December 1979.
44. Norman, op. cit.
45. Lewis, op. cit.
46. UN Security Council Distribution General S/13616 (1979).
47. United States Diplomatic and Consular Staff in Tehran, Provisional Measures, Order of 15 December 1979, *ICJ Reports 1979*, p. 8, para. 1.
48. United States Diplomatic and Consular Staff in Tehran, Judgement, Request for the Indication of Provisional Measures, Order of 15 December 1979, *ICJ Reports 1979*, p. 11.
49. Ibid., p. 11, paras 2 and 3.
50. Stephen Barber, 'US Sends warning to Russia', *Daily Telegraph*, 24 December 1979. (SALT-II was scheduled to be presented to the Senate for its approval of ratification early in the following year.)
51. Jane Rosen, 'US Told to Avoid Iran Row', *The Guardian*, 15 December 1979.
52. Ibid.
53. *Financial Times*, 24 December 1979.
54. 'US Delays Iran Sanctions Plan', *The Sunday Times*, 30 December 1979.
55. UN Security Council, Distribution General S/13735 (10 January 1980).
56. 'Iran Warns UN States of Boycott', *New York Times*, 15 January 1980.
57. *The Times*, 29 January 1980.
58. 'Gesture to Bani-Sadr: US Postpones Imposition of Sanctions against Iran', *International Herald Tribune*, 29 January 1980. In response to this statement, the students said: 'One of the characteristics of the revolution is that all the decisions should not necessarily be made through governmental channels. We do not agree with two governments.'
59. Ibid.
60. 'State of the Union: The Carter Doctrine', *The Economist*, 26 January 1980, p. 36.
61. Ibid., p. 33.
62. *International Herald Tribune*, 29 January 1980.
63. William Borders, 'US Allies asked to Back Iran sanctions, are Sympathetic but Cautious', *New York Times*, 9 April 1980.
64. Ibid.

65. Axel Krause, 'Allies Delay Response to Carter Hostage Bid', *International Herald Tribune*, 15 April 1980.
66. Richard Wallis, 'EEC Delays Sanctions Stand, Demands Iran Free Hostages', *International Herald Tribune*, 11 April 1980.
67. Ibid.
68. Ibid.
69. 'Europeans Convinced of Need for Strong Measures', *Financial Times*, 15 April 1980.
70. John Palmer, 'Unwilling to be Dragged into America's Quarrels', *The Guardian*, 11 April 1980.
71. 'Europeans Convinced of Need for Strong Measures', *Financial Times*, 15 April 1980.
72. David Tonge, 'Foreboding of the Western Allies', *Financial Times*, 21 April 1980.
73. Leonard Downie, Jr, 'US Calls on its Allies to Back Moves on Iran', *International Herald Tribune*, 9 April 1980.
74. *The Economist*, 19 April 1980, p. 48.
75. 'Nerves', *The Economist*, 26 April 1980, p. 13.
76. Ibid.
77. James Wightman, 'Thatcher's Fear on Iran Curbs', *Daily Telegraph*, 15 April 1980.
78. 'Europeans Convinced of Need for Strong Measures', *Financial Times*, 15 April 1980.
79. *The Times*, 10 April 1980.
80. *The Economist*, 26 April 1980, p. 13.
81. From the 'Full Text of Communiqué Issued by the EEC Foreign Ministers on 22nd April', Commission of the European Communities.
82. Ibid.
83. Ibid.
84. Section 1, sub-section (1) of the Iran (Temporary Powers) Bill.
85. Section 1, sub-section (2) (a) of the Iran (Temporary Powers) Bill.
86. Section 1, sub-section (2) (b) of the Iran (Temporary Powers) Bill.
87. 'Complaints of Cheating: Emergency Sanctions Debate', *The Times*, 20 May 1980.
88. Ibid.
89. Ibid.
90. John Wyles, 'UK Sanctions about Face', *Financial Times*, 21 May 1980.
91. 'The Sanctions Mouse that Squeaked,' *The Economist*, 24 May 1980.
92. 'Criticism at Number Ten', *The Times*, 21 May 1980.
93. Ibid.
94. Ibid.
95. 'Britain is to Act with Community on Sanctions against Iran', *The Times*, 20 May 1980.
96. 'More Bark than Bite', *The Economist*, 24 May 1980, p. 67.
97. *The Times*, 11 April 1980.
98. 'Japan Will Aid Neighbour State of Iran, Afghanistan', *Japan Times*, 21 April 1980.
99. Donald Kirk, 'Japan Outflanks Iran Oil Threat', *Observer News Service*, 24 April 1980.

100. Sam Jameson, 'US Offers to Help Japan Replace Iran Oil', *The International Herald Tribune*, 3 May 1980.
101. 'Japanese Refusing to Pay Higher Price for Oil from Iran', *New York Times*, 20 April 1980.
102. 'Japan Sets Freeze on Exports to Iran', *New York Times*, 23 May 1980.
103. 'Canada Issues Package of Sanctions', *The Times*, 24 April 1980.
104. 'Australia to Cut Iran Trade', *The Times*, 22 April 1980.

CHAPTER 9

1. 'Japanese Refusing to Pay Higher Price for Oil from Iran', *New York Times*, 20 April 1980.
2. Ibid.
3. 'Iranian Sanctions – Scarcely Worth Bothering to Bust', *The Economist*, 7 June 1980, p. 78.
4. *Tsukan Tokei* (Japanese Ministry of Finance, 1980).
5. *The Economist*, 7 June 1980, p. 77.
6. *The Economist*, 24 May 1980, p. 67.
7. Quoted in Shin Sasaki, 'Sogoizon Kankei no Naka no Iran Keizai Seisai', *Kokusai Mondai*, No. 246 (September 1980), p. 57.
8. Housing expenditure dropped by 10.9 per cent because many foreigners, mostly Westerners, left Iran.
9. *Middle East Economic Digest*, 18 July 1980, p. 23.
10. *The Economist*, 7 June 1980, p. 78.
11. Ibid.
12. *Middle East Economic Digest*, 16 May 1980, p. 27.
13. *Petroleum Intelligence Weekly*, 28 April and 19 May 1980.

CHAPTER 10

1. *Middle East Economic Digest* (hereafter *MEED*) 11 January 1980, p. 26.
2. 'How to use Sanctions', *The Economist*, 19 July 1980, p. 15.
3. *MEED*, 15 February 1980, p. 26.
4. *MEED*, 29 February 1980, p. 27.
5. Ibid.
6. Announcement by the Governor of the Bank Markazi on 18 May 1980.
7. *MEED*, 29 February 1980, p. 26.
8. *MEED*, 19 September 1980, p. 31.
9. *MEED*, 4 April 1980, p. 6.
10. *MEED*, 29 February 1980, p. 25.
11. *MEED*, 29 August 1980, p. 19.
12. *MEED*, 4 January 1980, p. 24.
13. *MEED*, 18 April 1980, p. 29.
14. *MEED*, 26 September 1980, p. 28.
15. *MEED*, 15 February 1980, p. 26.
16. *MEED*, 15 February 1980, p. 26.
17. *MEED*, 12 May 1980, p. 26.

18. *MEED*, 15 February 1980, p. 27.
19. *MEED*, 9 May 1980, pp. 25–6.
20. Ibid.
21. *MEED*, 29 February 1980, p. 26.
22. *MEED*, 18 April 1980, p. 24.
23. *MEED*, 25 April 1980, p. 20.
24. *MEED*, 6 June 1980, p. 31.
25. *MEED*, 18 April 1980, p. 30.
26. *MEED*, 18 January 1980, p. 24.
27. *MEED*, 21 March 1980, p. 26.
28. *MEED*, 19 September 1980, p. 32.
29. *MEED*, 18 January 1980, p. 24.
30. *MEED*, 8 February 1980, p. 27.
31. Ibid.
32. *MEED*, 15 February 1980, p. 27.
33. *MEED*, 21 March 1980, p. 26.
34. *MEED*, 2 May 1980, p. 25.
35. Hungarian National Radio, referred to in *MEED*, 8 August 1980, p. 20.
36. Announcement of the government of the Republic of Korea concerning developments in North Korea referred to in *MEED*, 29 September 1980, p. 29. North Korea needed 4.3–4.5 million tons of crude oil in 1980, of which the Soviet Union and China were to supply 1 million and 2 million tons, respectively.
37. *MEED*, 18 April 1980, p. 23.
38. *MEED*, 26 April 1980, p. 30.
39. From the statement by India's Petroleum Minister, Vecrendra Patil, in the Indian Parliament on 22 July 1980.
40. *Financial Times*, 3 May 1980.
41. 'Europeans Convinced of Need for Strong Sanctions', *Financial Times*, 15 April 1980.
42. *MEED*, 18 April 1980, p. 29.
43. *MEED*, 19 September 1980, p. 32.
44. *MEED*, 5 September 1980, p. 28.
45. *MEED*, 18 January 1980, p. 25.
46. The French Sugar Market Intervention Regulation Fund.
47. 'Iranian Sanctions – Scarcely Worth Bothering to Bust', *The Economist*, 7 June 1980, p. 77.

CHAPTER 11

1. 'Unit of Iranian Parliament Drafts Plan on Hostages', *New York Times*, 2 September 1980.
2. 'A Bogeyman Dies', *The Economist*, 2 August 1980, p. 28.
3. Case Concerning United States Diplomatic and Consular Staff in Tehran, Judgement, *ICJ Reports 1980*, p. 44.
4. Ibid., pp. 44–6.
5. 'Iran Drafts Terms for Release of the Hostages', *The Times*, 2 September 1980.

6. 'Khomeini Excites New Hope', *The Sunday Times*, 14 September 1980.
7. 'Tehran MPs Ruled out Talks on Hostages', *Financial Times*, 3 October 1980.
8. 'Tehran MPS in Uproar over Hostages', *Financial Times*, 1 October 1980.
9. 'Hostages Talks "if US repents"', *The Guardian*, 10 September 1980.
10. Bernard Gwertzman, 'Tehran Indicates it is Moving Closer to Hostage Decision', *New York Times*, 23 October 1980.
11. Ibid.
12. 'It Goes Back to AD 637', *The Economist*, 27 September 1980, p. 41.
13. William O. Beeman, 'Iran Has Iraq's Number', *New York Times*, 2 October 1980.
14. Ibid.
15. Quoted from Tehran Radio, 19 October 1980, by the *New York Times*, 20 October 1980.
16. 'War between Iran and Iraq', *Strategic Survey 1980–1981*, p. 50.
17. Eric Rouleau, 'Iranian Children Fighting in the Front Line', *The Guardian*, 16 October 1980.
18. Steven K. Hindy, 'Iraq Reports Bombers Set Tehran Fires', *International Herald Tribune*, 17 October 1980.
19. Praney B. Gupte, 'Fighting is Intense at Iranian Oil City', *New York Times*, 2 November 1980.
20. 'Abadan Isolated, Iraqis Claim', *Financial Times*, 17 October 1980.
21. Major-General Edward Fursdon, 'Iran Port Falls to Iraqis', *Daily Telegraph*, 25 October 1980.
22. David Cross, 'Russia Reassures US on Intentions in Gulf', *The Times*, 8 October 1980.
23. Drew Middleton, 'Iraqi Victory Claims: A Turning Point in Iran War?', *New York Times*, 5 November 1980.
24. Ibid.
25. *The Economist*, 27 September 1980, p. 42.
26. David Cross, 'US Tells Russians not to Interfere in Gulf', *The Times*, 24 September 1980.
27. *The Economist*, 27 September 1980, p. 42.
28. David Cross, *The Times*, 24 September 1980.
29. *The Economist*, 27 September 1980, p. 42.
30. Middleton, op. cit.
31. Ibid.
32. Henry Stanhope, 'Conflict Liable to Turn into Long War of Attrition', *The Times*, 23 October 1980.
33. *The Times*, 24 September 1980.
34. Richard Burt, 'Clash in Gulf: Bombs and Oil', *New York Times*, 25 October 1980.
35. Harold Jackson, 'US Unclear about Russian Stance on War', *The Guardian*, 8 October 1980.
36. Stanhope, op. cit.
37. Henry Jackson, 'Anxiety Grows in War', *The Guardian*, 16 October 1980.
38. Murray Ruberstein, 'Now that the Iranians Need the US', *New York Times*, 27 September 1980.

39. Ibid.
40. Middleton, op. cit.
41. 'Struggle for Power in Iran', *Strategic Survey 1980–1981*, p. 52.
42. *Middle East Economic Digest* (hereafter *MEED*), 14 November 1980, p. 33.
43. Ibid.
44. Announcement of the Petroleum Association of Japan in October 1980.
45. *MEED*, 14 November 1980, p. 33.
46. Hella Pick, 'US Petrol for Iran if the Hostages are Freed', *The Guardian*, 25 October 1980.
47. *MEED*, 14 November 1980, p. 33.
48. *Strategic Survey, 1980–1981*, p. 50.
49. *MEED*, 26 September 1980, p. 29.
50. *MEED*, 3 October 1980, p. 24.
51. *Keesing's Contemporary Archives*, 7 August 1981, p. 31, 016.
52. Reuter News from Tehran, *The Guardian*, 10 October 1980.
53. 'Tehran MPs in Uproar over Hostages', *Financial Times*, 1 October 1980.
54. Alex Brummer, 'US Warns Iranians on Hostages', *Financial Times*, 1 October 1980.
55. *Strategic Survey, 1980–1981*, p. 56.
56. Ibid.
57. *The Times*, 25 September 1980.
58. *Strategic Survey, 1980–1981*, p. 57.
59. Beeman, op. cit.
60. 'Iran Hopes for Iraq Coup as Exiles Plot Khomeini Fall', *The Sunday Times*, 16 October 1980.
61. Jane Rosen, 'UN Pins Hostage Hope on Radjai', *The Guardian*, 18 October 1980.
62. Bruce London, 'Iran Isolated "Because of Hostages"', *Daily Telegraph*, 14 October 1980.
63. 'Iranian Premier Due at the UN to Press Case against Iraqis', *New York Times*, 16 October 1980.
64. Ibid.
65. *The Sunday Times*, 16 October 1980.
66. Gwertzman, op. cit.
67. Richard Beeston, 'US Aid for Iran Hint if Hostages are Freed', *Daily Telegraph*, 22 October 1980.
68. David Buchan, 'Carter Backs Iran's "Integrity"', *Financial Times*, 21 October 1980.
69. *New York Times*, 23 October 1980.
70. Ibid.
71. Ibid.
72. Ibid.
73. 'Iran Calculated the Profits of a Deal over US Hostages', *The Sunday Times*, 26 October 1980.
74. Bernard D. Nossiter, 'Muskie Confers with Iraqi Aide; Gets Assurances', *New York Times*, 1 October 1980.
75. Joseph Fitchett, 'West Switches Tactics on Hormuz', *International Herald Tribune*, 30 September 1980.

76. The official statement issued on 26 September 1980, quoted by Patrick Brogan in 'US Consults Its Allies on How to Protect Oil and Shipping in Threatened Gulf', *The Times*, 27 September 1980.
77. Joseph Fitchett, 'West Quietly Makes Contingency Plans', *International Herald Tribune*, 2 October 1980.
78. 'Will the Fire Spread?', *International Herald Tribune,* 10 October 1980.
79. Joseph Kraft, 'A Defeat for US in Gulf', *International Herald Tribune*, 26 September 1980.
80. 'US Warns Iranians on Hostages' Safety', *The Guardian*, 24 September 1980.
81. Ibid.
82. Ibid. The radio did not identify the new locations.
83. 'US Fears War Could Hurt Hostages Effort', *International Herald Tribune*, 24 September 1980.
84. Ibid.
85. Shahran Chubin, 'The Soviet Union and Iran', *Foreign Affairs*, Vol. 61, No. 4 (Spring 1983), p. 937.
86. Ibid., p. 940.
87. David Cross, *The Times*, 8 October 1980.
88. 'Reagan Accuses Administration of "Grandstanding" on Iran Crisis', *New York Times*, 10 September 1980.
89. A.J. McIlroy, 'Letter on Hostages Scorned', *Daily Telegraph*, 11 September 1980.
90. 'US Sees Little Hope in Ayatollah's Speech', *The Guardian*, 15 September 1980.
91. Anthony Holden, 'Ayatollah Haunts US Election Campaign', *Observer News Service*, Washington, 17 September 1980, No. 40,491.
92. 'Captive Diplomats Return to Centre Stage', *Financial Times*, 24 October 1980.
93. Ibid.
94. David Cross, 'Mr Muskie is Cautious on Hopeful Signs for Hostages'. *The Times*, 20 October 1980.
95. *National Journal*, 7 November 1980, p. 1,877.
96. Quoted by Reuters, 16 September 1980. Ghotbazadeh had been Foreign Minister until the formation of the new Iranian government early in September.
97. William Safire, 'The Ayatollah Votes', *New York Times*, 27 October 1980.

CHAPTER 12

1. 'Algeria Wins its Spurs', *The Economist*, 24 January 1980, p. 22.
2. Ibid.
3. Anthony Sampson, *The Money Lenders* (London, 1981), p. 251–2.
4. 'President Carter Says All 52 Hostages are Alive and Well', *The Times*, 27 December 1980.
5. Ibid., p. 251.
6. Reprinted in *International Legal Materials*, Vol. XX, No. 1 (January 1981), pp. 224–8.

7. Reprinted ibid., p. 230.
8. *Middle East Economic Digest*, 23 January 1981, p. 10.
9. Ibid.
10. *The Economist*, 24 January 1981, p. 20.

Bibliography

Adler-Karlsson, Gunnar, *Western Economic Warfare 1947–1967: A Case Study in Foreign Economic Policy*, (Stockholm: Almqvist & Wiksell, 1968).

Akins, J.E., 'The Oil Crisis: This Time the Wolf is Here', *Foreign Affairs*, Vol. 51 (1973) pp. 463–80.

Albrecht-Carrie, René, *A Diplomatic History of Europe Since the Congress of Vienna*, (New York: Harper, 1958).

American Foreign Policy: Current Documents 1964 (Washington, DC, 1967).

Amerongen, Otto Wolff von, 'Economic Sanctions as a Foreign Policy', *International Security* (Harvard University), Vol. 5, No. 2 (Fall, 1980).

Baer, G.W., *The Coming of the Italo-Ethiopian War 1935–1936* (Cambridge, Mass.: Harvard University Press, 1967).

Baldwin, David A., 'The Power of Positive Sanctions', *World Politics*, Vol. 24, No. 1 (October 1971).

Barber, James, 'Economic Sanctions as a Policy Instrument', *International Affairs* (Royal Institute of International Affairs) July 1979.

Barber, James, and S. Michael 'Sanctions against South Africa – Options for the West', *World Politics*, April 1967.

Barker, A.J., *The Civilizing Mission: The Italo-Ethiopian War 1935–36* (London: Cassell, 1968).

Beloff, Max, *The Foreign Policy of Soviet Russia 1929–1941*, Vol. 1 (Oxford: Oxford University Press, 1949).

Bingham, T.H. and Gray, S.M., *Report on the Supply of Petroleum . . . to Rhodesia* (Foreign and Commonwealth Office, 1978).

Bonn, M.J., 'How Sanctions Failed', *Foreign Affairs*, Vol. 15, No. 2 (January 1937).

Bowett, Derek W., 'International Law and Economic Coercion', *Virginia Journal of International Law*, 1972, Vol. 16, No. 2 (1972).

Brownlie, I., *Principles of International Law* (Oxford: Clarendon Press, 1979).

Brzezinski, Zbigniew, *Power and Principle: Memoirs Of the National Security Adviser 1977–81* (London: Weidenfeld & Nicolson, 1983).

Bull, Hedley, *The Anarchical Society* (London: Macmillan, 1977).

Bullard, R., 'Behind the Oil Dispute in Iran', *Foreign Affairs*, April 1953.

Case Concerning United States Diplomatic and Consular Staff in Tehran, Judgment, *ICJ Reports 1980*.

Christopher, Warren, et al., *American Hostages in Iran* (New York: Yale University Press, 1985).

Chubin, Shahran, 'The Soviet Union and Iran', *Foreign Affairs*, Vol. 61, No. 4 (Spring 1983).

Churchill, Winston, *The Second World War*, Vol. 1: *The Gathering Storm* (Boston: Houghton Mifflin, 1948).

Crossman, Richard, *The Diaries of a Cabinet Minister*, Vol. 1: *Minister of Housing 1964–66*, (London: Hamilton, 1979).

Daoudi, M.S., and Dajani, M.S., *Economic Sanctions: Ideals and Experience* (London: Routledge & Kegan Paul, 1983).

Declaration of Events in Poland, approved at a special NATO Foreign Ministerial Meeting on 11 January 1982.

Direction of Trade Statistics (International Monetary Fund), 1979.

Doxey, Margaret P., *Economic Sanctions and International Enforcement*, 2nd edn (London: Macmillan, 1980).

Doxey, Margaret P., Economic Sanctions: Benefits and Costs', *The World Today*, December 1980.

Eckstein, Alexander, *Communist China's Economic Growth and Foreign Trade* (New York: McGraw-Hill, 1966).

Farrell, Barry, *Yugoslavia and the Soviet Union 1948–1956* (Hamden, Conn., Shoe String Press, 1956).

Patemi, N.S., *Oil Diplomacy* (New York: Whittier, 1954).

Fearon, Richard, 'Asset Freeze – United States Blocks Iranian Assets', Exec. Order No. 12, 170, 44 Fed. Reg. 65, 729 (1979), *Harvard International Law Journal*, Vol. 21 (1980).

Ford, Alan W., *The Anglo-Iranian Oil Dispute of 1951–1952*, (Berkeley, Calif., University of California Press, 1954).

Freedman, Robert Owen, *Economic Warfare in the Communist Bloc: A Study of Soviet Economic Pressure against Yugoslavia, Albania, and Communist China* (New York: Praeger, 1970).

Galtung, J., 'On the Effects of International Economic Sanctions', *World Politics*, Vol. XIX, No. 3 (April 1967).

Gonzalez, Edward, 'Castro, the Limits of Charisma', *Problems of Communism*, XIX (July–August 1970).

Goodrich, L.M., Hambro, E. and Simons, A.P., *Charter of the United Nations: Commentary and Documents* (New York: Columbia University Press, 1969).

Grieve, Muriel J., 'Economic Sanctions, Theory and Practice', *International Relations* (David Davies Memorial Institute of International Studies) III, No. 6 (October 1968).

Gross, Leo, 'The Case Concerning United States Diplomatic and Consular Staff in Tehran: Phase of Provisional Measures', *American Journal of International Law*, Vol. 74 (1980).

Halle, Louis J., *The Cold War as History* (London: Chatto & Windus, 1967).

Hamilton, F.E.I., *Yugoslavia: Patterns of Economic Activity* (New York: Praeger, 1968).

Hammond, Paul Y., *Cold War and Detente: The American Foreign Policy Process since 1945* (New York, 1975).

Hansard, Vol. 720, No. 3 (11 November 1965).

Harris, D.J., *Cases and Materials on International Law*, 2nd edn (London: Sweet & Maxwell, 1979).

Hilton, Ronald, 'Castrophobia in the United States', *The Yearbook of World Affairs 1964* (London, 1964).

Hoare, Samuel (Viscount Templeford) *Nine Troubled Years* (London, 1954).

House of Lords Debates, Vol. 99, Col. 352 (December 1965).

Huntington, Samuel P., 'Trade, Technology and Leverage: Economic Diplomacy', *Foreign Policy*, No. 32 (Fall 1978).

International Energy Statistical Review (National Foreign Assessment Center, USA) 30 January 1980.

International Legal Materials, Vol. XX, No. 1 (January 1981) pp. 224–8.

Kaser, M.C., *Comecon* (Oxford: Oxford University Press, 1965).

Keatley, Patrick, *The Politics of Partnership: The Federation of Rhodesia and Nyasaland* (London, 1963).

Kelsen, Hans, *Collective Security Under International Law* (Washington, DC, 1957).

Kennan, George F., *Memoirs*, Vol. I: *1925–1950* (Boston, Mass.: Atlantic Monthly Press, 1967) and Vol. II: *1950–1963* (London: Hutchinson, 1972).

Kissinger, Henry, *For the Record: Selected Statements 1977–1980* (London, Weidenfeld & Nicolson, 1981).

Knorr, Klaus, *The Power of Nations* (New York: Basic Books, Inc., 1975).

Larson, D. (ed.), *The Cuban Crisis of 1962* (Boston, Mass., 1963.).

Lillich, Richard B., 'Economic Coercion and the International Legal Order', *International Affairs* (Royal Institute of International Affairs) Vol. 51 (1975).

Longrigg, S.H., *Oil in the Middle East: its Discovery and Development*, 3rd edn (Oxford: Oxford University Press, 1968).

Losman, Donald L., 'The Effects of Economic Sanctions', *Lloyds Bank Review*, October 1972, p. 30.

MacDonald, R. St. J., 'The Organization of American States in Action', *University of Toronto Law Journal*, Vol. 15, No. 2 (1964).

MacKintosh, J.M., *Strategy and Tactics of Soviet Foreign Policy* (Oxford: Oxford University Press, 1962).

Mann, F.A., *Studies in International Law* (Oxford, Clarendon Press, 1973).

Mather, Ian, 'Iran May Face Sanctions Campaign', *Observer Foreign News Service*, No. 39,222 (13 November 1979).

Medlicott, William N., *The Economic Blockade*, Vol. 1 (London: HMSO, 1952).

Mottahadeh, Roy Parvis, 'Iran's Foreign Devils', *Foreign Policy*, No. 38 (Spring 1980).

Nyerere, Julius K., 'Rhodesia in the Context of Southern Africa', *Foreign Affairs*, April 1966.

O'Connell, D.P., *International Law*, 2nd edn (London: Stevens, 1971) Vol II.

'OECD Oil Statistics 1973', *Quarterly Oil Statistics* (OPEC).

Oppenheim, L. F., and Lauterpacht, H., *International Law*, Vol. 1, 8th edn (London: Longman, 1974).

Paust, Jordan J., and Blaustein, Albert P. (eds), *The Arab Oil Weapon* (New York: Oceana Publications, 1977).

Petroleum Intelligence Weekly, 28 April and 19 May 1980.

Plant, Steven E., 'Economic Warfare: Costs and Benefits?', *The Washington Quarterly* (Center for Strategic and International Studies, Georgetown University) Spring 1980.

Radcliff-Brown, A.R., 'Sanctions, Social', *Encyclopaedia of the Social Sciences*, Vol. 13 (New York, 1934) pp. 531–4.

Ramarzani, R.K., 'Iran's Revolution: Patterns, Problems and Prospects', *International Affairs*, Summer 1980.

Renwick, Robin, *Economic Sanctions* (Cambridge, Mass.: Center for International Affairs, Harvard University, 1981).

Report of a Committee of Privy Councillors, *Falkland Islands Review* (Franks Report) (London, 1983).

Roskill, Stephen W., *Hankey: Man of Secrets* (London: Collins, 1974).

Rouleau, Eric, 'Khomeini's Iran', *Foreign Affairs* (Fall 1980).

Royal Institute of International Affairs, *International Sanctions* (London, 1938).

Rubinstein, Alvin Z., 'The Soviet Union and Iran under Khomeini', *International Affairs*, Autumn 1981.

Salinger, Pierre, *America Held Hostage: The Secret Negotiations* (London: André Deutsch, 1981).

Sampson, Anthony, *The Money Lenders: Bankers in a Dangerous World*, (London: Hodder & Stoughton, 1981).

Sasaki, Shin, 'Sogoizon Kankei No Naka No Iran Keizai Seisai', *Kokusai Mondai*, No. 246 (September 1980).

Schlesinger, A. *A Thousand Days*, (Boston: Houghton Mifflin, 1965).

Schreiber, Anna P., 'Economic Coercion as an Instrument of Foreign Policy', *World Politics*, Vol. 25, No. 3 (April 1973).

Shamsedin, E.M., *Arab Oil and the United States: An Admixture of Politics and Economics*, University of South Carolina, No. 29 (April 1979).

Shihata, Ibrahim F.I., 'Destination Embargo of Arab Oil: Its Legality under International Law', *American Journal of International Law*, Vol. 68, No. 4 (October 1974).

Sick, Gary, *All Fall Down: America's Fateful Encounter with Iran* (London: I.B. Tauris, 1985).

Slater, Jerome, *The OAS and United States Foreign Policy* (Columbus, Ohio: Ohio State University Press, 1967).

Slater, Jerome, *Intervention and Negotiation: the United States and the Dominican Revolution* (New York: Harper & Row, 1970).

Smith, R.F., *The United States and Cuba: Business and Diplomacy 1917–60* (New York, 1961).

Statistical Year Book of the Trade in Arms and Ammunitions (League of Nations), 1935.

Storry, Richard, *Japan and the Decline of the West in Asia 1894–1943* (London: Macmillan, 1979).

Strategic Survey (International Institute of Strategic Studies) 1980–1981, 1981–1982 and 1982–1983.

Summary of Amendment of the Export Administrative Regulations, US Department of Commerce, 22 June 1982.

Szulc, Tad, and Meyer, Karl E., *The Cuban Invasion: Chronicle of a Disaster* (New York, 1962).

Taubenfield, Rita F., and Taubenfield, Howard J., 'The Economic Weapon: The League of the Nations', *American Society of International Law*, 1946.

Toynbee, A.J., *Survey of International Affairs 1935*, Vol. II: *Abyssinia and Italy* (Oxford: Oxford University Press, 1936).

Tsunoda, Jun, *Nichi-Bei Kosho* (Tokyo, 1960).

Ulam, Adam B., *Expansion and Co-existence: The History of Soviet Foreign Policy, 1917–1967* (New York: Praeger, 1968).

UN General Assembly, Resolutions: GA Res. 2131, 20UN GAOR, Supp. 14, UN Doc. A/6014 (1965); GA Res. 2625, 25 UN, GAOR, Supp. 28, UN Doc. A/8028 (1970); G.A. Res. 3171, 25 U.N. GAOR, Supp. 30, UN Doc. A/9030 (1974); GA Res. 3281, 29, UN GAOR, Supp. 31, UN Doc. A/9631 (1974).

UN Security Council Distribution General S/13616, 13652, 13659 (1979), S/13735, 13797, 13908 (1980).

UN Security Council Resolutions: 218 (23 November 1965) and 418 (4 November 1977).

'United States Diplomatic and Consular Staff in Tehran', Provisional Measures, 15 December, *ICJ Reports 1979*.

USSR Grain Situation (US Department of Agriculture, 13 December 1983).

Väyrynen, Raimo, 'A Case Study of Sanctions: Finland-the Soviet Union in 1958–59', *Co-operation and Conflict* (Nordic Studies in International Politics, March 1969).

Whiteman, M.M., *Digest of International Law*, Vol. 6 (Washington, DC, US Government Printing Office, 1968).

Index

237